SUGAR & SPICE

SUGAR
& SPICE

sweets & treats from around the world

GAITRI PAGRACH-CHANDRA

Photography by Yuki Sugiura

PAVILION

Contents

My Sweet Life

Sugar is in my blood, probably more so than in most people's. I don't mean that I suffer from any sugar-related affliction, but simply that it has always been a part of my life and it is a bond that goes back several generations. I was born and brought up in Guyana and my ancestors were indentured labourers who were recruited in India to fill the labour void created by the abolition of slavery. The connection of sugar and slavery is too deep and harrowing a topic to be dealt with here, so I shall confine myself to the remark that the indentured labourers were the fortunate ones; they worked extremely hard, but saw some reward for their labour. They were bound by contract to work on a specific plantation for a fixed number of years, after which they could either be repatriated or have the passage commuted to a land grant. Most of them stayed on, as the British colony had more to offer than the old country on the other side of the world. Sugar remained a mainstay of the country's economy, and with the passing of several generations and improved educational opportunities many were able to achieve admirable positions in the local sugar hierarchy. And so it was that I grew up on a series of sugar plantations, a comfortable little self-contained world that was a quaint mixture of British-inspired living combined with individual ethnicity. The sight of sugar cane in its various stages of growth as well as the tantalising aromas that accompany sugar production were part of my everyday life. Needless to say, as children we regularly sneaked into the factory and persuaded someone to hand out samples of cane juice, molasses or fresh sugar, but there was more to the sweetness of plantation life.

'The Club' was the centre of social life and while the building itself was different from plantation to plantation, the system remained unchanged. It was geared primarily around adult activities, and that was where our parents had a drink or two after an afternoon of bridge or a few strenuous sets of tennis, or simply as a prelude to dinner. If we happened to spot them as we passed by after a hard day's play, we joined them as unobtrusively as we could. There was always a games room with billiard and card tables; there was a little library with ancient novels and outdated copies of various English magazines. (They came by boat in those days.) Cool and shady verandas were plentiful as were comfortable armchairs set in conversational groups. These would be shoved to one side on Friday evenings when we had our weekly film show. The films themselves were real classics in the sense that we had seen some of them so often that we knew them by heart and never hesitated to predict the outcome vociferously to each other. John Wayne, Doris Day, Abbot and Costello, Jerry Lewis and company were all old friends, and if the elderly projector had a little glitch every so often, it simply meant an extra chance to collect refreshments.

But the reason I'm telling you about the club is because, for the children, it was the centre of sweets. There was no shop within our closed community, but the bar at the club was stocked with all kinds of chocolate, sweets, biscuits, nuts, ice cream and drinks. Until I was about eight or so, and we moved to another plantation, the club at Skeldon was absolutely my most favourite place and the barman was one of my most valued friends. This man's generosity knew no bounds. I had to pass the building on my way to or from our house and instead of one of my speedy rides on my tubby-tyred bike, I would pedal at a painfully slow pace, looking up anxiously at the side veranda that bordered on the bar. If he was there, we would have a short but extremely pleasing interchange, consisting of mutual greetings and the question of whether I wanted a bar of chocolate. Obviously, I never refused the offer and it was thrown down for me to catch. (Several years later I learned about bar tabs and monthly settlements.) But that wasn't all. The games room was an important place. The men played snooker and other games and used packets of cigarettes as stakes. My father played a lot of snooker and to make it better, he didn't smoke. Why was this better? He had his winnings handed out in chocolate bars. Life was good. Before I go on, let me share a tip with you. Chocolate, of course, softens incredibly fast in the heat of the tropics, so we used to keep the main stock in the refrigerator. However, the best way to eat it was to take a room temperature bar and remove the outer wrappers. Then we helped the foil-sealed bar to melt by holding it between hot little hands. When it reached the appropriate stage, a corner was torn off and the bar was applied to eager mouths and gently squeezed until there was nothing but crumpled foil left. Gross, I know, but so delicious.

Before we leave the delights of the Skeldon club, I just want to tell you how we were showered with sweets at Christmas parties. An enterprising parent or member of staff hit upon a way to keep us reasonably occupied while we waited with mounting suspense for Santa. (Santa was a profusely sweating father or other handy male who was bulked out and swaddled in the universally known outfit and driven in on the back of the red Land Rover that served as the plantation's fire engine.) We were herded into the games room and subtly grouped under the huge ceiling fans – and all of a sudden a shower of sweets flew all around us. As we scrambled to collect them, we never saw the hand that hovered by the fan switch just as we hadn't seen someone perched on a ladder painstakingly lining the flat blades of the fans with sweets.

Several years passed and many sweet treats were enjoyed, from imported toffees to local coconut drops and Indo-Guyanese sweets, which included the goodie bags my paternal grandfather received when he officiated as a *pandit* (Hindu priest) at religious ceremonies. It was time for a new phase. I left for university in Nova Scotia, ready to face whatever challenge was thrown my way, leaving behind a younger sister and parents who were comforted by the knowledge that the daughter of family friends lived there and could keep an eye on me. My years in Halifax provided me with a degree in political science and modern languages (which involved an excursion to Spain, but more about this shortly) as well as an increasingly more intimate relationship with 'real' Indian sweets. I should explain that the food taken by Indian indentured labourers to the Caribbean was quite basic fare and, while it was good, it had always been based on availability. Existing in isolation, it remained quite static until the late 1970s, when India started spending a lot of money on cultural enrichment for the diaspora in an attempt to re-connect them with their heritage. In Guyana, fresh and powdered milk were easily obtained, but until that time very few people made things like *paneer*, for instance, the soft fresh cheese that is such a wonderful base for any number of sweets.

Ahillya, the family friend, went most Sundays to the Hindu temple in search of spiritual refreshment and pleasant company. I often accompanied her, but I must admit that I was really drawn by refreshment of a more tangible kind. Traditionally, all those who attend temple services are fed a vegetarian meal, which is generally quite simple but amazingly tasty. My stomach was starved for spices and readily accepted whatever the ladies prepared. As they were almost all recently settled subcontinental Indians (as opposed to the Caribbean Indians I had grown up with), I learned new flavours all the time. Except for the weekends spent with Ahillya and her family, I existed on a diet of cafeteria food and our university cooks' idea of something really exotic was Chicken *Cacciatore* every few months. Those of you who have lived in foreign countries as students will readily identify with the joy I found in the vegetable curries, lentils and beans, rice and flatbreads at the temple. There was always something sweet as well, but I soon discovered that sweets played the leading role at shows and concerts. Forget the pallid popcorn dribbled with fake butter and sprinkled with gritty salt; this was the real thing. The shows were usually fundraisers and the ladies vied with each other to produce the most delectable mouthfuls imaginable. *Burfi*, *kalakand*, *peda*, *laddus*, *mohanthall*, *gulab jamuns* and much more were arranged in cardboard boxes and sold as snacks. It was absolute heaven and I have provided you with recipes for all these delightful things, so you can create your own boxes.

When I went to Salamanca in Spain, for a year as part of my language degree, I embraced the *turrones* (nougat) and various kinds of marzipan with great affection and steadily acquired even more tastes. But there is one that I fear I shall never quite manage: liquorice. I met my Dutch husband in Salamanca and we later made our home in Holland. Holland, in case you didn't know, is liquorice-land. There are literally dozens of kinds, in all shapes and sizes, in varying degrees of hardness, sweetness and saltiness, and added extras like bay leaf and honey are enjoyed as long as there is not too much adulteration of the pure liquorice flavour. Liquorice allsorts, known here as *Engelse drop* or English liquorice, are waved aside indulgently as lightweights. Nothing in liquorice strikes a chord and its apparently multiple charms are lost on me. People don't understand it; for my part, I don't understand how they can continue to suck and chew on liquorice when there is so much wonderful dark chocolate going begging. And so, dear reader, I went from a sweet-loving child to a sweet-loving woman and while my dimensions and proportions have undergone a little change over the years, and my palate has become more discerning, my enthusiasm for sweet treats remains undiminished. I continue to scour the world, from Turkey to North Africa, the Philippines and elsewhere, and there are many enchanting specimens which I shall now share with you.

Gaitri

Introduction

Ever since primitive man stumbled upon a honeycomb and tried its contents, people have steadily developed a taste for sweetness. Across the ages, honey made way for sugar, and sugar went from being a luxurious seasoning to a cheap household staple, but it never lost its charm and continues to hold us in its thrall. The first sweets were sold by apothecaries as remedies for chest and stomach complaints as well as other minor disorders, and ladies prided themselves on being able to create home cures based on sugar and herbs from their gardens. As time went by and sugar became more widely available, sweet-making began to thrive. By the eighteenth century it was quite prestigious to be a confectioner, but this was not only a case of being able to make small and tasty titbits, fabulous sugar sculptures were created by masters of the art.

At the root of it all lies sugar cane (*Saccharum officinarum*), which was domesticated between 8000 and 4000 B.C., most likely in Papua New Guinea. From there, it travelled to Southeast Asia, China and India as well as the Pacific Islands. Native species already existed in these places, but they were soon replaced with the choicer Papuan variety. Several nations have been involved in the development, cultivation and popularisation of both cane and sugar and no continent has escaped its touch. Papuans refined the cultivation, Chinese and Indians invented methods for producing sugar from the juice of the sweet reeds, Arabs took it westwards to the Mediterranean and Europe, Africans suffered enslavement to satisfy Europe's sweet tooth. It is a complicated story that is filled with enterprise, inventiveness, opulence, decadence, cruelty, atrocity and greed, all so tightly intertwined that it is best if we reflect on the product itself rather than its turbulent past. The production of beet sugar in commercial quantities started only in the early nineteenth century and while it is an ideal crop for temperate zones, it remains simply a sweetener, with none of the flavour of cane sugar.

This book is about sweet treats, but what is a sweet? Is it a toffee, a truffle, a tiny pastry drenched in syrup, a piece of marzipan or a slice of cake? It is all of these things and more, depending on where you happen to be. The common denominator is sugar (or, in rare cases, honey) and things developed around this key ingredient. You will find that sweets easily fall into one of five main categories. There are those that depend almost exclusively on sugar, e.g. boiled sweets and honeycomb; then there are the milk-based marvels such as fudge and *burfi*; next, we can identify nutty delights including marzipan; moving on, we arrive at chocolate in all its sumptuousness in truffles and brownies; and we close the list with flour confectionery in the form of cakes, biscuits and pastries. Naturally, there are many hybrids and a sweet can fall into more than one category at the same time.

Looking at the recipes, you may feel that a particular region is heavily represented in a specific category. This is not intended as a statement, but is simply a reflection of the culture. My quest was to give you the best there is. Spaniards, for instance, are uneasy around butter, but give them a handful or two of almonds and they will charm the taste buds right out of your mouth. North Africans constantly use nut bases and give them variety by adding a few drops of rose water here or orange flower water there. It can never be doubted that Indians know how to turn a pan of milk into a delectable treat, nor can anyone contest that Americans rule the brownie-making world. I had to do all of these the justice they deserve. For those of you who are wondering at the blatant omission of the wonderful world of filo and baklava, there is a valid reason: I dealt with those in great depth in my previous book, *Warm Bread and Honey Cake*.

I have tried out these treats on many people: friends, relatives, neighbours, people working around the house, even the colleagues of my husband and daughter. The one thing that became quite clear was that sweets make people's eyes light up, but at the same time they are very personal and can inspire strong likes and dislikes. There is no universal standard for appreciating sweets. It is a taste that is generally learned by exposure and experience, or acquired as a result of circumstances. Preferences will often depend on your geographic location and ethnic background. Wherever you live, you are bound to find a familiar favourite here, but I hope to tempt you to try many others that you may not yet know. I have given as wide a range as I could and even with the most basic skills, you will be able to find something to suit you.

Preparation times vary and things like fudge, for instance, require patience. But you'll have the pleasure of watching the ingredients blend and meld and metamorphose into something splendid. Others take just a few minutes, meaning almost instant gratification. All of the recipes have been well tested, but if things don't turn out the way they should, don't throw away your efforts prematurely. If you read the temperature on the thermometer wrongly, for instance, and your caramel doesn't reach the right setting stage, you can use it warm as a sauce or topping. Remember that commercial sweets are made up to precise formulas that will produce uniform taste, texture and appearance and cannot be compared on any level with the joy of homemade ones. It can take a try or two to get accustomed to boiling and working with sugar and a minor setback can happen on occasion. Approach things lightly and enjoy yourself. Sweet-making at home should be a pleasurable activity with a tangible reward at the end. Once you have made them, you can brighten up so many peoples' day. Single items, or boxes of assorted fudge, truffles or brownies all make good gifts, especially when well packaged. Don't forget to add a little card with storage advice and an indication of shelf life.

I have greatly enjoyed putting together this collection and I hope it will appeal. For those of you who like to have their food put into perspective, there is background information sprinkled throughout the book. For those who prefer to get straight down to business, do so, but take the time to read through the ingredients and method before you start, so that your products turn out as they should.

Enjoy!

Ingredients

Here are a few things you should know about the ingredients used in this book, given in alphabetical order.

Amarena cherries

Small, firm and flavourful cherries sold in jars with syrup. The best brands are Italian. The syrup can be used over ice cream and desserts when the cherries are gone.

Baking powder

This is usually a combination of bicarbonate of soda and an acid agent that is mixed to a special formula and sold as baking powder. Double-acting baking powder is fairly standard nowadays and although it works in two spurts, once when liquid is added and next when heated, it is still imperative that cakes be baked as soon as they are mixed. Biscuit doughs with baking powder that need to rest before baking have been designed with that in mind.

Bicarbonate of soda

On its own, bicarbonate of soda doesn't have much power and needs an acid to help it act. This will usually be provided in the recipe, so there is no need to take further action.

Butter

Unless otherwise stated, unsalted butter is used throughout this book. Do not substitute margarine; it lacks flavour and will not give the same result, because it may behave erratically, depending on its composition.

Cocoa

All of my recipes use premium quality alkalised cocoa. Alkalisation (a process also called 'Dutching') reduces the acidity and gives a deep colour and is standard in Europe. Non-alkalised cocoa is the norm in the United States and needs an acid ingredient to make it taste well in a cake. Readers should look for European-style cocoa.

Chocolate

The Before You Start section (see p.22) gives a lot of general information about chocolate, but here are the practicalities. Choose any good-quality chocolate that you like, but I would suggest something along the following lines as far as the percentage of cocoa solids go: dark chocolate 55–70%; milk chocolate at least 35%; and white chocolate at least 30%. If you deviate greatly from these, you can expect different results. Callebaut 55% is my standard dark chocolate and it is what I use when a recipe simply says 'dark chocolate'; it is easy-going and will allow itself to be put to almost any use. For truffles, Lindt 70% has a wonderful fruity flavour, but needs a little more attention. Green and Black's is also superb.

Chocolate Vermicelli

Also known as sprinkles, these are small, thin lengths of dark, milk or white chocolate and sometimes come as flattened flakes. They are good for decorating chocolates, especially truffles. Interestingly, the Dutch look down on them as decoration because they are usually eaten on bread. They come in a variety of flavours and qualities, including intensely dark.

Coconut

Only one recipe calls for fresh coconut, which can also be bought ready-grated and frozen. The others use unsweetened desiccated coconut that comes in fine or medium cuts. When a specific cut is required in the recipe, substituting another may alter the results, but there will no dramatic changes.

Cornflour

This is not to be confused with cornmeal, which is ground from the whole kernel. Cornflour is the starch extracted from corn and as it contains next to no gluten, it is often used to 'cut' flour, producing a more tender product.

Cream
Double cream is used in these recipes and it is interchangeable with whipping cream as long as the fat content is at least 48%. Use single cream (18% fat) only if specifically requested. Pasteurised cream from the chilling cabinet has a far finer flavour than UHT (ultra heat-treated) cream, which has a longer shelf life.

Crystallised petals
Crystallised rose and violet petals add fragrance and colour to whatever they adorn. Whole petals are eye-catching but quite expensive and the more economical fragments are usually large enough to decorate chocolates. Note that both kinds are hard and solidly coated with sugar; they are not simply petals that have been dipped in egg white and passed through sugar.

Eggs
The eggs called for weigh between 60 g/2$\frac{1}{5}$ oz and 65 g/2$\frac{1}{4}$ oz in the shell, yielding a net weight between 50 g/1$\frac{3}{4}$ oz and 55 g/2 oz. A few grams will not affect the overall outcome in a cake, but for recipes where a weight is given for egg whites, do stick strictly to that. The egg whites in nougat and marshmallows are uncooked and although it is quite rare for whites to be infected with salmonella, they could form a potential health risk for vulnerable groups such as young children, pregnant women, the elderly and those whose immune systems are under strain. Small cartons of pasteurised egg whites are becoming increasingly available in large supermarkets. This will be a safer option, but it is up to you to choose what to do.

Flour
Unless otherwise stated, this refers to wheat flour. I use plain flour. This allows the raising agent to be added as required and it does not contain any salt, as some kinds of self-raising flours do.

Flower waters
Rose water is distilled from the petals of roses, and orange flower water from the flowers of bitter oranges. Both have a distinctive and fragrant perfume and combine well with sweet things. Buy wisely and choose pure products, as there are many inferior brands on the market that are synthetic and nasty tasting. Indian grocers will sometimes steer you in the direction of *kewra* extract or essence as a substitute for rose water. However, *kewra* extract is made from the flowers of the screwpine (*Pandanus tectorius*) and has a different flavour.

Ghee
Ghee is clarified butter widely employed in Indian dishes. It contains less moisture than butter, making it less prone to spitting and burning when heated in a pan. Vegetable ghee is simply a nice name for margarine, so beware.

Glucose syrup (see Liquid glucose)

Gold and silver leaf
Sold in tiny vials or in books between sheets of tissue paper, these are pure forms of the metals and are edible although without apparent flavour. They are hammered down from small nuggets to an almost unbelievable thinness. Buy from a reliable source to ensure pureness; there have been cases in India of aluminium being substituted for silver. Indian grocers stock silver leaf (called vark), which is abundantly employed as a decoration for sweets. Gold leaf, which is more expensive, is available from good stockists of cake decorating materials and makes an extremely elegant decoration for chocolates and cakes.

Golden syrup and corn syrup
Golden syrup is a golden-coloured flavourful by-product of cane sugar refining that is used in sweets and cakes as

well as on its own as a sweetener. Unless actively encouraged to do so in the recipe, do not substitute corn syrup of any kind. The two syrups are very different in composition and arbitrary substitution can have unexpected – usually negative – results. Even when substitution is possible, the proportions may vary. Because golden syrup is often used in the UK as a substitute for corn syrup, many believe that it works both ways, and that golden syrup can be replaced with corn syrup. It may work in recipes with a soft baked filling, such as Pecan Pie (the American original uses corn syrup in any case), but many hard sweets such as brittle and honeycomb need golden syrup to achieve the characteristic flavour and texture. Where possible, I have given alternatives in the recipes, but I urge readers most fervently to look for Lyle's Golden Syrup. It can be found in many large supermarkets, in international groceries and most certainly online. Amazon carry it in both tins and bottles.

Gram flour
Often referred to by its Indian name *besan*, gram flour is made from chickpeas. Toasting brings out a pleasant nutty aroma that makes it delicious in sweets. It is generally used in its natural form in savoury dishes. Indian brands are best for these recipes.

Green tea powder
This is *matcha*, a very fine powdered tea that is best known as Japanese tea ceremony tea. It gives marvellous colour and flavour to sweets and baked treats. It is quite expensive, but a little goes a long way. You will not be able to achieve the same effect if you try to turn green tea leaves into powder at home.

Honey
The oldest sweetener known to man is not quite immune to human intervention. There is pure natural honey that is totally untampered with and there is 'pure' honey made by bees who have been fed large amounts of sugar to speed up production and eliminate the need to forage. Then there is thickened sugar syrup sold by the unscrupulous as honey. Obviously, pure and natural honey is to be used. I use runny golden to amber-coloured honey unless otherwise stated.

Hundreds and thousands
These are called coloured sprinkles in the US, but they are not exactly the same as they are tiny sticks. Hundreds and thousands are minute sugar balls coated with bright colours and make a simple but attractive decoration.

Liqueurs and spirits
Use sipping quality ones that you would also enjoy in a glass. They have the strongest flavour in uncooked preparations such as truffles. Cooking will make the alcohol evaporate, leaving flavour without an alcoholic kick. Maraschino is very often sold in tiny bottles, so you can use it up very quickly as needed, with little loss of flavour.

Liquid glucose
Liquid glucose is a thick clear syrup that is valued in sweet-making because it retards crystal formation and allows a smooth texture to develop. It is not quite the same in composition as light corn syrup, but can be substituted if absolutely necessary.

Milk
When simply 'milk' is called for, you can use either full cream milk with a fat content of 3–4%, or semi-skimmed milk with a fat content of 2%. Take the advice given in the recipe into account – for instance, using pasteurised whole milk rather than homogenised or UHT (ultra heat-treated) milk for making *paneer*. Evaporated milk has had almost half of its moisture removed, leaving a concentrated cream-coloured product with a slightly caramelised taste. It is not sweetened, unlike condensed milk whose sticky texture is due to its being cooked with sugar until thick and concentrated. Powdered milk (called dry milk by some) comes in full cream and fat-free variants that are widely used in Indian sweets. The two are not interchangeable, so use the kind specified.

Molasses (see Treacle)

Nuts
Buy your nuts as freshly as you can from a reliable source. Walnuts are best bought in the shell, unless you

use large amounts at a time. Choose French walnuts above Indian and Chinese. They are worth the expense. When selecting pistachios, try to get attractive green ones. Good-quality ground almonds will be finer than you can achieve at home and flaked almonds are best bought. Cashews have more flavour if you toast them just before use, so buy raw nuts from an Asian grocer or health food shop. See the Nice and Nutty chapter (p.128) for more information about nuts. The Before You Start section (p.22) will also tell you more about how to deal with the nuts.

Rice flour
There is a clear distinction between glutinous and non-glutinous rice flours and the two are not interchangeable. Glutinous rice flour gives a gummy texture and is used primarily in Asian food. Non-glutinous rice flour is used in this book. It is the 'regular' kind that you will find on a Western supermarket shelf. It makes looser-textured cakes and biscuits.

Semolina
Coarsely milled durum wheat that comes in fine, medium and coarse grades. It holds its shape well after cooking and retains moisture, adding bite and texture to products.

Silver balls
These balls of sugar are coated with a fine layer of edible silver and come in various sizes. They have no clear flavour apart from sugar and are used for decoration.

Starch wafers
Also known as edible wafer paper, starch wafers are made from various kinds of starches and are very useful for lining tins when making sticky confectionery. Sweet shops sell coloured versions, but plain white gives the best effect.

Stem ginger
Comes in jars, preserved in syrup. The pieces are usually the size of a finger joint and, as it is a natural product, strength varies. It is usually chopped very finely before being added.

Sugar
Given the choice, I would always choose cane sugar above beet sugar, as it has so much more flavour. However, in Europe we generally have to make do with the beet sugar that lines supermarket shelves, with the exception of demerara sugar. Real demerara sugar has very hard golden crystals and does not dissolve easily. This makes it unsuitable for creaming with butter, but it is very good in sweets when you take the time to handle it as it should be. Granulated sugar is the coarsest of the other sugars, followed by caster sugar, which has slightly smaller crystals. Icing sugar is ground to a fine powder and dissolves almost instantly. Each kind of sugar has been chosen for its special characteristics, so do not interchange them in the recipes, except in rare cases where absolutely necessary, such as substituting granulated sugar for unreliable brands of demerara sugar. (Please also see Before You Start, About Sugar, p.22.)

Treacle (dark)
Dark treacle is known as molasses in some countries. Like golden syrup, it is a by-product of cane sugar refining, but unlike its clearer and sweeter sister, dark treacle is extremely deep in colour and has a pleasantly pungent, earthy flavour with a restrained sweetness. It gives a unique flavour to sweets and cakes.

Vanilla
I find that with vanilla, you get what you pay for, so it is well worth spending a little extra on this most delectable of flavourings as it will add life to your sweets. Choose natural extracts or fresh soft pods. The main kinds are Tahitian, Madagascar and Mexican and each has its own flavour characteristics.

Vinegar
A few of the sweets require vinegar. Use a neutral-tasting natural product.

Sweet-making Equipment

To make life easier for you, I have provided a list of equipment at the beginning of some chapters, but here is a summary:

Sugar thermometer
This is the only way to guarantee success with mixtures that need to be cooked to a specific temperature. See p.22 for details on using a sugar thermometer and a few tips on how to check the stages manually.

Chocolate thermometer
A chocolate thermometer is required for tempering chocolate. It is easier to read than a sugar thermometer, as it has a narrower and more clearly defined range.

Dipping forks
If you plan to dip truffles and chocolates in melted chocolate, dipping forks are highly recommended. Round ones with a simple loop are good for truffles and forks with long and thin tines will work well for other shapes. A dining fork can be used if necessary, but you will not have quite such a neat result as the tines are thick and close together and will retain more chocolate than necessary.

Saucepans
Each recipe tells you what size saucepan to use and whether it should be coated or not. While coated pans are excellent for sticky mixtures such as many Indian sweets, other mixtures are best cooked in uncoated pans with a very heavy base. That way, you can monitor colour changes better and the contents will be less likely to burn.

Double boiler
Chocolate needs to be melted slowly and carefully, especially if it is to be used as a coating. A double boiler does the best job. If you don't have one, improvise by using a saucepan topped by a heatproof bowl that fits snugly on top, so that no steam can escape and spoil the chocolate.

Spatulas, spoons and scrapers
Wooden spoons and spatulas and silicone spatulas are called for. Wooden spoons are an all-purpose aid for very liquid mixtures, but spatulas are good for scraping the bases of pans. Silicone spatulas are useful for their flexibility to scrape things that are in danger of sticking to the sides of pans. Flexible plastic scrapers are good for any number of jobs, especially those that involve removing or spreading sticky mixtures.

Whisk
A small wire whisk is useful for stirring mixtures that have a tendency to become lumpy and will also give a smoother finish than a spoon when blending other ingredients such as chocolate and cream.

Silicone mat
A silicone mat is a wonderful non-stick aid that can replace baking parchment or greaseproof paper in many cases and can also be used to roll out anything from pastry to marzipan.

Baking parchment and greaseproof paper
Useful for lining tins for both sweets and cakes, baking parchment is coated with silicone, making release easy. It can be used with hot or cold mixtures. Use greaseproof paper for cold or cool mixtures, or the wax coating will melt and stick firmly to the product as it cools.

Clingfilm
This is absolutely essential for wrapping and also for rolling marzipan and pastry in a mess-free and safe way.

Rolling pin
I use plain wooden rolling pins that have become seasoned with use. A working length of about 30 cm/12 in will cover most possibilities.

Palette knife
A large offset palette knife will serve most purposes. A small one is useful for decorating smaller items neatly.

Metal ruler
A ruler is absolutely essential for measuring diameters, heights and widths. A metal one is very hygienic in the kitchen, as it can be washed after use.

Tins for moulding
The recipes tell you what size to use for which purpose. A 20-cm/8-in square tin and small, medium and large loaf tins will take you quite far. The base measurements are more important than the volume in most cases. Here are some indications:
Small: 8.5 x 17 cm/3 x 7 in.
Medium: 10 x 20 cm/4 x 8 in.
Large: 10.5 x 29 cm/4 x 11 in, or 11.5 x 23 cm/4½ x 9 in.

Heavy-duty electric mixer
A heavy-duty freestanding electric mixer makes quick work of cake batters and is also needed for some sweets such as marzipan and nougat. Hand-whisking can replace it in some cases, but always check the advice in the recipe.

Hand-held stick blender
This is one of the most useful tools to have in the kitchen. It is extremely easy to use as it can be immersed into any bowl of mixture. It gives unbeatably smooth results for sauces, fudge, etc., but will not introduce much air and is less suitable for whipping cream.

Food processor
A food processor is an ideal tool for grinding nuts finely or chopping chocolate. Failing that, you can try a hand-held rotary grater for nuts and a regular coarse grater for chocolate.

Scales and measuring equipment
I cannot stress enough how important good digital scales are; they are the only way to ensure accuracy.

I am not a fan of volume measurements as they can be very hit-or-miss, depending on how you use them, e.g. spooning flour into a cup or dipping the flour from a canister with the cup. Liquid measures are fine, as are measuring spoons for small amounts of dry ingredients and liquids. When things like syrup and honey are given by weight, an easy way to measure them is to put the container on the scales and use the tare function to set it at 0. After that you simply have to keep count of how much you have removed. For instance, removing 25 g/1 oz will register as -25 g/-1 oz. If you don't have a tare function, you can do it by mental arithmetic.

Wrapping and packaging for presentation
Attractive presentation can give great satisfaction. Think of truffles in coloured cases packed in a pretty cardboard box or peppermint creams in foil wrappers or neat stacks of biscuits in paper cases in a tin. Here are some of the items you might like to consider:

* Foil sweet wrappers
* Squares of greaseproof paper
* Foil or paper cases in various sizes
* Pretty tins for biscuits
* Decorated waxed cardboard boxes
* Food grade cellophane bags and pouches
* Food grade roll of cellophane

Stockists
A quick surf on the internet will soon find any online suppliers or cake decorating shops in your neighbourhood and many items are now stocked in the baking section of good supermarkets. Check shops that carry articles for kids' parties too; they often have colourful waxed cardboard boxes in various sizes, intended for carry-home treats. I have used Jane Asher and Squires Kitchen's mail order services and find them to be prompt and efficient. They stock all kinds of exciting articles including thermometers, gold and silver leaf, flower waters and pretty packaging materials.
www.janeasher.com
www.squires-shop.com

Baking Equipment

As baking is familiar to most people, there is no list at the beginning of the relevant chapters. Instead, here is some information to help you on your way.

Oven

I find electric ovens to be the most reliable kind. Always preheat the oven to the required temperature and place the rack so that the article to be baked will sit in or just under the centre of the oven. The temperatures given here should work with both conventional and fan-assisted ovens, as the times are quite short. Browning tends to occur a little earlier in a fan-assisted oven. Cooking times are indications and what will work to the minute in one oven will need less or more time in another. That is why I always try to describe what to look for, such as colour, firmness, etc.

Electrical appliances

Other appliances (mixers, blenders and food processors) are discussed in Sweet-making Equipment on p.19.

Scales and measuring equipment

See Sweet-making Equipment on p.19.

Whisks

The most useful whisk in my kitchen is a balloon whisk. It allows a lot of air to enter whisked mixtures and is also the best instrument for folding dry ingredients into wet, keeping the mixture light.

Cutters

Plain and serrated round cutters are useful for cutting out tartlets. Always wash and dry them well after use so that they do not rust. You may need to flour or dust them with icing sugar when cutting out sticky doughs and marzipan.

Baking tins

Each recipe specifies what kind of tin to use. Good-quality ones will not warp. Note that dark tins will cook faster than light or uncoated ones. Always prepare them as advised, even if they are non-stick.

Cake testers

Simple thin bamboo skewers or wooden toothpicks are best for testing for doneness. Special non-stick testers are useless, as their non-stick properties will prevent the batter from sticking to them, cooked or not.

Wire racks

If baked goods are not allowed to cool properly on a wire rack, they will go soggy from the condensation that builds up.

Before You Start

About weights and measures

I urge you in the strongest of terms to use metric weights. These are not only extremely precise, but they also show you the proportions at a glance. Imperial weights are the next best thing, but it is not that easy to weigh out quarter ounces. Volume measurements make me uneasy. 100g is always 100g, and a pound is always a pound. When it comes to volume, a cup is what the cook makes of it. If flour is dipped from a bag and the crown swept off with a knife, it can weigh 10-20% more than a cup into which flour is spooned. Similarly, a reader will immediately understand that 100g of ground blanched almonds is exactly the same as 100g of blanched almonds that still have to be ground. Using cups the reader must be careful to read what is intended: is it 1 cup of already ground blanched almonds or 1 cup of blanched almonds, still to be ground? Careless reading can cause unnecessary problems. If you use volume measurements, note that the 'dip and sweep' method has been used in the conversions in this book.

About sugar

Sugar is such a plain and simple ingredient, but there can be pitfalls. Although each recipe tells you what kind of sugar to use for the promised result, it is an unfortunate fact of life that sugar can vary, depending on its origin and method of production. I have never had any trouble with granulated, caster and icing sugars, but demerara sugar now comes in many guises. Real demerara sugar is a joy. It is unrefined cane sugar that has hard, pale golden crystals with a flavour that veers towards caramel. However, it dissolves more slowly than other types and if you rush things and bring it to the boil before it dissolves completely, it will re-crystallise erratically and give hard flecks to your sweets. An even greater problem is the authenticity of demerara sugar and the creative new ways of labelling. I strongly suspect some types of being tampered with. Avoid any demerara sugar that is too moist; particularly avoid 'dark' demerara sugar, which is so syrupy as to lean towards muscovado. These will make your sweets sandy-textured. If in any doubt, substitute granulated sugar for demerara.

Boiling Sugar

A **sugar thermometer** is really the only fail-safe way to ensure the correct temperature and stage of the sugar. Buy a good one and put your trust in it. I like a flat clip-on model, with the bulb neatly encased so that it does not touch the base of the pan and give you a reading for the pan rather than its contents. The clip is usually adjustable and once you attach it to the pan, it stays in place so that you can constantly monitor the temperature. The stages are usually also printed on the flat metal backing in both Celsius and Fahrenheit, leaving little room for error. Whatever thermometer you choose, make sure that it is a sugar thermometer and not an ordinary cooking one, and read the manufacturer's instructions carefully. Unless your thermometer is digital, bend down to read it from the front – don't look down from above, which may give you a false reading.

To check the accuracy of your thermometer, put it in a pan of boiling water and see if it registers 100°C/212°F. If you can't use a thermometer, guidelines for hand-testing follow and the names of the stages are very descriptive. You may get some deviation as to texture, so be prepared for that. Milk mixtures are not usually cooked beyond firm ball stage. Chewy caramels and toffees go from firm to hard ball stage. Brittles go from soft to hard crack. Follow the directions in each individual recipe.

Thread (110–112°C/230–234°F): Press some of the mixture between your thumb and forefinger, then extend your fingers. The mixture should stretch in a thread.

Soft ball (112–115°C/234–240°F): Pour a little of the mixture into a bowl of very cold water. If you press it between your thumb and forefinger, it should stay together as a very soft whole without dissolving or falling apart immediately.

Firm ball (118–120°C/245–248°F): Pour a little of the mixture into a bowl of very cold water. If you press it between your thumb and forefinger, it should form a firmly pliable whole.

Hard ball (121–130°C/250–265°F): Pour a little of the mixture into a bowl of very cold water. If you press it between your thumb and forefinger, it should stay together as a hard and barely pliable ball that will not crack when pressed.

Soft crack (132–143°C/270–290°F): Pour a little of the syrup into cold water. It will harden into threads but will still be flexible.

Hard crack (149–154°C/300–310°F): Pour a little of the syrup into cold water. It will harden into brittle threads that break when you try to bend them.

Caramel (158–170°C/320–340°F): The syrup will darken in colour. The sugar breaks down and re-forms crystals in a different way. Strange though it may sound, the darker the colour, the softer the caramel.

Use a **saucepan** that is uncoated so that you can see the changes of colour. The saucepan should be quite large, holding at least four to five times the amount you put in. Sugar syrups bubble merrily but fairly modestly; fudge can be quite tempestuous, rising volcanically from time to time. See Creamy Creations (p.80) for more specific information on milk and sugar mixtures.

Follow the instructions in the recipe regarding **stirring**, or you can get very unexpected results. If you don't allow the sugar to dissolve, for instance, before boiling it to the required stage, you may find that it all crystallises on the surface, looking like a desert landscape, and it will be next to impossible to break up all the crystals in time for it to cook to the right consistency.

Simple sugar mixtures tend to cook a lot faster than those enriched with milk and butter. Enriched or not, the mixture 'pauses'. Just when you think that things are moving along nicely, it pauses quite stubbornly and may even make a slight downward movement before continuing to climb again in the right direction.

! Attractive though it is to allow children to see things like honeycomb foam, keep them away from the actual process, as hot sugar can inflict severe burns if treated carelessly and accidental spills do happen to even the most careful cook.

Preparing Nuts

Each recipe tells you whether the nuts should be toasted or not, and if you should leave them whole, chop or grind them.

To toast nuts, preheat the oven to 180°C/350°F/Gas Mark 4. Scatter the nuts in a single layer on a baking sheet with sides. Give the sheet a shake a few times during the process. The exact toasting time depends on how well toasted you want the nuts to be and toasting is meant to bring out the flavour. If you allow them to become too brown, they will have an unpleasantly bitter taste. Use the following guidelines based on whole skinless nuts, but rely on your sight and sense of smell. Allow them to cool before using, unless the recipe explicitly states otherwise.

Almonds 10–12 minutes

Cashews 8–10 minutes

Hazelnuts 10–12 minutes

Pine nuts 5 minutes

Pistachios 7–10 minutes

Walnuts and pecans with skins 10–12 minutes (although I find them better and sweeter untoasted)

Macadamias are crisp enough to use as they are

You can also toast nuts in a dry frying pan, but timing depends on the pan, heat and type of nuts. I generally use the frying pan only for pine nuts. Keep shaking the pan until the nuts reach the desired stage. The drawback with this method is that the nuts are prone to developing dark spots where they come into contact with the pan and do not colour as evenly as in the oven.

Grinding is best done in a food processor and if you add a small amount of the sugar or flour from the recipe (don't add extra!), you will be able to grind finer and drier as some of the oil will be absorbed.

Chopping is best done by hand so that you can monitor the size of the pieces. A large knife and a chopping board will work well, but if you have one, a mezzaluna and a shallow wooden bowl (used to chop fresh herbs) work even better, as the nuts don't fly all over the place.

Melting and tempering chocolate

Chocolate needs to be **melted** for a number of recipes. Chop it into small pieces to ensure even melting. If you are handy with the microwave method, use it by all means and remember to use short bursts rather than prolonged heating. I don't care for this method, as it can scorch the chocolate and it heats less evenly. Slower and more even melting over hot water on the stove is better. If you don't have a double boiler, improvise one with a saucepan and a heatproof bowl that fits snugly over it so that steam will not escape and fall onto the chocolate. The water should be barely simmering and the bowl should not touch the water. Leave to melt, stirring as necessary, and remove from the heat. If the chocolate is to be combined with cream (for truffles and glazes), the cream is usually heated in a pan and the finely chopped chocolate is added off the heat and left to melt before being stirred until smooth.

Melted chocolate will be fine for most things, but if you want a crisp and shiny finish, you will need to **temper** it. I'll provide you with some facts and views as well as a way to temper chocolate manually, and leave you to decide whether it is for you.

Essentially, tempering chocolate means putting it into a good frame of mind so that it will set with a crispness and attractive sheen. This can happen only if the cocoa butter melts completely and is evenly distributed. Tempered chocolate will also contract on cooling, so tempering is absolutely necessary for moulded chocolates or you will have a hard time prising them out of their moulds. Professional chocolatiers use machines that will do it all and end up with great results. Hand tempering has got to be the most frustrating culinary process known to man. It sometimes seems that every possible element joins the conspiracy to sabotage all one's careful monitoring. And you don't discover it until you have dipped an entire batch. The dipped chocolates glisten up at you very desirably and bit by bit they set. If you have been successful, they will keep on glistening, but in a dry way. The odd renegade or two are not so hard to take; they can be eaten as samples. But when you see a pattern, like a gilded abstract painting appear, dejection sets in. The first time it happens, you tell yourself that it is actually quite a nice pattern. But you know that you would prefer to have no pattern. I cling to the consoling belief that hand-tempering does not sit well with my philosophy that sweet-making should be enjoyable and rarely bother with it. There are many methods, some involving several stages of heating and cooling, others requiring some of the chocolate to be worked on a marble slab. I use the following method on the rare occasions that I bother to temper. I have found that larger quantities work better than smaller ones and it will be hardly worth your while to use less than 500 g/1 lb 2 oz. The excess can be re-melted later for other uses.

You will need a **chocolate thermometer**. A sugar thermometer will not work as the range is wider and that makes it difficult to get a precise reading. Chop the chocolate finely. Melt 80 per cent of the quantity in the pan or bowl above barely simmering water and allow dark chocolate to reach 45°C/113°F (milk chocolate 32°C/90°F and white 30°C/86°F). Remove the pan or bowl immediately and put it on a wooden surface or a mat. Thoroughly stir in the remaining 20 per cent, then allow the temperature to decrease to 30–32°C/86–90°F (milk chocolate 30°C/86°F and white 28°C/82°F). If you need to dip a lot of chocolates, put the bowl of tempered chocolate over a pan of warm (not hot) water to keep the temperature stable.

Caramels, Toffees and More

Makes 16 clusters of a satisfying size

175 g/6 oz/scant 1 cup demerara sugar

150 g/5½ oz/½ cup golden syrup or
light corn syrup

2 tbsp water

200 ml/7 fl oz/generous ¾ cup double cream

⅛ tsp salt

125 g/4½ oz/1¼ cups walnuts, coarsely chopped

250 g/9 oz/9 squares dark chocolate,
tempered or simply melted (see p.25)

Soft caramel with chunky bits of walnut, together
with thin trails of dark chocolate, make these
clusters irresistible. Packaged in pretty cases
or paper cups and arranged in an attractive
box or tin, they make a good gift - if you can
bear to part with them. Tempered chocolate will
give a shinier and crisper finish, but you can
simply melt the chocolate.

Caramel Nut Clusters

Put the sugar, syrup and water into a large heavy-based uncoated saucepan and stir over low heat until the sugar dissolves completely. Undissolved sugar will make your caramel grainy. Attach a sugar thermometer to the pan, increase the heat and leave to boil without stirring until it reaches 120°C/248°F (firm ball stage). It will take about 4–5 minutes.

Meanwhile, heat the cream in a small saucepan and have it standing by. Stir in the hot cream as soon as the sugar reaches the correct temperature, stirring constantly. It will hiss and spit in the beginning. Once the cream is well incorporated, leave the mixture to continue boiling without stirring until it reaches 120°C/248°F once again. This will take about 15–18 minutes (or longer for corn syrup), but rely on the thermometer and keep a close watch. Take the pan off the heat, remove the thermometer and stir in the salt and walnuts. Leave the mixture to rest for about 15 minutes, or until it thickens enough to hold its shape when scooped out.

Use 2 dessertspoons to scoop out and drop 16 clusters onto a sheet of baking parchment or directly into your cupcake cases. They should spread only minimally. Leave to cool.

When the clusters have cooled completely and set into soft caramel, they can be dipped or decorated. To dip: loosen them from the baking parchment. Prick a cluster with a cocktail stick or lay one on a dipping fork and dip it into the melted chocolate to coat. Tap the stick or fork several times on the edge of the bowl so that excess chocolate falls back into the bowl. Return the coated cluster to the baking parchment. Pull out the cocktail stick and neaten the tiny hole it leaves. Coat the other clusters in the same way. As you near the end, you may need to use a small spoon to help coat the tops. Alternatively: use a spoonful of melted chocolate to trail thin zig-zag lines over the tops of your caramel clusters. Leave to set.

Makes about 24

125 g/4½ oz/generous ⅓ cup dark treacle

125 g/4½ oz/generous ⅓ cup golden syrup
or light corn syrup

75 g/2¾ oz/¼ cup + 2 tbsp granulated sugar

25 g/1 oz/2 tbsp (¼ stick) butter, flaked

125 g/4½ oz/1⅓ cups desiccated coconut,
preferably medium cut, plus about
40–50 g/1½–1¾ oz/scant ½–½ cup extra
desiccated coconut, for rolling

generous ¼ tsp ground cinnamon

¼ tsp freshly grated nutmeg

Trinidadians have a much-loved homely confection that is known as 'tooloom' or 'touloum'. It is made from local molasses (dark treacle), sugar and freshly grated coconut, cooked together for a while until the mixture reaches the right consistency, then rolled into balls. I decided to go for a quick and easy hybrid that is in the style of 'tooloom', using desiccated coconut. It is supposed to be a sticky toffee, so don't overcook the mixture or you will end up with coconut-coated hockey pucks. Conversely, if a trial toffee spreads too much, knead a few extra tablespoons of coconut into the warm mixture before continuing to shape the balls.

Coconut Toffees

Put the treacle, syrup, sugar and butter into a medium uncoated heavy-based saucepan and stir over low heat until the butter melts and the sugar dissolves completely. The butter will melt quite quickly, but it will take a while for the sugar to dissolve properly. Attach a sugar thermometer to the pan, increase the heat and bring to the boil. Leave to boil just until it reaches 112–113°C/234–235°F (soft ball stage), then remove immediately from the heat. This can go extremely fast and the golden syrup version can get there in about 3–4 minutes, so keep a sharp eye on the thermometer. To hand-test, drop a little of the mixture into a bowl filled with cold water. If you can press it together into a soft ball, it is ready.

Working quickly or the toffee will harden, stir in the coconut and spices. Mix well for a minute or so, then leave to stand for about 5 minutes. Give the mixture a good stir and scrape it out onto a corner of a silicone mat or sheet of baking parchment. Leave to stand for a few minutes until cool enough to handle but still soft. Scatter the extra coconut onto the mat or baking parchment.

Using a small dessertspoon or a large teaspoon, dip spoonfuls of the toffee mixture, working from around the edges inwards. Roll into truffle-sized balls between your palms, moistening them lightly with water if necessary. Roll the balls in the coconut and set to one side as you continue to roll the rest. They are very attractive as they are, served on a pretty plate, but you can also make them more special by putting them in foil sweet cases or cups.

My mother-in-law grew up in a sweet shop - or the next best thing - and remained an ardent supporter of the confectionery industry until her death. Her parents owned a delicatessen in The Hague, specialising in fine groceries, sweets, chocolates and nuts. Chocolate-coated toffees were one of her favourites and she kept them with the rest of her stash in a small cupboard conveniently situated next to her armchair. Letting ourselves in through the back door and calling out to announce ourselves, we would often receive a thick response as she hastily disposed of the remnant in her mouth. We now live in that house, but I keep CDs and DVDs in that cupboard and leave the sweets downstairs in the kitchen, because I could so easily fall into the same trap. She would have enjoyed these soft caramels, which are far easier on the teeth than her toffees were, although this caramel is firmer than the Caramel Nut Clusters (see p.29).

Makes about 24

225 g/8 oz/generous 1 cup caster sugar

185 g/6½ oz/½ cup golden syrup or light corn syrup

2 tbsp water

250 ml/9 fl oz/generous 1 cup double cream

¼ tsp salt

¾–1 tsp vanilla extract

30 g/1 oz/2 tbsp (¼ stick) butter, flaked

250 g/9 oz/9 squares melted or tempered dark chocolate (see p.25), for dipping (optional)

Caramels

Line a large loaf tin with baking parchment.

Put the sugar, syrup and water into a large uncoated heavy-based saucepan and stir over low heat until the sugar dissolves completely. Undissolved sugar will make your caramel grainy. Attach a sugar thermometer to the pan, increase the heat and leave to boil without stirring until it reaches 120°C/248°F (firm ball stage). It will take about 4–5 minutes (corn syrup may need extra time).

Meanwhile, heat the cream in a small saucepan and have it standing by. Stir in the hot cream as soon as the sugar reaches the correct temperature, stirring constantly. It will hiss and spit in the beginning. Once the cream is well incorporated, leave the mixture to continue boiling without stirring until it reaches 122°C/252°F this time. This will take a little longer than 25 minutes, but rely on the thermometer and keep a close watch. Take the pan off the heat, remove the thermometer and stir in the salt, vanilla and butter. Pour into the loaf tin and leave to set.

Cut the caramel when completely set. You can cut them into squares and wrap in cellophane, or first dip them in chocolate (see Totally Truffles p.150). Unwrapped or uncoated caramels will eventually spread at room temperature so store in an airtight container in a cool place. They will keep for about a week. Don't refrigerate the chocolate-coated ones, or they will discolour.

Makes about 32 small squares

200 g/7 oz/1 cup granulated sugar

75 g/2¾ oz/scant ¼ cup golden syrup

50 g/1¾ oz/3½ tbsp butter, plus extra for greasing

50 ml/1¾ fl oz/scant ¼ cup double cream

100 ml/3½ fl oz/scant ½ cup very strong coffee

These candies are said to have been invented in the latter half of the eighteenth century by Baron Hendrik Hop from The Hague. His fondness for coffee bordered on addiction and he gladly believed in the medicinal properties that were ascribed to it in those days, supposing it to relieve his gout. Eventually, he drank so much coffee that he developed a stomach complaint and his doctor forbade its use, and the sediment in a forgotten cup of sweet coffee inspired him to approach a local sweet maker with the request for a coffee-flavoured sweet. Another variant suggests that the addiction was so great that he longed for coffee while travelling around in his coach on diplomatic business. As it was not practical to drink liquids in a moving vehicle, he had the sweets made as a substitute. Sweets and legends live on and there is even a small museum in The Hague dedicated to Baron Hop and his creation. The coffee flavour here will depend on the strength of your brew.

Coffee Blocks
Haagsche Hopjes

Line a small loaf tin (with a base measurement of approx. 10 x 15 cm/4 x 6 in) with baking parchment.

Put all of the ingredients into a large uncoated heavy-based saucepan and stir over low heat until the butter melts and the sugar dissolves completely. Attach a sugar thermometer to the pan, bring to the boil and leave to boil without stirring until it reaches 130°C/265°F (just past late hard ball stage and approaching soft crack stage). It will take about 25–30 minutes from the time it comes to a rolling boil, but rely on the thermometer.

Remove the thermometer and pour the mixture into the loaf tin. It will bubble up quite a lot, but keep on pouring steadily. Leave to cool until firm enough to cut.

Lift the block out of the tin and place on the work surface. Cut into about 32 squares with a greased knife and leave to cool completely, spaced well apart.

Store in an airtight container in a cool place, or they will stick together. You can also wrap them individually in small squares of greaseproof paper and store in a jar. They will keep for a week or two, but will become softer and stickier as time goes by.

Makes about 16

150 g/5½ oz/1 cup blanched almonds

large pinch of saffron strands

1 tbsp boiling water

200 g/7 oz/1 cup caster sugar

50 g/1¾ oz/scant ¼ cup runny honey

3 tbsp neutral-tasting oil (e.g. peanut or sunflower)

25–30 g/1 oz/scant ¼ cup pistachios, coarsely chopped

This Iranian treat looks like brittle but has more of a toffee texture. It is surprisingly easy - and quick - to make. If you don't have saffron strands, use a ¼ tsp ground saffron. And if you don't have that either, leave it out and call it Almond Toffee Clusters. On no account is it to be replaced with something like turmeric. It may have the same colour, but your beautiful toffee will taste like curry. Note too that my timings and temperatures will not work if you substitute butter, so do use the oil, even if your inner feeling tells you that butter is so flavourful. It is, but it will also behave differently.

Saffron and Almond Toffee Clusters

Sohan Asali

The almonds can be lightly toasted for added crunch, but that is up to you. Leave them to cool if toasted, then chop them coarsely. There will be fine bits and even a little powder in between, but leave it all in. It will add body to the mixture.

Leave the saffron strands to steep in the boiling water, or add the ground saffron to the water.

Put the sugar, honey and oil in a medium uncoated heavy-based saucepan and stir over medium–high heat to dissolve the sugar crystals. It will be a thick paste at first but will become liquid as it gets hotter. Attach a sugar thermometer to the pan and continue to stir. When the mixture reaches 100°C/212°F, stir in the almonds. It should take about 5 minutes to get there, but rely on the thermometer. Leave to cook further, stirring constantly, until the thermometer registers 130°C/265°F (just about to pass from hard ball to soft crack). This takes a minute or so, so be watchful. Pour in the saffron liquid while stirring. It will spit, but continue to stir until it reaches 130°C/265°F again. This will take another minute. Immediately take the pan off the heat and remove the thermometer.

Spoon about 16 tbsp of the beautiful golden mixture onto a sheet of baking parchment and decorate immediately with the chopped pistachios, pressing to embed them. Leave to cool completely. Store in a glass jar for up to a week, with small squares of baking parchment in between to discourage sticking.

The Lingering Quality of Treacle

Growing up in the former British colony of Guyana left us with a taste
for many British treats. When I was a child, we always had a huge tin of
Quality Street (an extremely popular brand of British sweets containing a
mix of toffees and chocolates) in the house; not one of those miserly little
ones that you could get in the supermarket, but one that would have done a
sweet shop proud. That tin was a source of joy to my sister and me and our
mother wisely kept it out of the kitchen storeroom. What she didn't know was
that we knew that it was kept on the highest shelf in one of the cupboards
that lined the corridor to the bedrooms. If the tin was at the front of the
shelf, I could reach it by climbing onto a lower shelf. If it got pushed to
the back, I couldn't touch it. In that case we made use of our trusted
accomplice: our father. We trusted him, not because he was our father, but
because he liked all the sweets in the tin that we didn't, like the soft
centred strawberry and coconut ones. My sister liked almost everything
else and my favourites were the green foil-covered chocolate
triangle, the large pointed purple one filled with caramel and
a nut, and the dark toffee in the amber-brown wrapper.
There was something about that toffee that made it
different from other toffees. Looking back,
it must have been the treacly flavour.

Makes at least 24 pieces

250 g/9 oz/1¼ cups demerara sugar

125 g/4½ oz/generous ⅓ cup dark treacle

60 g/2¼ oz/¼ cup (generous ½ stick) butter

1 tbsp water

1½ tsp white wine vinegar

sunflower oil, for oiling

These treacle toffees are quite simple to prepare at home if you have 15 minutes or so to spare. They are hard and brittle until you put one in your mouth and allow it to exude treacly goodness onto your tongue, softening towards the end into one last bit of chewiness.

Treacle Toffee

Generously line a small–medium loaf tin with baking parchment.

Put all of the ingredients (except the oil) into a large uncoated heavy-based saucepan and stir over low heat until the butter melts and the sugar dissolves. The butter will melt quite quickly, but it will take a while for the sugar to dissolve properly. Be patient and keep at it, as undissolved sugar will make your toffee grainy. Attach a sugar thermometer to the pan, increase the heat and, stirring constantly, leave to boil until it reaches 125°C/257°F (hard ball stage). This will give a very firm toffee and 130°C/265°F a harder one. Beyond this you will end up with a more break-teeth toffee. The entire process should take about 20 minutes, but rely on the thermometer and keep a close watch.

Pour the mixture into the loaf tin and leave it to firm up. Once it is firm enough to be cut, use a thin metal spatula to mark small squares right down to the bottom. Oil the spatula before each downward movement.

Now you can take one of two options. Option one is for those who are inclined towards neat presentation. Remove the paper with the toffee and use the oiled spatula to separate the pieces, allowing them to harden without touching each other.

Option two is for those who long for the nostalgia of bygone days, before health and hygiene rules and regulations caused block toffee to disappear from the counters of sweet shops. Leave the toffee to cool and harden in the tin. Once it becomes brittle, put it into a thick plastic bag and tap it with a kitchen mallet or small hammer, or just slap it against the work surface to break the toffee into pieces. Some pieces will break along the markings and others will shatter where they like. However you serve it, it is absolutely delicious.

Store in an airtight container between layers of greaseproof paper.

Quantity made will depend on the thickness

200 g/7 oz/generous ½ cup runny honey

100 g/3½ oz/½ cup granulated sugar

250 g/9 oz/2 cups toasted sesame seeds

Here is something with a nice chewy texture that could become a brittle if cooked to hard crack stage. This kind of simple confection has been made and eaten for countless centuries. When the Arabs introduced sugar from the Far East to the Western world, it gradually began to replace some or all of the honey in existing recipes. It is quick and easy to make and very wholesome. And I must say that the entire sheet lying on the mat looks very pretty, like a well-aged mosaic.

Chewy Sesame Strips

Put the honey and sugar in a medium uncoated heavy-based saucepan and stir over low heat until the sugar dissolves completely. Increase the heat and let it come to a rolling boil. Lower the heat, attach a sugar thermometer to the pan and cook until it reaches 134°C/273°F (soft crack stage). It will take about 5–6 minutes. Immediately take the pan off the heat, remove the thermometer and stir in the sesame seeds.

Scrape the mixture out onto a silicone mat or large sheet of baking parchment and quickly flatten it with a spatula. Top with another sheet of baking parchment and flatten with a rolling pin, rolling gently back and forth to achieve a thickness of ¼–½ cm/⅛–¼ in.

Remove the top sheet of parchment; it doesn't matter if there is some sugar mixture clinging to it. Use a straight-sided bench scraper or blunt knife to mark into rows about 3 cm/1¼ in wide, then again at right angles 5–6 cm/2–2½ in apart, to create bars. Press deeply and if using a knife and a silicone mat, be careful not to cut through it. Work fast, as the sugar will start to set. Leave to cool.

Once cool, transfer the mixture to a hard surface. Use a large knife to cut the bars apart along the depressions. The mixture is sticky, so press hard to cut right through.

Store in a tin lined with greaseproof paper, with sheets between each layer to prevent the pieces from sticking to each other. They will keep for several weeks.

**Makes a 20 x 20cm/8 x 8 in square,
to be broken into shards as desired**

150 g/5½ oz/¾ cup caster sugar

75 g/2¾ oz/scant ¼ cup golden syrup

1¾ tsp bicarbonate of soda

Honeycomb, known as 'hokey pokey' in New Zealand,
and several other names, is made from three
storecupboard staples, none of which is honey. The
name simply refers to the texture and appearance,
which is light, airy and crisp. It is perhaps best
known in the form of the mass-produced chocolate-
coated confectionery (Crunchie) bar and is quick and
easy to make at home, even without the aid of a
sugar thermometer. I enjoy preparing it because it
makes me feel like an alchemist when it starts
frothing and changes so completely after the
bicarbonate of soda is added. It can be eaten as
it is, mixed into ice cream, trifles and other
creamy desserts, or used as a crisp last minute
decoration straight from the freezer.

Honeycomb

Generously line a 20 x 20 cm/8 x 8 in baking tin with baking parchment.

Put the sugar and golden syrup into a large uncoated heavy-based saucepan.

Sift the bicarbonate of soda onto a saucer and set aside.

Stir the sugar and syrup over low heat until the sugar dissolves, then increase the heat slightly and bring to the boil. Watch it closely and try not to stir unless absolutely necessary. Lower the heat if necessary. It will take about 3–4 minutes to reach the right consistency and the desired deep amber colour. Be alert. The difference between the perfect consistency and disaster in the form of overcooking can be mere seconds. Err on the side of undercooking if anything at all. Brown syrup will mean a crisp but burnt and nasty-tasting mouthful.

As soon as the syrup turns dark amber, remove the saucepan from the heat and quickly stir in the bicarbonate of soda. Stop as soon as it is mixed in, or you will deflate the mixture. Pour the mixture into the prepared tin. It will not fill the tin, but allow it to find its own way and do not stir or level it. Leave to cool completely.

The honeycomb can be kept in an airtight container for several days and can also be frozen for later.

Makes a 20 x 20cm/8 x 8 in square, to be broken into shards as desired

200 g/7 oz/generous ½ cup golden syrup	
100 g/3½ oz/½ cup demerara sugar	
20 g/¾ oz/1½ tbsp butter	
1 tbsp water	
2 tsp white wine vinegar	
2½ tsp bicarbonate of soda	

This is a harder and more robust version of the previous honeycomb. It takes a little longer to prepare and will require a sugar thermometer. It appears all over the world in many versions. In Ireland there is a yellow coloured honeycomb toffee that is graphically referred to as 'Yellowman' or 'Yellaman'. It is a treat that is centuries old, still made and enjoyed by many, and has always had a special association with fairs, especially the 'Lammas' fairs held around late July and August. In America it appears as 'sponge candy' and 'sea foam' among other names. The most peculiar version I have ever eaten is the Spanish one called 'carbón' (coal). Colouring is added to make the mixture black and it does look quite realistic. It was often given to naughty children at Christmas time as a caution.

Yellowman Honeycomb

Generously line a 20 x 20 cm/8 x 8 in tin with baking parchment.

Put the golden syrup, sugar, butter, water and vinegar into a large uncoated heavy-based saucepan.

Sift the bicarbonate of soda onto a saucer and set aside.

Stir the ingredients in the saucepan over low heat until the butter melts and the sugar dissolves then increase the heat slightly and bring to the boil. Attach a sugar thermometer to the pan, lower the heat a little and leave to boil without stirring until it reaches 132°C/270°F (soft crack stage). It will take about 10–12 minutes from the time it comes to a rolling boil, but rely on the thermometer and keep a close watch.

Take the saucepan off the heat, remove the thermometer, then sprinkle on the bicarbonate of soda and quickly stir it in. It will foam up a lot more than the simple honeycomb recipe. Stop as soon as it is mixed in, or you will deflate the mixture.

Pour the mixture into the tin and do not stir or level it. The mixture will almost fill the tin, but will subside a little as it cools. Set aside to cool completely and do NOT mark it into squares; the pressure of the knife deflates it. It has to be broken randomly.

The honeycomb can be kept in an airtight container for several days and can also be frozen for later.

Makes about 36

25 g/1 oz/2 tbsp (¼ stick) butter, plus extra
for greasing

150 g/5½ oz/¾ cup granulated sugar

50 g/1¾ oz/scant 2½ tbsp dark treacle

generous ¼ tsp salt

2 tbsp water

2 tbsp white wine vinegar

I am stumped as to how to translate 'boterbabbelaar'. My hefty and usually reliable dictionary hesitatingly suggests 'bulls-eye'; its component parts simply mean 'butter' and 'chatterbox'. I'll just describe it and leave it up to you to call it what you like. These boiled confections are a traditional homemade speciality of the southern Dutch province of Zeeland, and family recipes abound even though they are now also manufactured commercially. Sugar, vinegar, salt and a modest amount of butter are the main ingredients, with a secret touch here and there, such as the stock cubes I saw in one recipe. Dark treacle is often an optional ingredient, particularly when granulated sugar is used instead of the soft, syrupy brown sugar that appears to be unique to Holland. They are very easy to make, with no real pulling involved either, but you will need to stretch the fairly hot mixture into a rope before it cools.

Boterbabbelaars

Grease a baking sheet with butter.

Put all of the ingredients into a medium uncoated heavy-based saucepan and stir over low heat until the butter melts and the sugar dissolves completely. Attach a sugar thermometer to the pan, bring to the boil and leave to boil without stirring until it reaches 130°C/265°F (just past late hard ball stage and approaching soft crack stage). It will take about 15 minutes from the time it comes to a rolling boil, but rely on the thermometer.

Remove the thermometer and pour the mixture out onto the baking sheet. It will bubble a bit and then spread out in a thin layer. Leave it to cool slightly; it should be warm and pliable.

Grease your hands with butter and roll the mixture up loosely. Use a pair of kitchen scissors to cut it into 3 portions and quickly stretch each portion with a massaging motion to make a rope with the thickness of an average-sized pinkie finger. Snip at 2 cm/¾ in intervals and leave to cool on the baking sheet.

They will keep for a week or two, but will become stickier as time goes by.

Brittles with Crunch and Zing

**Makes 1 large sheet, to be broken
into pieces**

1 tbsp neutral-tasting oil (e.g. sunflower), plus
extra for oiling (optional)

350 g/12 oz/1¾ cups granulated sugar

50 ml/1¾ fl oz/scant ¼ cup water

150 g/5½ oz/1 cup blanched almonds, toasted

100 g/3½ oz/⅔ cup pistachios, toasted

Nut brittles are one of the oldest forms of
confectionery and are still made and eaten all
over the world. This one is in the traditional
crisp Middle Eastern style, without fuss or
frills. The nuts used are subject to personal
taste and availability and vary from humble
peanuts and sesame seeds to costlier but
irresistible macadamias and pistachios.
I have used a mixture of almonds and pistachios
here, but feel free to make your own single
flavours or combinations. Toasted nuts make
the best brittle and are even better if added
slightly warm.

Pistachio and Almond Brittle

Oil a baking sheet, if using, and set aside.

Put the sugar and water in a large uncoated heavy-based saucepan and stir over low
heat to dissolve the sugar crystals. They should all be dissolved before the mixture
comes to the boil, or they will re-crystallise. Attach the sugar thermometer, if using,
to the pan and bring to the boil, without stirring, over medium heat until it reaches
150°C/302°F (hard crack stage). It will be dark amber and will spin several thin,
hard, brittle threads when you lift it with a spoon.

Remove immediately from the heat and quickly stir in the oil followed by the nuts.
Scrape the mixture out onto a silicone mat or the oiled baking sheet in as flat a layer
as you can get it, but work fast because the sugar will set. Leave the odd straggler in
the saucepan to fish out later, rather than try to get every scrap out.

Break into pieces to serve.

**Makes 1 large sheet, to be broken
into pieces**

generous ½ tsp bicarbonate of soda

½ tsp ground cinnamon

½ tsp ground cayenne pepper

¼ tsp ground ginger

¼ tsp ground coriander

250 g/9 oz/1¼ cups demerara sugar

75 g/2¾ oz/scant ¼ cup golden syrup

3 tbsp water

25 g/1 oz/2 tbsp butter, flaked

½ tsp salt

50 g/1¾ oz/scant ½ cup pumpkin seeds,
lightly toasted

50 g/1¾ oz/⅓ cup sunflower seeds,
lightly toasted

125 g/4½ oz/generous ¾ cup unsalted
roasted peanuts

The unexpected spiciness from the cayenne pepper comes as a surprise and contrasts nicely with the background sweetness in this brittle. You can vary the amount to suit your taste and some people might even like it to have more of a kick. It makes an interesting and delicious end to an Asian meal, to accompany your tea or coffee. For those who prefer sweeter spices, try the Spiced Peanut Brittle (see p.50). Golden syrup adds both texture and flavour and is highly recommended, but you can substitute the same weights of granulated sugar for both demerara sugar and golden syrup.

Spicy Peanut and Seed Brittle

Sift the bicarbonate of soda with the ground spices and set aside.

Put the sugar, golden syrup, water, butter and salt into a large heavy-based saucepan and stir over low heat to melt the butter and dissolve the sugar crystals before the mixture comes to the boil. Increase the heat slightly once the sugar has dissolved and lower it as soon as it comes to a rolling boil. Attach a sugar thermometer to the pan and leave to boil, without stirring, *just until* it reaches 142°C/288°F (high soft crack stage). It will take 15–20 minutes once it starts to boil, but keep an eye on it as it can move very fast towards the end and a few seconds can make a big difference.

Immediately take the pan off the heat, remove the thermometer and quickly stir in the bicarbonate of soda and spice mixture. The mixture will foam. Stir in the seeds and/or nuts quickly but thoroughly and use a silicone spatula to scrape out onto a silicone mat or large sheet of baking parchment. Top with another sheet of baking parchment and flatten with a rolling pin. Work fast because the sugar will start to set.

Remove the top sheet of baking parchment; it doesn't matter if there is some sugar mixture clinging to it. Use a blunt knife to mark the mixture into diamond shapes, making lines about 3 cm/1¼ in apart. Press deeply and if using a silicone mat, be careful not to cut through it.

Leave to cool, then break into pieces to serve. Store leftovers in an airtight container. The brittle will keep for a few weeks in a cool dark place.

**Makes 1 large sheet,
to be broken into pieces**

½ tsp ground cinnamon

½ tsp ground cardamom

¼ tsp ground ginger

¼ tsp ground white pepper

generous ½ tsp bicarbonate of soda

250 g/9 oz/1¼ cups demerara sugar

75 g/2¾ oz/scant ¼ cup golden syrup

3 tbsp water

25 g/1 oz/2 tbsp butter, flaked

½ tsp salt

250 g/9 oz/1²⁄₃ cups unsalted roasted peanuts

This version uses sweeter spices than the Spicy Peanut and Seed Brittle (see p.49), in combination with a little white pepper. This is not as bizarre as it might seem. Dutch spice cakes and biscuits almost always include some white pepper, once so prized a spice and now so commonplace an ingredient. There is something cosy and warming about this brittle that makes it hard to stop at one piece. Golden syrup adds both texture and flavour and is highly recommended, but you can substitute the same weights of granulated sugar for both demerara sugar and golden syrup.

Spiced Peanut Brittle

Sift the bicarbonate of soda with the ground spices and set aside.

Put the sugar, golden syrup, water, butter and salt into a large heavy-based saucepan and stir over low heat to melt the butter and dissolve the sugar crystals before the mixture comes to the boil. Increase the heat slightly once the sugar has dissolved and lower it as soon as it comes to a rolling boil. Attach a sugar thermometer to the pan and leave to boil, without stirring, *just until* it reaches 142°C/288°F (high soft crack stage). It will take 15–20 minutes once it starts to boil, but keep an eye on it, as it can move very fast towards the end and a few seconds can make a big difference.

Immediately take the pan off the heat, remove the thermometer and quickly stir in the bicarbonate of soda and spice mixture. The mixture will foam. Stir in the nuts quickly but thoroughly and scrape out onto a silicone mat or large sheet of baking parchment. Top with another sheet of baking parchment and flatten with a rolling pin. Work fast as the sugar will start to set.

Remove the top sheet of baking parchment and use a blunt knife to mark the mixture into diamond shapes, making lines about 3 cm/1¼ in apart. Press deeply and if using a silicone mat, be careful not to cut through it.

Leave to cool, then break into pieces to serve. Store leftovers in an airtight container. The brittle will keep for a few weeks in a cool dark place.

Caramel
The Amber Gem

Well-made hard caramel is a thing of great beauty: brittle, translucent, amber-coloured and almost like a jewel - sometimes quite literally. Our daughter spent several months at university in the Lithuanian capital Vilnius, as an exchange student. When we went to visit her, we saw a small city of contrasts. Poverty and affluence existed almost side by side and a wrong turning from a shopping street that wouldn't be out of place in Milan or Paris could suddenly lead to an eerily derelict neighbourhood that had so far escaped the zeal for renovation. It is a city of hills and the simple and natural beauty of the views can be breathtaking. One thing that I had asked to be put high on the itinerary was an amber shopping trip, as Baltic amber has ranked as some of the most beautiful in the world since ancient times and comes in a wide range of colours and textures. Judy had done her homework well and we came away with some amazing modern designer pieces as well as more traditional ones with lovely traces of fossilised life shimmering on the inside of the almost transparent beads. Our shopping was done mainly in a few fairly elegant shops, but we still enjoyed browsing for bargains at pavement stalls. Surprised to see Judy surreptitiously bite an amber necklace (or rather, shocked at the germs it held!) I received an explanation: she was checking to see if it was real amber or caramel. Apparently, it was quite the thing among unscrupulous vendors to cook hard caramel and shape them into beads to pass off on unsuspecting tourists. The shops are a safer bet, and they even slip a small certificate of authenticity into the little linen bag that comes with your purchase. As they grab the certificate at random from a pile in the drawer, it is hard to say exactly what it is they are certifying, but it does inspire confidence.

**Makes 1 large sheet,
to be broken into pieces**

250 g/9 oz/1¼ cups granulated sugar

75 g/2¾ oz/scant ¼ cup golden syrup

4 tbsp water

50 g/1¾ oz/3½ tbsp butter, flaked

generous ½ tsp bicarbonate of soda, sifted

150 g/5½ oz/1 cup toasted, salted macadamias,
coarsely chopped

I like to keep a stash of this in the freezer, as it comes in handy for quick and unexpected desserts. Try it on its own, break a large shard to accompany good vanilla ice cream, or mix small pieces into the ice cream just before you eat it. Macadamia nuts have a rich buttery flavour and this brittle brings it out well. The texture is slightly aerated, making it crisp but yielding to the bite. I use salted toasted macadamias, as they are easiest to come by and they add a delicious contrast to the underlying sweetness. If you have only unsalted macadamias, add a pinch of salt with the nuts. Only golden syrup will give the desired result, so do try your best to get some.

Buttery Salted Macadamia Brittle

Put the sugar, golden syrup, water and butter into a large heavy-based saucepan and stir over low heat to melt the butter and dissolve the sugar crystals before the mixture comes to the boil. Increase the heat slightly once the sugar has dissolved and lower it as soon as it comes to a rolling boil. Attach a sugar thermometer to the pan and leave to boil, without stirring, until it reaches 140°C/284°F (the upper regions of soft crack stage). It will take 15–20 minutes once it starts to boil, but keep an eye on it.

Immediately take the pan off the heat, remove the thermometer and quickly stir in the bicarbonate of soda. The mixture will foam. Stir in the nuts thoroughly; the foam will subside. Scrape the mixture out with a silicone spatula onto a silicone mat or large sheet of baking parchment, top with another sheet of baking parchment and flatten with a rolling pin. Work fast, as the sugar will start to set. The thickness of the brittle depends on the size of the nuts.

Leave to cool, then break into pieces to serve.

Store leftovers in an airtight container, with baking parchment or greaseproof paper between the layers to prevent them from sticking to each other.

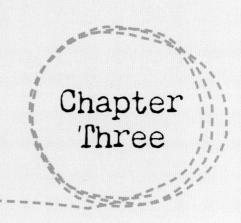

Chapter
Three

Delights from Near and Far

Chocolate-coated Peppermint Creams

Plain peppermint creams have delighted generations of children, both in the making and eating. These chocolate-coated after-dinner treats are a little more sophisticated, but still very easy to make. The peppermint extract called for is widely available. You will find that most older recipes call for peppermint oil and it is truly excellent for sweet-making, with a very pure and concentrated flavour. The only trouble is finding it. I have had absolutely no success in recent years. If you are lucky enough to locate a source, check that it is food grade. You will need a few drops only, so make up the liquid shortfall with more cream, or water.

Makes just over 24

250 g/9 oz/scant 2¼ cups icing sugar, plus extra for dusting

2 tsp peppermint extract, or to taste

scant 3 tbsp double cream, or as needed

250 g/9 oz/9 squares melted or tempered dark chocolate (see p.25), for dipping

Sift the icing sugar into a bowl. Add the peppermint extract and cream. (Note that the strength and flavour of peppermint extract can vary, so add a little at first and taste. If you end up using a different amount than stated above, adjust the amount of cream accordingly.) Knead well to make a smooth, firmly malleable dough. If necessary, add a little icing sugar to make it firmer or a few drops of extra cream to make it softer.

Dust a silicone mat or pastry board with icing sugar and roll the dough out to an even thickness of about 7.5 mm/generous ¼ in, dusting as needed. Use a 3.5-cm/1½-in plain round cutter to cut out rounds and transfer them carefully with a metal spatula to a sheet of greaseproof paper dusted with icing sugar. Re-roll and cut out the trimmings. Neaten the rounds if necessary and leave to dry, uncovered, at room temperature for an hour or so. The tops should feel dry to the touch.

Transfer the rounds, dry side down, to a wire rack, then use a soft pastry brush to remove excess sugar and any other loose particles from the top and sides, or they will fall off into the dipping chocolate. Leave to dry for a few hours, changing their position once or twice, then decorate as desired.

Using a dipping fork, dip the rounds in melted chocolate, turning them over to coat well, then tap sharply on the side of the bowl before passing it across the rim to remove excess chocolate. Deposit gently onto a second sheet of greaseproof paper and leave to harden. To make the little faces, half-dip each disc into the melted chocolate. Deposit gently onto the waxed paper. Put the remaining melted chocolate into an icing bag fitted with a plain small tip. Pipe a variety of faces under the chocolate caps and allow to harden. They can be wrapped in squares of coloured foil or placed in paper sweet cases or simply served on a plate. Keep well wrapped for up to a week at a constant cool temperature to discourage discolouration.

Variation

If you aren't going to dip the peppermint creams, you can tint them in one or more pastel shades, such as pink or green and cut out various shapes, decorating them as you wish. Leave them to air dry on both sides until dry to the touch before storing between sheets of greaseproof paper in a container.

The English-speaking world recognises this Mediterranean treat as 'nougat', its French name. Italians refer to it as 'torrone' while Spaniards call it 'turrón'. Nuts are the star attraction and nougat is made with all kinds, such as almonds, pistachios and hazelnuts, although rarely with walnuts. You do need to have a heavy-duty freestanding electric mixer, as there is a lot of continuous whisking involved, some of it simultaneously with the syrup boiling. The mixture is stiff and sticky and less powerful motors might not be up to the job. If you can, leave it to set for 24 hours so that the flavours can mingle and the texture becomes firmer.

**Makes 1 large rectangle
to be cut as desired**

1 egg white
200 g/7 oz/1 cup caster sugar
75 g/2¾ oz/scant ¼ cup runny honey
50 g/1¾ oz glucose syrup
50 ml/1¾ fl oz/scant ¼ cup water
1½ tsp rose water OR 1 tsp orange flower water OR ½ tsp vanilla extract
125 g/4½ oz/generous ¾ cup pistachios, lightly toasted
125 g/4½ oz/generous ¾ cup almonds with skins, lightly toasted

Soft Pistachio and Rose Water Nougat

The nougat is very sticky, so line the mould or large loaf tin with sheets of edible wafer paper, cut to fit. Lacking that, use baking parchment.

Whisk the egg white to stiff peaks in a heavy-duty electric mixer. A single egg white is sometimes a problem in large mixer bowls. In that case, I usually whisk it briskly by hand first until it foams, giving it more volume for the mixer to catch.

Put the sugar, honey, glucose syrup and water in a medium heavy-based uncoated saucepan and stir over low heat until the sugar dissolves completely. Attach a sugar thermometer to the pan, increase the heat and bring to the boil. Leave to boil without stirring until it reaches 125°C/257°F. It will take about 5 minutes from the time it comes to the boil.

Quickly remove the thermometer and pour a third of the syrup in a steady stream onto the egg white, with the motor running at low–medium speed. Avoid pouring directly onto the whisk. Leave it running.

Attach the thermometer back onto the pan of syrup and continue to cook until it reaches 147–148°C/297–298°F (approaching hard crack stage). Remove the thermometer and pour in a steady stream over the egg white mixture. Again, avoid pouring directly onto the whisk. Once all the syrup is in the bowl, increase to medium–high speed and whisk for 8 minutes. Stop the motor and add the liquid flavouring, then whisk for another minute.

Fold in the nuts with a sturdy spatula. Use a plastic scraper to transfer dollops of the mixture to the loaf tin. It is extremely sticky, so use a table knife to help scrape the mixture off the scraper. Flatten as well as you can, top with more edible wafer paper and flatten further into a neatish block of even thickness.

Leave the nougat to set uncovered for 4–6 hours, then store in an airtight container at room temperature for up to 10 days. Cut into squares or bars as required.

Turrón
Sweetest of Legacies

Turrón is a Spanish delicacy that is eaten in awe-inspiring amounts in the festive period surrounding Christmas – an ironic timing, given the assumption that it is in all likelihood a legacy from the Moors who occupied southern Spain centuries ago. The word covers a multitude of variants. Some types are related to nougat, others are brittles and marzipan-like confections, or even fudges. Several theories are offered for the origin of the name, the simplest being that it derives from the verb *turrar*, meaning 'to toast'. The Moorish connection pops up in the mention of *turun* in the 11th-century treatise *De medicinis et cibis semplicibus*, written by an Arab physician. Least likely is the popular myth that tells of sweet-making competitions organised by trade guilds in the 18th century, one of which was won by Catalan pastry cook Pablo Turrons for his wonderful new confection. If he really did exist, who is to say that his surname wasn't the result of the family business? The written word is far older and even appears in Spanish literature in 1541, in *Los Lacayos Ladrones* (*The Thieving Lackeys*), a play by Sevillan playwright Lope de Rueda. In it, the protagonist Dalagón spends his time dishing out physical punishment to his servants, who have been surreptitiously helping themselves to the stash of *turrón de Alicante* that he had hidden in his desk.

In its older and more traditional forms, this delicious treat consists of little more than honey, sugar and nuts, and it is truly amazing how much variety a few basic ingredients can provide, both in flavour and texture. Crunchy *Alicante turrón* is made from a honeyed syrup, egg whites and whole toasted Marcona almonds. For the softer *Jijona turrón* the toasted almonds are ground very finely and the mixture is shaped into smooth slabs. *Agramunt turrón* is like a darker version of that of Alicante, but generally uses hazelnuts and is made into small discs instead of the more usual rectangles. These three types now enjoy protected status, although copies and variations abound. *Turrón de yemas*, enriched with egg yolks, is more like marzipan than traditional *turrón*, and creamy walnut *turrón* could almost be mistaken for fudge. Chocolate has also become a very popular ingredient and even crisp amber-hued nut brittles known as *guirlache* often have the word *turrón* tacked beguilingly onto their name. Walking into a *confitería* or a well-stocked department store in December, one is spoiled for choice. Counters groan under the weight of the gigantic slabs of all shades and textures, plain or studded with nuts and vibrantly coloured candied fruit, waiting to be cut to order and taken to grace family tables across the country.

Nowadays, mass production dominates and the ingredients simmer in large vats in closely regulated factories, making the *turronero*'s work simpler than before, and producing a uniformly consistent product. Some of the best still comes from the handful of artisan *turroneros*, including the dwindling number of convents that specialise in confectionery as a much-needed extra source of income. Recipes for home cooks first appeared in the *Manual de Mujeres* (*Ladies' Manual*), published anonymously in the 16th century, and it is not difficult to make these delectable sweets in the comfort and convenience of your own kitchen. I hasten to add that they will not be replicas of the commercial versions that are made using precision equipment, but they are delicious in their own right.

Makes 1 large rectangle to be cut as desired

3 egg whites

175 g/6 oz/generous 1 cup blanched almonds, toasted and very finely ground

175 g/6 oz/generous ¾ cup caster sugar

175 g/6 oz/½ cup runny honey

Eating this soft-textured 'turrón', with its honey and toasted almonds, is like taking a bite of the past and it has remained unchanged for centuries. It is the homemade version of Jijona-style 'turrón', but it is coarser in texture and less oily than the commercially produced kind, which is difficult to replicate in a domestic kitchen without professional specialist equipment. This one is easy to make without a thermometer, which is more of a hindrance than help while stirring. Toast the almonds until dark golden brown for the most flavour.

Toasted Almond Nougat

Turrón Blando de Almendras

Line a large loaf tin with baking parchment.

Whisk the egg whites to stiff peaks in a heavy-duty electric mixer. Stir in the ground almonds to make a paste and set aside.

Put the sugar and honey in a medium heavy-based uncoated saucepan and stir over low heat until the sugar dissolves completely, then bring to the boil. When it reaches a rolling boil, stir in the paste, lower the heat and cook for about 15 minutes over low heat until quite stiff. Stir constantly to prevent it from catching. The mixture will become more and more difficult to stir as it thickens.

Scrape it out into the loaf tin and level the top with a plastic scraper or with lightly moistened hands.

Leave the nougat to cool and set uncovered for 4–6 hours, then store in an airtight container at room temperature. Leave the slab whole and cut into squares or bars as required. It will keep for a few weeks and is best after a few days of maturation.

Makes 1 large rectangle to be cut as desired

1 egg white

200 g/7 oz/1 cup granulated sugar

200 g/7 oz/generous ½ cup runny honey

100 g/3½ oz/⅔ cup whole hazelnuts, toasted

100 g/3½ oz/⅔ cup whole almonds, toasted

This nougat has a lovely honey flavour.

Almond and Hazelnut Nougat

The nougat is sticky and will want to cling to the mould with all its might, so line a mould or large loaf tin with sheets of edible wafer paper, cut to fit. Lacking that, use baking parchment.

Whisk the egg white to stiff peaks in a heavy-duty electric mixer. A single egg white is sometimes a problem in large mixer bowls. In that case, I usually whisk it briskly by hand first until it foams, giving it more volume for the mixer to catch. Switch off the mixer.

Put the sugar and honey in a medium heavy-based uncoated saucepan and stir over low heat until the sugar dissolves completely. Attach a sugar thermometer to the pan, increase the heat and bring to the boil. Leave to boil without stirring until it reaches 140°C/284°F (soft crack stage). It will take 5–10 minutes from the time it comes to the boil and can vary depending on the honey, so keep an eye on the thermometer.

Remove from the heat and unclamp the thermometer. Switch on the mixer again, allowing it to run at a low speed. Pour the syrup in a steady stream over the egg white. Avoid pouring directly onto the whisk. Once all the syrup is in the bowl, increase to quite a high speed and whisk for 6 minutes. It will be very stiff.

Fold in the nuts with a sturdy spatula and use a plastic scraper to transfer dollops of the mixture to the loaf tin. It is extremely sticky, so use a table knife to help scrape the mixture off the scraper. Flatten as well as you can, top with more edible wafer paper and flatten further into a neatish block of even thickness.

Leave the nougat to cool and set uncovered for 4–6 hours, then store in an airtight container at room temperature for up to 10 days. Leave it whole and cut into squares or bars as required.

Makes 36 cubes

350 g/12 oz/1¾ cups granulated sugar

20 g/¾ oz glucose syrup

175 ml/6 fl oz/¾ cup water

2 egg whites

30 g/1 oz/generous ¼ cup icing sugar

15 g/½ oz/scant 2 tbsp cornflour

5 tbsp boiling water

15 g/½ oz/scant 2 tbsp powdered gelatine

1½ tbsp rose water

Marshmallows are all about texture, if one is perfectly honest, and young and old enjoy a mouthful of this springy, spongy and bouncy confection. They have been around at least since the nineteenth century and were originally made using the mucilaginous root of a plant called marsh mallow (Althaea officinalis). Nowadays gum Arabic is used by professional confectioners, but a simple version can be made at home with gelatine, egg whites and a flavouring. This version uses rose water, in the French style. It needs to be whipped for a very long time, so a heavy-duty freestanding electric mixer is almost essential.

Marshmallows

Line a 20 x 20-cm/8 x 8-in baking tin with baking parchment.

Put the sugar, glucose syrup and water in a medium heavy-based uncoated saucepan and stir over low heat until the sugar dissolves completely. Attach a sugar thermometer to the pan, increase the heat and bring to the boil. Leave to boil without stirring until it reaches 125°C/257°F. It will take about 20–25 minutes from the time it comes to the boil, so you can do the other preparation while it boils.

Whisk the egg whites to stiff peaks in a heavy-duty electric mixer, then switch off the motor. Mix the icing sugar and cornflour together and dust the base of the tin with a layer of the mixture.

Pour the boiling water into a small bowl and sprinkle on the gelatine. Stir with a wire whisk to dissolve it properly. Add the rose water and set aside. By this time, the syrup should be nearly ready. As soon as it reaches 125°C/257°F, take the pan off the heat and remove the thermometer. Pour in a little of the gelatine mixture, stirring well with the whisk. It will froth up a lot, so wait a few seconds for it to subside before pouring in the rest and stirring well with the whisk. Switch the mixer back on at a medium speed and pour the syrup very slowly and steadily over the whites. It will swell. Avoid pouring directly onto the whisk. Once all the syrup is in the bowl, increase to fairly high speed and whisk for another 12–15 minutes until the mixture is thick and glossy and soft peaks hold their shape.

Scrape the mixture into the tin and leave to set at room temperature for about 2 hours.

Sift the rest of the icing sugar mixture over a sheet of baking parchment and invert the set marshmallow over it. Do this gently, or you will end up with a cloud of sugar in your face and all over the work surface. Cut into squares and press the cut sides into the powder to coat well.

Keep in an airtight container and eat within a few days, which shouldn't be a problem, as I managed to eat a whole row while portioning the last batch.

Turkish Delight
Lokum

Known at least since the mid-nineteenth century in England, first as 'lumps of delight' and later as Turkish Delight, this sweet is called 'lokum' in Turkey. Its original name was 'rahatü'l-hulkum', an Arabic expression meaning 'throat's ease' that was corrupted in colloquial speech, becoming 'rahat-lokum', then 'latilokum' and finally 'lokum'. Recipes appeared in Turkish manuscript books from the late nineteenth century onwards and while specific amounts were given in some cases, instructions could be quite vague, depending on a certain amount of knowledge and skill on the maker's part. 'Lokum' remains a confection that is best made by specialists. In Turkey wheat starch is used instead of cornflour and many variations and combinations are made, including versions with mastic (which makes it chewy), clotted cream or nuts. Liquid flavouring is added sparingly in the form of oil of rose, violet, lemon, bitter orange and so on. Using oil instead of waters or extracts means that a drop or two is sufficient for an entire batch and the texture will not suffer. There are even special scissors with half-moon shaped blades designed to cut the slabs into lumps.

Turkish delight takes a long time to cook and it is no wonder that people outside of Turkey have taken to using gelatine to make it set quickly and effectively. My friend and oracle Nevin has warned me against using gelatine, as it is not the authentic way. Furthermore, if I persisted in going ahead with gelatine, I was to call it 'A Sweet', never Turkish Delight. I have used her straightforward traditional method as a basis here, and before we get to the actual recipe (on the following page), let me share the advice given by another friend: stirring without interruption in the same direction is crucial for a good result.

Makes about 36 cubes

about 200 g/7 oz/scant 2¼ cups desiccated coconut
500 g/1 lb 2 oz/2½ cups granulated sugar
125 g/4½ oz/scant 1 cup cornflour
½ tsp cream of tartar
1 tsp lemon juice
600 ml/1 pint/2½ cups water
75 g/2¾ oz/½ cup pistachios, toasted or untoasted
50–75 g/1¾–2¾ oz/⅓–½ cup hazelnuts, toasted and coarsely chopped
25–50 g/1–1¾ oz/⅛–⅓ cup pine nuts, toasted

Turkish Delight

Lokum

Generously line a large loaf tin with baking parchment. Scatter a good layer of coconut over the base of the loaf tin and set aside.

Put all of the ingredients, except the remaining coconut and other nuts into a large uncoated heavy-based saucepan and place over medium heat. Stir with a wooden spatula to dissolve the cornflour and sugar. Keep stirring, as the cornflour will suddenly start to set and turn into small lumps. Switch to a wire whisk and use it to stir the mixture for a few minutes until it is smooth. It will look like glue and should have no lumps at all. Switch back to the wooden spatula and keep stirring gently, making sure that the sides and bottom are constantly being scraped. This is a lengthy process, but it is important to keep it moving. After about 20 minutes it will start to rise and fall with a hissing sound. You will be only about halfway. It needs to cook for a further 20–30 minutes to achieve the right texture. When about 40 minutes have passed from the time it started to get lumpy, you can start testing. Put a teaspoonful of the mixture into a bowl of cold water. Under the water, press it together with your fingers and try to flatten it. If it is pliable and doesn't fall apart when you do this, it is ready. If the mixture is too soft, it needs to be cooked further. (A thermometer is no help – you have to test it manually. Note that the test described is not soft ball stage on a sugar thermometer; this is a completely different mixture.)

Remove the pan from the heat and stir in the nuts. Scrape the mixture out into the tin. Do it in dollops to get it well distributed. Flatten the top as well as you can with the spatula and scatter another good layer of coconut over it. Use your hands to press the block and flatten the top; don't worry, as the coconut will prevent burns.

Leave to cool, preferably overnight. If you press it with a finger, it should feel springy and there should be no indentation in the surface. Cut into cubes. Put the rest of the coconut in a shallow bowl and press the uncoated sides in it to coat. They will be softer than most commercial products, which have a tendency to be rubbery. Keep on a plate or sweet dish and cover only with something like a mesh dome. If they are not allowed to breathe, they will sweat. They are best eaten within a week.

Moors and Christians

The Moors may have been expelled from al-Andalus several centuries ago, but much evidence of their Spanish sojourn remains all over Andalucia, in place names, architecture and food. They have blended seamlessly into the Catholic landscape in more ways than one and Medina Sidonia illustrates this beautifully.

The houses of Medina Sidonia cling tightly to their hillside as they glisten whitely in the blazing Andalucian sun. It is a lovely place to visit, with many points of historic interest and all of the picturesque quaintness of the region. What makes it so special to me, though, is that it is the acknowledged confectionery capital of the province of Cádiz – and justly so. In addition to the traditional pastry and sweet shops, the Augustinian sisters at the convent of San Cristóbal have their own little *pastelería-confitería* leading off their main courtyard. Reluctantly, I broke the serene silence by pressing the buzzer and a smiling young nun appeared almost immediately. Wrought iron grillwork separated us, but formed no barrier to a friendly chat, during which I learned that she was from Kenya. Finding it almost impossible to choose, I decided to take her advice and buy an assorted box. This was put into a rotating metal contraption set into the wall and given a twirl so that I could remove my box and replace it with money. Among the treasures within were several sweets that could have just come from an Arab market: melt in the mouth *Amarguillos* (see p.146), Pine Nut Clusters (see p.142), heavily spiced honey and nut *alfajores* and more. But the sweets that are most traditionally associated with convents, particularly those in wine-producing regions, are those made with egg yolks, and the Augustinian sisters had turned them into works of art. They came in various shapes and sizes, covered with chocolate or fondant and some were even flavoured with *aguardiente*, a strong Spanish brandy. My own versions follow, but first let me tell you why egg yolks feature so prominently in their sweets.

Egg whites were often used in wine clarification in the Iberian Peninsula, particularly in sherry and port, resulting in gluts of egg yolks. These were obligingly given to local convents, where the nuns put them to good use by turning them into delicious sweets, which they sold to supplement their meagre means. Many Spanish traditions were taken to the Philippines by the colonisers and clergy who followed on their heels and egg candies are one of the many culinary legacies. There was no wine production to provide excess yolks, but there was the unique local custom of using egg whites in the mortar of large buildings, such as churches, so the yolks once again made their way into convents.

These confections are immensely popular in Spain, Portugal and the Philippines. I know what you're thinking and normally, I would be the first person to agree with you, as I don't like eggy-tasting things. Next time you have several yolks left over from meringues or something else, do give these egg candies a go. You may even find yourself having to make meringues to use up the extra whites. There are a few variations at the end of the recipe.

Makes 12

6 egg yolks

grated zest of ½ a lemon (preferably organic)

125 g/4½ oz/½ cup + 2 tbsp caster sugar

2 tbsp water

50 g/1¾ oz/½ cup finely ground almonds

2–3 tbsp granulated sugar

Egg Candy
Yemas / Bolinhos de Ovos

Put the egg yolks in a medium heavy-based uncoated saucepan and stir in the lemon zest. Put the caster sugar and water in a small saucepan and stir over low heat until the sugar dissolves. Attach a sugar thermometer to the pan, increase the heat and bring to the boil. Leave to boil without stirring to 110°C/230°F (thread stage).

Remove the thermometer and pour the syrup over the egg yolks, stirring constantly. Place the mixture over low heat and cook for a further 3–5 minutes until well thickened.

Stir in the almonds and remove from the heat. Scrape the mixture out onto a plate and spread it out a little to cool.

Scatter the granulated sugar on a second plate. Take large teaspoonfuls of the mixture and roll into balls between your palms. Roll around in the sugar to coat and place them in paper cases.

Keep refrigerated and serve chilled or at room temperature. They are even better next day and will keep for a few days.

Variations

The nuns at San Cristóbal had a whole array of variations, which you might also like to try. In that case, omit the step of coating the candies with sugar, or the chocolate will not stick. For Snowy Egg Candies (*yemas nevadas*) flatten the balls into discs and leave them to air dry for an hour or two before dipping them into melted fondant (their way) or white chocolate (even better). If you make a dark chocolate version, you can add a few drops of very strong brandy to the mixture first, but don't let it get too soft. Another way is to pipe the mixture out into thin sticks with a 1-cm/½-in plain nozzle, then leave them to air dry for an hour or two before dipping.

Makes about 16 squares

300 g/10½ oz/1½ cups granulated sugar

250 ml/9 fl oz/generous 1 cup water

175 g/6 oz/scant 2 cups desiccated coconut,
preferably medium cut

125 g/4½ oz/½ cup full-cream powdered milk

30 g/1 oz/2 tbsp ghee or soft butter

¼–½ tsp cardamom or 1 tsp vanilla extract

red or green food colouring (optional)

This recipe is quite simple and uses powdered milk and desiccated coconut to create what might be called coconut ice with an Indian accent. The texture will depend on the cut of coconut you use and a medium cut will make it nice and chewy. If you don't care for the bold flavours of ghee and cardamom, use butter and vanilla extract instead. The mixture is creamy white, but part or all of it can be tinted pink or green if you like.

Easy Coconut Burfi (or Coconut Ice with an Indian Accent)

Line a large loaf tin for a thick layer or line a 20-cm/8-in square tin for a thinner layer with baking parchment.

Put the sugar and water in a large uncoated heavy-based saucepan and stir over low heat until the sugar dissolves completely. Attach a sugar thermometer to the pan, increase the heat and bring to the boil. Leave to boil without stirring until it reaches 110°C/230°F (thread stage).

Immediately take the pan off the heat and remove the thermometer. Stir in the remaining ingredients thoroughly. If you would like to colour part of the mixture, scrape half of the white mixture into the tin, then quickly mix the food colouring into the remaining half. Use it to top the white mixture and level it. Leave to set slightly, then mark it into squares, all the way down to the bottom.

When completely set, store in an airtight container at cool room temperature. It will keep for several days.

Makes 10

butter, for greasing (optional)

225 g/8 oz/1⅛ cups demerara sugar

4 tbsp water

225 g/8 oz/scant ⅓ cup finely grated coconut (fresh or frozen)

1.5 cm/⅝ in piece of ginger, grated OR large pinch of grated orange zest OR ¼ tsp vanilla extract (optional)

This is coconut ice the way it is traditionally made in many Caribbean households. The brown sugar gives it a homely colour, and flavourings vary from fresh ginger to orange peel and vanilla extract. You can use the freshly grated zest of an orange, but dried orange peel used to be quite standard. When I was growing up in Guyana, every household had a twirl of orange peel suspended from a handy nail in the kitchen to dry. The peel was pared artistically so that it remained whole and formed a pretty spiral, and pieces were broken off as needed. I should also mention that some people do not hold with all this thermometer business. My mother, for instance, chucks all of the ingredients into a cast-aluminium wok and stir-fries them until the sugar starts to border on burning. She calls it nice caramelisation.

Caribbean Coconut Drops

Sugar Cakes

Grease a baking sheet, if using and set aside.

Put the sugar and water in a large uncoated heavy-based saucepan and stir over low heat until the sugar dissolves completely. Attach a sugar thermometer to the pan, increase the heat and bring to the boil. Leave to boil without stirring until it reaches 110°C/230°F (thread stage), then remove the thermometer.

Stir in the (thawed) coconut and any flavouring you are using. It will spit a little. Increase the heat and cook until all of the liquid has evaporated. Continue to cook until the mixture feels heavier to stir. It should be sticky enough to stay together if you press a little onto a plate. It will take about 10 minutes, or a little longer after the coconut is added and you may need to play around a bit with the heat so that the mixture does not burn.

Spoon out 10 neat heaps onto a silicone mat or greased sheet and press any scattered fragments back onto the cakes. Press the tops with the back of a spoon to flatten slightly. When they have set, they should feel firm to the touch and the tops will have a whitish tinge. Undercooking will give floppy, chewy cakes and overcooking will result in a dry, loose mixture that cannot be shaped.

When completely set, store in an airtight container at room temperature. They will keep for several days.

**Makes 15 small discs 3.5 cm/1½ in
in diameter, 2 cm/¾ in high, or a
larger number of smaller confections**

100 g/3½ oz/scant ¾ cup plain flour

50 g/1¾ oz/scant ¼ cup full-cream
powdered milk

75 g/2¾ oz/¼ cup + 2 tbsp caster sugar

20 g/¾ oz Rice Crispies (about 8 tbsp)

100 g/3½ oz/7 tbsp butter, melted with
⅛ tsp salt

¼ tsp vanilla extract

Filipinos are adept at adapting foreign foods into uniquely local specialities. Spanish colonisers introduced many new foods, and the 'polvoron' biscuit, a Christmas speciality in Spain, changed character over the centuries. First, it evolved from a baked biscuit to a moulded sweet. With the arrival of the Americans, dairy products flooded the market. Butter soon replaced lard and powdered milk was added for richness. People took to adding extra flavourings, among others 'pinipig', which are flattened grains of young rice that are cooked into porridge or fried until crisp. It was a logical step to Rice Crispies after that. Oval metal moulds are used locally to create the shapes. A spring moves an inner plate, neatly pressing out the sweets. A silicone mat with small round shapes will give the Western cook a similar effect.

Toasted Flour and Rice Crispies Sweets

Polvoron

Put the flour in a hot, dry non-stick frying pan or wok and toast over medium heat, stirring constantly. The flour should darken to golden brown and give off a pleasant aroma. Don't skimp on this step, or your candies will have an undercooked taste and lack depth. It will take up to 20 minutes and you may need to turn down the heat slightly after 12 minutes or so. Keep it moving so that it cooks evenly without getting scorched.

Transfer the toasted flour to a mixing bowl and stir it for a minute or two to remove any lumps. Add the powdered milk and sugar and mix well. Stir in the Rice Crispies, pour in the butter and add the vanilla. Combine well, then spoon the mixture into a sheet of small simple silicone moulds and tamp down well to compact it. This is important, or your sweets will crumble. You can fill the moulds halfway if you prefer smaller sweets, and shape a second batch after the first batch has been unmoulded. When the moulds are full, invert them carefully and apply even pressure with your fingers to unmould each shape. If you have any badly crumbled shapes, you can re-mould the mixture and tamp it down better this time. Leave to cool.

When the sweets are completely cool, wrap them in squares of coloured foil. Alternatively, wrap them in twists of greaseproof paper. In the Philippines they use *papel de Japón* – Japanese paper – which is like thin greaseproof paper and comes in many bright colours. Whatever you use, make sure that it is food grade. They will keep in a cool place for at least a week.

Anticipation has a powerful effect where food is concerned, and a description is often enough for us to make up our minds. If I tell you that these Indian confections are made from gram flour, I'm quite sure that reactions will range from a polite "Oh?" to a not so polite "Eugh!" Forget the description and just taste them. They are delicious as well as being rich in protein and gluten-free. I tried them out on the house painters, Dutch countrymen with conservative eating habits. They cautiously sniffed and poked and nibbled, and came to the satisfied conclusion that they were nutty 'zandkoekjes', a loose-textured shortbread. The 'laddus' are usually left plain or topped with the ubiquitous chopped pistachios, but a pinch of silver leaf makes a lovely decoration. You might also like to try the Gram Fudge (see p.97), which has a different composition and an even more delightful flavour.

Makes 10-12 small balls

75 g/2¾ oz/⅓ cup (generous ½ stick) butter, plus extra for greasing

125 g/4½ oz/1⅓ cups gram/chickpea flour (besan)

¼ tsp ground cardamom

100 g/3½ oz/scant 1 cup icing sugar, sifted

edible silver leaf, to decorate (optional)

Gram Sweets
Besan ke Laddu

Grease a flat plate and set aside.

Melt the butter in a non-stick frying pan or wok, add the gram flour and fry over medium heat for 10–12 minutes, stirring constantly. The flour should darken slightly and the raw and sharp smell you start out with will change to a pleasant, nutty aroma. Don't skimp on this step, or your *laddus* will have an undercooked taste instead of the intended nuttiness. The texture will change from lumpy and loose to a fairly smooth, stiffish paste.

Transfer the paste to a mixing bowl and stir in the cardamom. Stir gently for a minute or two to reduce the temperature, then add the icing sugar, mixing well until it is free of lumps. It will be loose and grainy.

Dip a generous soup spoonful (the kind of spoon you eat your soup with, not a serving spoon) and deposit it in one palm. Clench your fist tightly several times, shifting the position of the mixture a few times. You need to compress it really well, or it will crack when you try to shape it. Use both palms to press back and forth into a neat crack-free ball; rolling will make it disintegrate. Arrange on the flat plate and decorate with small pieces of silver leaf. Leave to cool.

When the *laddus* are completely cool, transfer them to paper cases. Serve at room temperature. Store any leftovers in a cool place in an airtight container for a few days.

Makes 16 large squares

100 g/3½ oz/7 tbsp butter, plus extra
for greasing

125 g/4½ oz/scant ¾ cup medium semolina

⅛ tsp salt

100 g/3½ oz/½ cup granulated sugar

400 ml/14 fl oz/1¾ cups milk, preferably
full-cream

toasted almonds, pine nuts, cashews,
pistachios, dried cranberries, etc.,
to decorate (optional)

'Halva' or 'helva' simply means 'sweet thing' and you will find it made with all kinds of ingredients. Flour and semolina 'halvas' are popular from North Africa to Turkey to India and come in many variants. You will see them presented in various ways, cut into shapes or made into impressively high mounds, artistically decorated with nuts and dried fruit. This simple recipe takes less than 15 minutes to prepare. Try to get a medium semolina, as the finer types give it a closer texture. The optional nuts can be used whole or chopped as a decoration, singly or in whatever combination you like; a few cranberries will add a touch of brightness. It is particularly delicious eaten warm, when the butteriness is at its most pronounced.

Simple Semolina Halva

Grease a flat plate and set aside.

Melt the butter in a large shallow non-stick pan, add the semolina and salt and fry over medium heat for 4–5 minutes, stirring constantly. The butter will froth a bit; fry until the semolina darkens slightly. Don't skimp on this step, or your halva will have an undercooked taste instead of the intended nutty butteriness.

Stir in the sugar and add the milk after a minute or so. Keep on stirring until all of the milk has been completely absorbed, about 2 minutes, and continue to stir for a further 3–4 minutes. The mixture will be like lumpy dough, so keep on turning it over to cook evenly and to avoid browning in spots.

Turn the mixture out onto the flat plate and pat it firmly into a block, about 2 cm/¾ in thick. It is best eaten fresh. Serve warm if you can (but not so hot that the butter burns your mouth!) in small cubes each decorated as desired, or cut it into larger squares, diamonds or triangles and decorate as desired. It is easily re-heated in the microwave, or well wrapped in foil in the oven. The melting butter will give it a delicious flavour and looser texture. When cold, it is more solid in consistency.

Professionally produced sesame 'halva' uses soapwort to produce its characteristic texture and this ingredient is not something even the most zealous shopper will readily find, let alone know how to use. But don't despair. Here is an easy and tasty way to make homemade sesame 'halva' and the recipe is easily halved for small households. The syrup is cooked to soft ball stage, giving a soft and succulent sweet. My tasters and I like it best this way, and cooking the syrup up to hard ball, as is often suggested, will make your 'halva' dry and crumbly. Once set, it can be cut into cubes or squares and presented on a plate. They look even more attractive in coloured foil cases. If you want to get really fancy, you can even press the mixture into small silicone moulds, the kind that are used for making chocolates. It must be pliable enough for you to press out the moulded shapes.

Makes 24 small squares

250 g/9 oz/1¼ cups granulated sugar

100 ml/3½ fl oz/scant ½ cup water

300 g/10½ oz/1⅓ cups sesame paste (tahini)

75–100 g/2¾–3½ oz/½–⅔ cup pistachios, coarsely chopped

Sesame and Pistachio Halva

Line a large loaf tin with baking parchment.

Put the sugar and water in a medium heavy-based uncoated saucepan and stir over low heat until the sugar dissolves completely. Attach a sugar thermometer to the pan, increase the heat and bring to the boil. Lower the heat slightly and boil without stirring until it reaches 114°C/237°F (soft ball stage). It will take about 10 minutes.

While the syrup is boiling, stir the sesame paste well before weighing; there is always a layer of oil that rises to the surface. Weigh it out into a bowl and add the pistachios. Set aside.

When the syrup reaches the correct temperature, remove the thermometer and pour the syrup over the sesame paste. Stir thoroughly for a minute or so to combine well. Scrape the mixture out into the loaf tin and leave to cool and set for a few hours.

Cut into squares as needed. Store in an airtight container for up to a fortnight.

Peanut Butter Halva

Working on the principle that if sesame paste could make *halva*, then so could peanut butter, I tried it and it works very well. Though – or perhaps because – plainer in flavour than the sesame version, this one has proved very popular with children and quite a few adults too. It is basically the same as Sesame and Pistachio *Halva* (above), substituting 300 g/10½ oz/1⅓ cups smooth peanut butter for the sesame paste (tahini) and pistachios. Pour the prepared syrup over the peanut butter and stir briefly until combined. This sets firmer than the sesame version, so mark it into cubes or squares when half set, for a neat finish.

An embarrassment of guavas

I'm sure some of you may be wondering why there are no recipes for fruit pastes and cheeses in this collection. To start with, there were so many other delicious things begging for room, but that is only part of it. Let me explain.

Walking into a Colombian bakery in New Jersey one hot summer day, I was assailed by a vague stirring of nostalgia. I couldn't quite place it at first because it wasn't as if the products on display were all old and familiar friends. Suddenly, it came to me. It was the smell of guava. Most of the rolls and pastries that didn't have caramel spread (*dulce de leche*) had a guava paste filling. There were mini Swiss rolls, crescent-shaped yeast turnovers, doughnuts and more, all bursting with the rich brown paste. A familiar feeling of helplessness began to blunt the nostalgia as my mind dredged up the corresponding memories.

One of the houses we lived in when I was growing up had a garden with more than a dozen guava trees and after the initial excitement at the numerous varieties, shapes and flavours, it always seemed like hundreds. They may have had proper horticultural names but to us children, the local visually suggestive names like 'Red Man' and 'White Lady' used to describe the flesh were more common. We started eating them long before they ripened properly and our stomachs were impervious to indigestion. This natural bounty began to pall very rapidly as the season progressed. We could never manage to successfully strip the trees, however much we climbed and tore at the fruit or however vigorously we shook them. Birds delighted in the riper fruit, which dangled in the higher branches and insects of all shapes and sizes buzzed greedily around or burrowed their way in for a taste. Then the half-eaten and well-pecked guavas would fall to the ground where the relentless tropical heat soon converted them to a mushy mess and the originally pleasant and pervasive fruity smell soon staled to stench as decay set in. There was seemingly no escape. The kitchen was full of large vessels with guava jelly, jam and cheese in varying stages of preparation, as well as the 'gifts' blithely – and perhaps a tiny bit maliciously – sent by others. Even if we gave away basket-loads to friends (often similarly afflicted), there was still a mountain left to cook. My palate soon became so saturated that it ceased to appreciate the nuances and much as I loved sweet things, I came to regard them simply as cooked guava of varying thickness. To this day, I haven't quite come to terms with fruit pastes.

Chapter
Four

Creamy Creations

Technical advice

Milk

Milk is one of the most delicious bases for making confectionery, and different cultures have found ways of their own to create a glorious array of tempting delicacies. The milk itself can be used in various stages – fresh, dried or evaporated – and the type and form of milk is important for the result. Fresh milk, for instance, will make good sweets and fudges, but when some of the moisture is allowed to evaporate, it becomes creamier and fuller tasting. Reducing it further, to a dough-like texture much loved by Indians, it becomes sublimely rich. Don't worry, you won't be asked to do this! There are shortcuts and tricks to create the effect without the lengthy procedures that are usually involved.

Each recipe specifies what type of milk to use. These are: fresh full-cream milk, dried (powdered) milk, sweetened condensed milk and evaporated milk. In some cases, paneer, a soft fresh cheese is required (see p.98).

Sugar

The recipes all state what kind of sugar you should use, and success and timing both depend on that. Try not to interchange. In Europe we have less choice in sugars than in the United States. In the case of granulated and caster, these recipes have been tested with the common beet product available in the average supermarket. Demerara is, of course, the delicious hard golden brown cane sugar from my homeland, now produced in other countries. Nostalgia aside, it gives excellent results and is more stable and predictable than beet sugar. Whatever sugar you are using, allow it to dissolve properly for the best results.

Liquid glucose

This is a clear liquid with the consistency of treacle. It inhibits the formation of crystals, giving a smooth and silky texture to fudge. It is highly recommended and can easily be bought in the baking section of large supermarkets and online.

Sugar thermometer

An accurate sugar thermometer is highly recommended for consistent results in fudge making. See p.22 for more information, as well as how to test manually.

A note on cooking Indian-style sweets

I find that milk sweets with a high proportion of liquid to sugar, such as Indian-style sweets, can be nerve-wracking if one relies on the sugar thermometer. This is the reason why I tell you what to look for instead. With these sweets, I have often had the mixture reach the desired consistency before the correct stage has been indicated by the thermometer, with lots of dancing and skipping of the mercury in between. Common sense is your best guide and more soothing to the nerves. Each recipe specifies the desired consistency and characteristics. Have a bowl of very cold water standing by and pour a little of the mixture into it; wait for it to settle and press together to see if it forms a soft ball, the first stage of proper setting. If it falls apart before you can press it together, it needs more time. For background information on Indian sweets, see pp.92–3.

Saucepans

Always use a heavy-based saucepan in the size specified for milk mixtures. Even constant stirring will not prevent the contents from burning in a thin saucepan. Use the size specified, even though the ingredients appear to be so little. The mixture bubbles and swells from time to time, so you will need the space. Where a small saucepan is specified, using a large one can mean that the thermometer will not give an accurate reading as the level of liquid is too low. Non-stick pans are fantastic for sticky and doughy mixtures; this is usually indicated in the recipe.

To stir or not to stir: a burning question

Fudge mixtures take quite long to cook to the desired consistency, so make sure you have at least 45 minutes at your disposal. To stir or not to stir is a question to which there is no simple yes or no answer. It depends on the proportion of sugar to milk, the heat and the pan itself. If you don't stir, the texture will usually be finer. But as the mixture can also stick and burn quite easily, stirring is recommended in many cases. If you follow the instructions given in the individual recipes and do not deviate from the list of ingredients, you can expect what is promised. If not, you'll have to take your chances as to the outcome. As a rule of thumb, fudge mixture in a very heavy-based saucepan can be left undisturbed for the first 10 minutes, but it becomes trickier after that. Use a flat-edged wooden spatula that scrapes the base well and enables you to get into the corners. Spoons are less effective.

Moulding

Most people like their fudge nice and thick. The tin you use will determine the thickness. For instance, large loaf tins measuring about 23 x 11 cm/9 x 4¼ in at the base will give a lovely chunky thickness, 30 x 10 cm/12 x 4 in will give a fairly thick fudge. A 20 x 20-cm/8 x 8-in square tin, which most people have in their kitchen, will give a thin layer. Whatever tin you use, it will still be delicious, so treat this information as a guideline. Lining the tin makes unmoulding easier. A trick to decrease the size of your 20 x 20 cm/8 x 8 in tin: line it with baking parchment or foil; never use greaseproof paper, as the heat will make it stick to both pan and mixture. Bring one end up 5 cm/2 in from the side of the tin and fill the empty space with scrunched up paper or foil. If you want a perfect edge, cut a piece of cardboard and position it between the lining and the filling material.

Makes 18 thick squares

50 g/1¾ oz/3½ tbsp butter, flaked, plus extra for greasing (optional)
450 g/1 lb/2¼ cups granulated sugar
250 ml/9 fl oz/scant 1 cup evaporated milk
25 g/1 oz liquid glucose
scant ¼ tsp salt
¾–1 tsp vanilla extract
75–100 g/2¾–3½ oz/¾–1 cup walnuts, coarsely chopped

This is my standard recipe for good old-fashioned fudge. I like to add walnuts, but you can leave them out if you prefer. The liquid glucose is highly recommended, but you can still make the fudge without it; it will just be a little less smooth in texture.

Fudge with Walnuts

Grease or line a large loaf tin with baking parchment.

Put the sugar, milk and liquid glucose in a large heavy-based saucepan and stir over low heat to dissolve the sugar completely, then increase the heat to medium. Once it comes to a rolling boil, attach a sugar thermometer if you are using one, and lower the heat. Leave the mixture to boil, stirring gently with a wooden spatula for the first 10 minutes or so, then more energetically as it starts to thicken. Make sure that you keep on scraping the bottom and corners of the pan, and shift the thermometer from time to time to get in behind it. Leave it to boil to 112°C/234°F (just passing from thread to soft ball stage).

Take the saucepan off the heat and remove the thermometer. Add the flaked butter and sprinkle on the salt, and leave it for a minute or two until the butter melts. Add the vanilla and beat vigorously for about 2–3 minutes, then stir in the walnuts thoroughly and scrape the mixture out into the loaf tin. Level the surface and leave to set.

As soon as the fudge is firm enough, mark it into squares and unmould when completely set. It will keep for at least 2 weeks, but gets harder after a few days.

Makes 24 squares

300 g/10½ oz/1½ cups demerara sugar

125 g/4½ oz/½ cup + 2 tbsp granulated sugar

200 ml/7 fl oz/generous ½ cup evaporated milk

50 g/1¾ oz liquid glucose

25 g/1 oz/2 tbsp butter, flaked

scant ¼ tsp salt

50 g/1¾ oz/1¾ squares good white chocolate, finely chopped

½ tsp vanilla extract

75 g/2¾ oz/½ cup pecans, coarsely chopped

Brown sugar and white chocolate give this soft-textured fudge a caramel undertone and the pecans add a pleasant crunch and sweetly nutty flavour. You can substitute walnuts if you don't have pecans, or even leave them out altogether for a plain version, but to my mind, they really add a lot.

Pecan Caramel Fudge

Line a large loaf tin with baking parchment for a thick layer.

Put the sugars, milk, liquid glucose, butter and salt into a large heavy-based uncoated saucepan and stir over low heat to dissolve the sugar and melt the butter, then increase the heat slightly to medium. Once it comes to the boil, attach the sugar thermometer if you are using one, and lower the heat. Leave it to boil to 112–114°C/230–237°F (soft ball stage), stirring occasionally for the first 10 minutes and constantly and gently after that.

Take the saucepan off the heat and remove the thermometer. Scatter in the white chocolate and leave to stand for 2–3 minutes to melt the chocolate and reduce the temperature slightly.

Stir in the vanilla and mix vigorously with a wooden spoon for a minute or so to blend in the chocolate. Use a hand-held stick blender (best tool for the job) or hand-mixer and beat well for a minute. If you don't have either of these implements, beat very vigorously by hand for 4–5 minutes.

Stir in the pecans thoroughly, scrape the mixture out into the loaf tin and level the surface. Mark into squares when partially set, cutting all the way to the bottom. Unmould when completely set. It will keep for at least 2 weeks, but gets harder after a few days.

Makes 18 thick squares

25 g/1 oz/2 tbsp butter, flaked, plus extra for greasing (optional)

40 g/1½ oz candied orange peel

30–40 g/1–1½ oz stem ginger (in syrup), drained

400 g/14 oz/2 cups granulated sugar

150 ml/5 fl oz/generous ½ cup evaporated milk

50 ml/1¾ fl oz/scant ¼ cup full-cream or 2% milk

35 g/1¼ oz liquid glucose

¼ tsp salt

¾ tsp vanilla extract

rounded ¼ tsp ground cardamom

Stem ginger, the kind that comes in olive-sized chunks in jars with syrup, gives this fudge a pleasant kick. If some of your eaters don't care for ginger, sprinkle it over the top of part of the fudge instead of stirring it into the mixture. That way, you'll be able to satisfy both factions. For the best flavour, leave it to mature for a day before eating. The ginger will be quite potent when just set, but will mellow nicely by the following day.

Preserved Ginger and Orange Fudge

Grease or line a large loaf tin with baking parchment.

If the orange peel has a white, sugary coating, rinse with warm water and pat dry. The sugar crystals will give a grainy texture. Chop the orange peel to the size of an orange pip or corn kernel. Chop the ginger half that size and set aside.

Put the sugar, milks, liquid glucose, butter and salt into a large heavy-based uncoated saucepan and stir over low heat to dissolve the sugar and melt the butter, then increase the heat slightly to medium. Once it comes to a rolling boil, attach the sugar thermometer and lower the heat. Leave the mixture to boil, stirring occasionally with a wooden spatula for the first 10 minutes or so, then constantly and increasingly more energetically as it starts to thicken. Make sure that you keep on scraping the base and corners of the pan, and shift the thermometer from time to time to get in behind it. Leave to boil to 112°C/234°F (just passing from thread to soft ball stage). This can take up to 30 minutes from the time it comes to the boil.

Take the saucepan off the heat and remove the thermometer. Stir in the vanilla and cardamom. Use a hand-held stick blender (best tool for the job) or hand-mixer and beat well, for just over a minute with the stick blender, or 2 minutes with the mixer. If you don't have either of these implements, beat very vigorously by hand for 4–5 minutes. Stir in the ginger and orange peel thoroughly, then scrape the mixture out into the loaf tin and level the surface. Mark into 18 squares when partially set, cutting all the way to the bottom.

Unmould when completely set and store in an airtight container for a day before eating.

Makes at least 24

50 g/1¾ oz/3½ tbsp butter, flaked, plus extra
for greasing (optional)

500 g/1 lb 2 oz/2½ cups granulated sugar

300 ml/10 fl oz/scant 1¼ cups evaporated milk

100 g/3½ oz/3½ squares dark chocolate
(e.g. 70% cocoa solids), coarsely grated or
very finely chopped

large pinch of salt

1 tsp vanilla extract

75 g/2¾ oz/¾ cup untoasted walnuts OR
toasted hazelnuts, coarsely chopped (optional)

This fudge is soft-textured and can be made to suit your taste, as the cocoa content of your chocolate will determine its flavour. One with about 55% cocoa solids will obviously be less intense than one that has 85%. The walnuts are optional, so leave them out if you prefer, or substitute coarsely chopped toasted hazelnuts. The specified tin will make a nice thick layer that can be cut into small cubes, which can be put into paper or foil cases for an attractive presentation.

Creamy Chocolate Fudge

Grease or line a large loaf tin with baking parchment for a thick layer.

Put the sugar, milk and butter into a large heavy-based uncoated saucepan and stir over low heat to dissolve the sugar and melt the butter, then increase the heat slightly to medium. Once it comes to the boil, attach the sugar thermometer and lower the heat. Leave the mixture to boil to 110°C/230°F (thread stage), stirring gently from time to time so that it does not catch. Cooking it all the way to soft ball stage will harden the texture unnecessarily; the chocolate will help it to set.

Take the saucepan off the heat and remove the thermometer. Scatter the chocolate over the mixture and leave to stand for a minute or two. Give it a stir to distribute the chocolate and leave to stand for another minute or two. Stir in the salt and vanilla and beat vigorously with a wooden spoon for 2 minutes. Stir in the walnuts or hazelnuts, if using, and scrape the mixture out into the loaf tin. Level the surface and leave to set.

Unmould it as soon as it has set and cut into cubes. It will keep for at least 2 weeks, but gets harder after a few days.

This soft-set fudge was a childhood staple and I deliberately don't call it peanut butter fudge. The amount of peanut butter is quite small, improving the texture and adding a slight nuttiness without coming to the foreground. Growing up on a plantation is like being part of a large extended family and there is never Mr This or Mrs That, only Aunties and Uncles. Auntie Bernice and Uncle Bernie (really!) had no offspring of their own and lavished time and affection on all the plantation children. As if by magic, the most beautifully decorated birthday cakes appeared for our parties and sweet treats were always forthcoming. Auntie Bernice's fudge had something special and at the time we never bothered to analyse it, we simply ate and enjoyed it. Years later, as she watched her mother-in-law prepare the original recipe, my sister figured out that it was the peanut butter, a fairly unobtrusive amount of it. Because of the large proportion of milk to sugar, it is best made by sight and feel, so you don't need a sugar thermometer, just patience and a good spatula.

Makes 24 squares

25 g/1 oz/2 tbsp butter, plus extra for greasing (optional)

350 g/12 oz/1¾ cups demerara sugar

350 ml/12 fl oz/generous 1⅓ cups evaporated milk

50 g/1¾ oz/scant ¼ cup smooth peanut butter

¾ tsp vanilla extract

Soft-set Plantation Squares

Grease or line a medium loaf tin with baking parchment.

Put the sugar and milk in a large heavy-based uncoated saucepan and stir over low heat to dissolve the sugar completely. Increase the heat slightly to medium. Once it comes to the boil, lower the heat. Leave the mixture to boil, stirring from time to time for the first 5 minutes, then more intensively as time goes by, not forgetting the sides and corners of the pan. Scrape down the sides regularly. The mixture will look granular, but that is normal. About 20–25 minutes after it comes to the boil, keep a keen eye on the mixture, as it will start to thicken. Keep stirring. After 25–30 minutes it will be very thick. Pour a little into a bowl filled with cold water. If you can press it into a soft ball between your thumb and forefinger without having it dissolve or fall apart immediately, it is ready. It will be no more than 98°C/208°F on a sugar thermometer if you use one – and this is not a typo!

Remove the saucepan from the heat. Stir in the butter, peanut butter and vanilla and beat vigorously with a wooden spatula for 2 minutes, then transfer the mixture to the loaf tin. Level the top quickly and leave to set before cutting into small squares. It will keep for 10 days, but note that it is a very soft confection, far softer than traditional fudge.

Makes 18 squares

50 g/1¾ oz/3½ tbsp butter, flaked, plus extra
for greasing (optional)

400 g/14 oz/2 cups caster sugar

100 ml/3½ fl oz/scant ½ cup milk

175 g/6 oz/½ cup condensed milk

½–1 tsp vanilla extract

Tablet is very similar to fudge, but it has a grainier texture. I would call it sandy, but in a good way, as this characteristic actually allows it to dissolve on the tongue, leaving a very rich and creamy aftertaste. This one is quite pale in colour and is good plain. If you feel you must add to it, crystallised ginger, dried figs, candied orange peel or nuts will work well. This might sound like a modern idea, but tablet's documented history can be traced back at least to the early eighteenth century. It was made from a simple base of mainly sugar and water, but with flavourings such as fresh oranges, rose, cinnamon and ginger.

Today, instead of water, much of the liquid consists of various mixtures of milk, cream and condensed milk. See 'Borstplaat' on p.107 for a Dutch variant to tablet.

Scotch Tablet

Grease or line a large loaf tin with baking parchment.

Put the sugar, butter and milk in a large heavy-based uncoated saucepan and stir over very low heat to dissolve the sugar completely. This takes a good 10 minutes or so, but be patient; it makes a difference to the texture. Increase the heat slightly and when it comes to a rolling boil, stir in the condensed milk and bring to the boil again. Attach a sugar thermometer to the pan and lower the heat. Leave the mixture to boil, stirring gently but thoroughly with a wooden spatula while it cooks. It is quite a lively mixture and it will bubble and seethe merrily. Make sure that you keep on scraping the bottom and edge of the pan, and shift the thermometer from time to time to get in behind it. Leave to boil to 114°C/237°F (soft ball stage).

Take the saucepan off the heat and remove the thermometer. Add the vanilla and whip with a hand-held stick blender for about 2 minutes (3 minutes with a hand-held mixer) or beat vigorously for at least 5 minutes with the spatula. Pour immediately into the loaf tin. It will be quite liquid. Level the surface and leave to set.

As soon as it is firm enough, mark it into squares and unmould when completely set. It will keep for at least 2 weeks.

Milk: a truly divine ingredient

It is no secret that the exalted status enjoyed by the cow in India is largely due to the creature's ability to produce wonderfully nourishing milk in addition to other useful items that can be used as fuel, fertiliser and the like. Dairy products have been known in the Indus valley since at least 2500 BC and have traditionally been used by all of the religions that make up the population of the subcontinent: Hindus, Muslims, Jains and Buddhists.

Although cows' milk was predominant in the past, milk from other animals was also valued, both as food and as a remedy for a number of ailments. Milk from goats and donkeys was supposed to be good for infants, while rarer antelope's milk was a remedy for bronchitis. Sheep's milk alleviated both bronchitis and gout and mare's milk was known to be strengthening. Over the ages, milk has been used as a drink and to make desserts, porridges and confections. The cream gives butter, usually clarified to make rich ghee, which will keep far better in a warm climate, and the resulting buttermilk makes a refreshing beverage. Yogurt and other curds made by light fermentation are still a cooling element in fiery southern Indian food. When cut with an acid agent, milk curdles and produces soft cheese-like *paneer*, which is eaten in savoury preparations or used to make all kinds of delicious sweets. This cutting of milk is surrounded by a faint shroud of mystery, as it was supposedly prohibited by Hinduism; by all accounts, the technique was introduced by the Portuguese and has been accepted practice ever since, leading to an even greater diversity in milk-based sweets.

We might consider dried, evaporated and condensed milk to be modern convenience foods, but Indians have long practised all kinds of milky arts. Jains, who were required by their religion to strain the milk through a muslin cloth before use, took to soaking lengths of muslin in milk and drying it, then reconstituting it as needed. Others have perfected techniques to concentrate the goodness found in milk to make sumptuously rich and delicious delicacies. It is not a random process and each stage is intended for a specific use. The milk can be reduced to half, one-third, one-sixth or one-eighth of its original volume. When only one-eighth remains, it is almost unrecognisable from its original state and becomes more of a dough in which the sugar has caramelised gently to produce a sweet undertone. This is the product that is prized by sweet makers and it is known by several names, chiefly *khoa*, *khoya*, *mava* or *mawa*. In India, where there is an abundance of good professional sweet-makers, many people will just pop out and get some tasty ready-made titbits. Home cooks who want to make a particular delicacy involving *khoa* can also step into a shop and buy it. Modern cooks, especially those living outside of India, often concoct mixtures of powdered and condensed milks, mixed with solids such as *paneer*, to dispense with the need for *khoa,* and the results can be very effective.

Copious quantities of sweets are eaten in India, and many of those involve dairy products in some form. Even gods have a special attachment to both milk and sweets. Krishna, often depicted as a chubby blue-skinned urchin, is described as being the bane of milkmaids' lives because he stole their milk and curds, leaving trails of broken and overturned pitchers in his wake; he was also known to be partial to sweets such as the fudge-like *pedas*. Ganesh, the elephant-headed god of ample girth, had a great weakness for sweets of all kinds, and is generally portrayed holding a sweet in one hand. Temple offerings include ghee, milk and sweets and they are incorporated into countless Hindu rituals. Ayurvedic medicine even prescribes certain sweets as a form of medication in a few cases and special herbs and spices are added to make them beneficial to specific groups, such as nursing mothers or convalescents. Eaten as a snack or dessert, Indian sweets are the loveliest kind of indulgence, and definitely worth the effort involved. Making them yourself means that you will be able to ensure that the best quality products are used. They steadfastly remain one of my many weaknesses.

Subcontinental Indians most often speak of 'peda' and Guyanese Indians prefer 'pera'; it is one of the most popular members of the family of fudge-like sweets. While Indian versions are very soft and often enriched with nuts, the Guyanese kinds vary from hard caramel-coloured balls to softer discs kept moist and white by the addition of powdered milk. I remember very well the older version my grandmother used to make, using fresh milk from her own cows, cooked slowly in a cast-aluminium wok we call a 'karahi', until it became thick, with wood smoke from the clay fireplace and rich creamy aromas mingling freely. Then she scooped it up with a spoon and formed small balls between her palms, dipping them in cold water at frequent intervals to relieve the heat – I would say pain – from the mixture. In spite of all the care and love that went into that kind, I still prefer the softer type and this recipe is a hybrid of my own, combining Indian influences with the way my mother makes hers.

Makes 32 balls or discs, or 24 squares

butter, for greasing

400 g/14 oz/2 cups demerara sugar

350 ml/12 fl oz/generous 1⅓ cups evaporated milk

75 g/2¾ oz/generous ½ cup full-cream powdered milk

75 g/2¾ oz/generous ¾ cup finely ground pistachios

100 g/3½ oz/generous ¾ cup finely chopped pistachios (if making balls)* OR whole pistachios to decorate squares and discs

* For the best effect, chop the pistachios finely and sift out any powder, or the powder will coat the balls and prevent the larger pieces from sticking.

Pistachio Milk Sweets

Pista Peda / Pistachio Pera

Grease a 30 x 10-cm/12 x 4-in rectangular tin, such as a large loaf tin if making squares OR a shallow bowl and a large flat plate if making discs and balls.

Put the sugar and milk in a large heavy-based uncoated saucepan and stir over low heat to dissolve the sugar completely, then increase the heat slightly to medium. Once it comes to the boil, lower the heat a little and leave to boil until it thickens and darkens slightly, stirring occasionally at first and continuously as it thickens. Leave to cook for 20–25 minutes from the time it comes to the boil, but start keeping a closer eye on it after 15 minutes or so. It has reached the correct consistency when you can see the base of the pan as you stir the mixture. This means that when you pull

the spoon across the bottom of the pan, the mixture does not immediately cover the base again as it did when it was thinner. Note that the mixture itself will still be fairly runny and may even look slightly grainy. Remove the saucepan from the heat and beat in the powdered milk, followed by the 75 g/2¾ oz/generous ¾ cup ground pistachios. Beat vigorously for 3–4 minutes; it should thicken, making it more and more difficult to beat.

Pour the mixture into the tin if making squares. Press a whole pistachio into each square before a thin skin forms, or it will wrinkle. Mark the block as soon as it sets sufficiently.

For discs and balls, pour the mixture into the shallow bowl. Leave the mixture to become firm enough to shape, then dip up a small dessertspoonful and shape into a ball between greased palms. Put the chopped pistachios in another shallow bowl and roll the balls around to coat with the nuts. For discs, simply flatten the balls into thick discs and decorate immediately with a whole pistachio. Arrange on buttered plates and leave to dry for an hour or so before covering with clingfilm.

Serve at room temperature and eat within a few days. I freeze them too, with no noticeable loss of flavour. In that case, pack them into sturdy containers, with baking parchment or greaseproof paper between the layers.

Makes about 15 pieces

125 g/4½ oz/9 tbsp (generous 1 stick) butter

250 g/9 oz/2¾ cups gram/chickpea flour (besan)

¼ tsp ground cardamom

300 g/10½ oz/1 cup sweetened condensed milk

slivered pistachios, flaked almonds or silver leaf, to decorate

Chickpeas are an extremely popular food in India, both whole as a pulse and in flour form. Whole, they are made into delicious curries or re-fried with fragrant spices to make a drier dish. Gram (chickpea) flour is also widely used to create an array of spicy savoury snacks, from simple soft-textured fritters such as 'vada' to crisp 'sev', deep-fried sticks made from a well-seasoned batter. And amazing though the thought may seem to the uninitiated, gram flour is used to make delectable confectionery. It provides both texture and flavour, with an attractive background nuttiness that is enhanced by toasting the flour before use.

This easy Indian sweet is high on my list of favourites and I find it hard to stop at one piece. It is neither too sweet nor over-rich. Recipes vary and some traditional ones can be quite complicated, requiring many steps and ingredients. This one is very simple and can be whipped up in less than half an hour to satisfy a sudden craving. It also keeps well for several days. Get your chickpea flour from an Indian grocer (where it is called 'besan') if you can. It will be fresh and cheap.

Gram Fudge
Mohanthal

Melt the butter in a non-stick frying pan or wok, add the gram flour and fry over medium heat for 10–12 minutes, stirring constantly with a wooden spatula. The flour should darken slightly and the raw and sharp smell you start out with will change to a pleasant, nutty aroma. Don't skimp on this step, or your fudge will have an undercooked taste instead of the intended nuttiness. The texture will change from large lumps to fine breadcrumbs. Lower the heat slightly and immediately stir in the cardamom and condensed milk with a silicone spatula, scraping down the sides to ensure even cooking and absorption. Keep stirring until the mixture holds its shape and looks like soft pastry. It will take only a minute or two to reach that stage and overcooking will give a drier texture.

Scrape the mixture out onto a sheet of baking parchment and shape it into a slab, about 15 x 20 cm/6 x 8 in and 2 cm/¾ in thick. If using nuts, press them into the surface. If using silver leaf, cover the entire surface or apply it randomly in small pieces.

Cut the fudge into diamonds or squares and serve at room temperature.

Leftovers will keep in a cool place in an airtight container for several days.

Recipe I will make just over 200 g/7 oz;
Recipe II will make scant 250 g/9 oz and
Recipe III will make about 325 g/11½ oz.
Actual yield depends on the creaminess of the
milk you use. I prefer to have a little left over
rather than risk not having enough.

Recipe I
1.25 litres/2 pints/5 cups full-cream milk
----
60 ml/2 fl oz/¼ cup fresh strained
lemon juice

Recipe II
1.5 litres/2½ pints/6⅓ cups full-cream milk
----
70 ml/2¼ fl oz/generous ¼ cup fresh strained
lemon juice

Recipe III
2 litres/3½ pints/8 cups full-cream milk
----
90 ml/3 fl oz/⅓ cup fresh strained
lemon juice

'Paneer' is a soft fresh Indian cheese that forms the basis for many milk sweets as well as savoury dishes. For sweet-making, it is usually drained and used almost immediately, but savoury preparations, especially those that involve cubing and frying, require the cheese to be pressed overnight to compress it. It is very simple to make at home and there is minimal work involved: whole milk, lemons and some patience and you're in business. Use pasteurised milk, not sterilised ultra heat treated (UHT). The latter is often stabilised to such an extent that it will not curdle as desired. Besides just curdling the milk, the lemon adds a delicious tang that cuts the richness of sweets made with this 'paneer'.

Paneer for sweets

Line a large sieve or colander with a piece of muslin and hang it above a large bowl.

Put the milk in a saucepan and heat it to boiling point. Remove the pan from the heat and stir in the lemon juice. The milk will start to curdle and separate into curds and a watery green-tinged liquid, the whey. After a few minutes, when the liquid is quite clear and the curds have clumped together, pour the contents of the saucepan into the sieve. The bowl will fill up with the whey. Discard this and leave the *paneer* to stand for 2–3 hours (or overnight) until all possible moisture has drained out, making sure that the sieve hangs free of liquid at all times.

Once the *paneer* has drained properly and there is no moisture on the top, pick the muslin up and give it a twist to squeeze out any remaining liquid. The *paneer* can now be used for making sweets or it can be refrigerated for later. It is best used within a few days. If chilled, put it into an airtight container to avoid absorbing other smells.

Makes about 12 pieces

175 g/6 oz *paneer* (see Recipe I, p.98)

40 g/1½ oz/scant ⅓ cup full-cream powdered milk

75 ml/2½ fl oz/5 tbsp milk

30 g/1 oz/2 tbsp soft butter or ghee

100 g/3½ oz/½ cup caster sugar

¼ tsp ground cardamom

chopped pistachios, gold or silver leaf, crystallised violets, crystallised rose petals, silver balls, etc., to decorate (optional)

'Burfi' comes in a range of textures and compositions and this one has a richly creamy flavour and a good body that moulds well. It is not something to be made on the spur of the moment, as you will need to prepare the 'paneer' a few hours beforehand, but it is certainly worth the effort. Traditional recipes call for 'khoa' or 'mawa'. These are names for the same highly concentrated milk base with the consistency of a soft and sticky dough that is such a popular ingredient in Indian sweet-making. It is made by reducing milk to an eighth of its original volume, which is a time-consuming process and is usually done professionally. This recipe uses a quick shortcut with extra milk solids. Traditional decorating options stop at gold and silver leaf or chopped pistachios. A few more suggestions are given below and if you use a different option on each piece, you can create an attractive Bollywood presentation.

Burfi

Put the *paneer*, powdered milk and milk in a bowl and mash together until well mixed. Scrape the mixture out into a non-stick wok or large saucepan, add the butter or ghee and place over medium heat. Keep stirring the mixture to prevent it from catching and lower the heat if necessary. It will gradually change from liquid to something resembling very soft dough in 13–15 minutes.

Remove the pan from the heat and stir in the sugar and cardamom. Leave to stand for a few minutes until the sugar dissolves, then put it back over the heat. Keep stirring just until you see some butter separating. This will take only a minute or two. Transfer immediately to a flat plate and shape it into a neat slab, about 2 cm/ ¾ in thick.

Decorate as desired and leave to set; sugar decorations are best added before serving or the colour may bleed.

Serve in small squares or other shapes. Refrigerate any leftovers; well wrapped, the *burfi* will keep for at least a week. Bring to room temperature for serving.

Makes about 12–18 pieces

275 g/9¾ oz *paneer* (see Recipe III, p.98)

200 g/7 oz/⅔ cup sweetened condensed milk

¼ tsp ground cardamom

2 tbsp chopped pistachios OR a small piece of silver leaf, to decorate

'Kalakand' can best be described as a stovetop cheesecake. It is served in squares like fudge and makes a delicious dessert after a spicy meal or an accompaniment to a cup of tea. It isn't as sweet to the taste as you might expect it to be with the condensed milk and has a pleasantly lemony undertone from the 'paneer'. Once you have the 'paneer', it doesn't take very long to cook. Brightly coloured pistachios or edible silver leaf make an attractive decoration.

Stovetop Cheesecake
Kalakand

Line a 1.25-litre/2-pint/1-quart loaf tin with baking parchment.

Put the *paneer*, condensed milk and cardamom in a bowl and mash together until smooth. Scrape the mixture out into a non-stick frying pan or wok and place over medium heat. Stir constantly to prevent it from catching and lower the heat if necessary. Keep the sides of the pan clean with a wooden or silcone spatula. At first you will have a fairly thin and glistening mixture, but as the moisture evaporates it will gradually become thick and matte. It should take about 12–15 minutes to reach the right consistency. It will look and feel like a soft dough that stays together and the colour will be just a shade more creamy than when you started.

Scrape the dough out into the loaf tin and quickly level the top. If using pistachios, sprinkle them on and press lightly to embed. If using silver leaf, wait until it cools and sets, then press on small pieces randomly.

It will keep refrigerated for several days, but serve at room temperature, in squares.

Makes 16 generous squares

30 g/1 oz/2 tbsp butter, plus extra for greasing

200 g/7 oz vermicelli, preferably medium thick

1 litre/1¾ pints/4 cups milk, preferably full-cream

100 g/3½ oz/½ cup granulated sugar

30 g/1 oz/generous ⅛ cup sultanas

¼ tsp ground cardamom

⅛ tsp freshly ground nutmeg

1 tsp vanilla extract

6 red glacé cherries, cut into eighths

Vermicelli cake or 'sewain' is Guyanese comfort food at its soothing best and despite its particular association with the Muslim holiday of Eid it is a great favourite with young and old of all religions and races. It is Mughal in origin and is one of the many foods that were taken by the Indian indentured labourers to the Caribbean, where its Indian name of 'seviyan' was simplified to 'sewain'. It comes in varying consistencies, from a fairly liquid dessert that is served in bowls to the cake type that is given here, which is always considered more special than the runnier version. Although it bears a superficial resemblance to Jewish 'lokshen kugel' (noodle pudding), 'sewain' is creamier and more fragrantly spiced and it is cooked entirely on the stove.

Vermicelli Cake

Seviyan / Sewain

Grease a 20 x 20-cm/8 x 8-in baking tin.

Put the vermicelli in a bowl and break it up roughly. If it comes in short lengths, this step won't be necessary.

Heat the butter in a large wide pan, ideally a non-stick wok, and add the vermicelli. Use 2 wooden spatulas to toss the vermicelli around in the butter until a few of the strands are dark golden brown and the vermicelli gives off a pleasant aroma. Pour in the milk and add the sugar and sultanas. Bring to the boil, then lower the heat and simmer for 10–15 minutes, stirring gently and almost continuously, and scraping down the sides of the pan as necessary with a wooden spatula. The volume of liquid will reduce considerably. The vermicelli should be cooked through and generously coated with a thick creamy sauce.

Stir in the remaining ingredients and transfer to the tin to set.

Once it has set, it can be cut into squares to serve either lukewarm or cold. Lukewarm, the texture will be softer and creamier; and cold, it will be firmer. Both are delicious; it is a matter of personal preference. If you are not serving it within a few hours, cover it well and refrigerate. Individual portions can be warmed briefly in the microwave. It will keep for a few days, or I have also frozen it successfully for a month.

For the milk dumplings

125 g/4½ oz/scant 1 cup skimmed milk powder

70 g/2½ oz/½ cup plain flour

1 tsp baking powder

⅛–¼ tsp ground cardamom (optional)

60 g/2¼ oz/¼ cup (generous ½ stick) cold butter, cubed

about 160 ml/5½ fl oz/generous ⅔ cup milk (more as needed)

corn, sunflower or peanut oil, for deep-frying (purists may use ghee)

For the syrup

375 g/13 oz/scant 2 cups granulated sugar

375 ml/13 fl oz/scant 1¾ cups water

¾ tsp lemon juice

rose water, for sprinkling (optional)

The 'gulab jamuns' of my childhood were made with full-cream powdered milk, but now, Indian ladies around the world seem to have switched unanimously to skimmed milk powder, on the grounds that it makes a lighter 'gulab jamun'. While homemade versions rely on powdered milk, professional sweet makers in India tend to use the milk dough base of 'khoa' (described on p.93), often frying them in pure ghee, the clarified butter that is a much loved but exceedingly rich frying medium. Although some have switched to oil, purists remain undaunted by the prohibitive price of ghee and steadfastly disregard any possible connection to heart trouble. A few drops of 'kewra', a highly scented rose-like essence distilled from the flowers of the Pandanus tectorius, are sometimes sprinkled over the dumplings. It can be overwhelming to the uninitiated, and rose water makes an excellent substitute. 'Gulab' means 'rose' and the name translates roughly to 'rose plums', but this step is purely optional, as the dessert is perfect without any extra embellishment. Although they can be eaten at any time of the day with tea or coffee, they are particularly good as the finale of a spicy Indian meal when the creamy taste and fragrant syrup will soothe the palate and extinguish any residual fires lurking in your mouth.

Milk Dumplings in Syrup

Gulab Jamun

The technique for the dumplings is like making pastry. Mix the dry ingredients together in a bowl. Rub in the cold butter well with your fingertips until the mixture looks like fine breadcrumbs. Add the milk and mix well with a wooden spoon or plastic scraper. It will look quite wet and gloopy, but that is how it is meant to be at this stage. Bring it together as neatly as you can into the centre of the bowl and cover with clingfilm. Leave to rest for about 15 minutes while you prepare the syrup. For the syrup, put the sugar, water and lemon juice in a saucepan and bring slowly to the boil while stirring to dissolve the sugar. Leave to simmer without stirring for 5 minutes, then remove from the heat and set aside.

By this time your bowl of previously gloopy mixture should have absorbed the liquid and will look and feel like pastry. Shape the mixture into 18 neat and smooth balls and set aside. Cracks will open up while frying. If you find it impossible to shape the mixture into crack-free balls, you will need to knead in extra milk, a few drops at a time.

Heat enough oil for deep-frying in a deep pan. The oil should not be too hot, or the dumplings will darken very fast, before the centres cook. Have a roomy dish standing by. (If the dish is too small, the dumplings will bump into each other and lose their roundness.) Deep-fry the dumplings in small batches until brown and cooked through, giving them a slight nudge so that they flip over to cook on the other side. Take into account that they will expand exponentially as they cook. You can cook one first to get an idea of the cooking time, size and heat. Break it open to see if it is cooked and has no hard core. If necessary, lower the heat and prolong the cooking time for the rest. Remove with a slotted spoon and put in a wide shallow dish, about 26 cm/10½ in in diameter.

When all have been deep-fried, pour the warm syrup over them. Allow them to absorb as much syrup as they can, turning them over after 30 minutes or so.

Drain them and keep in an airtight container in the refrigerator. Serve them at room temperature in small bowls, about 2–3 per portion. If you are presenting them as part of a buffet, you can put them individually in foil or paper cases. Sprinkle with rose water just before serving, if you desire.

Dutch Fondant Fudge

Borstplaat

Makes a thin sheet about 10 x 30 cm/4 x 12 in

300 g/10½ oz/1½ cups caster sugar
----
100 ml/3½ fl oz/scant ½ cup double cream
----
30 ml/2 tbsp milk
----
1 tsp vanilla extract
----
food colouring (optional)

'Borstplaat' is cousin to Scotch Tablet (see p.91) and it dates from medieval times, when sugar was a highly prized commodity and an extravagance, used sparingly (if at all) during the year as a seasoning or for medicinal purposes. In its original form of water, sugar and herbs, it started out as many other confections did: as a medicinal lozenge sold by apothecaries, perhaps for chest complaints as the word 'borst' means 'chest'. For the feast of St Nicholas on 5 December, caution was thrown to the wind by those in a position to do so and sugary treats were in great demand. More than one traditional song firmly encourages good behaviour in children, with the promise of sweet treats to come: for instance, 'wie zoet is krijgt lekkers, wie stout is de roe': 'sweet [children] will get delicious treats, naughty ones the stick'. 'Borstplaat' remains primarily a December tradition. This version is the colour of old ivory and made in a single sheet, but you will also find it in pastel colours, poured into small heart-, wreath- or animal-shaped moulds. It is made far thinner than either tablet or fudge and is also sweeter.

Generously line a large loaf tin with baking parchment or use individual small shapes.

Put all of the ingredients, except the food colouring if using, in a medium heavy-based uncoated saucepan and stir over very low heat to dissolve the sugar completely. This takes a good 10 minutes or so, but be patient; it makes a difference in the texture. Bring to the boil and attach a sugar thermometer to the pan. Keep stirring the mixture gently but thoroughly with a wooden spatula while it cooks. It is quite a lively mixture and it will bubble and seethe merrily. Make sure that you keep on scraping the bottom and corners of the pan, and shift the thermometer from time to time to get in behind it. Leave to boil to 116°C/241°F (upper soft ball going on to firm ball stage). It cooks a lot faster than either fudge or tablet.

Take the saucepan off the heat and remove the thermometer. Add any colouring now and beat vigorously for about 2 minutes with the spatula. You will feel the mixture thicken and it will start to settle and feel grainy around the sides and on the bottom of the pan. Pour immediately into the loaf tin or individual moulds. It will be very liquid. Leave to set.

As soon as it is firm enough, mark the sheet into squares and unmould when completely set, or break into shards when hard. It will keep for 2 weeks.

Makes about 24 squares

butter, for greasing

160 g/5¾ oz sweet dried mangoes

100 g/3½ oz/½ cup + 50 g/1¾ oz/¼ cup granulated sugar

325 g/11½ oz *paneer* (see Recipe III, p.98)

90 g/3¼ oz/generous ¼ cup sweetened condensed milk

flakes of dried mango, to decorate

If you like cheesecake, you will like this Indian-style sweet, which can be called a mango 'burfi', fudge or cheesecake. Indians will tell you about their gorgeous Alphonso mangoes, Filipinos about Carabao, Guyanese about Buxton Spice, and so on. Those of us who live outside of mango-growing regions have to make do with what our local supermarkets offer - and a pretty poor offering it can be too, so I tried using rehydrated dried mangoes for cooking, on the basis that only the best are selected for drying in the country of origin. Taste the mangoes if you can and select a sweet kind, as there are also tarter types on the market. Neither fresh nor canned fruit will give a good result here, and there will be far too much liquid. Despite the separate steps, this recipe is quite simple.

Mango Moons

Grease a plate or tray about 20 x 20 cm/8 x 8 in.

Rehydrate the mangoes in the microwave or on the stovetop. Put them in a bowl or saucepan and cover generously with water. Microwave on high (1000 watts) for 4–5 minutes, or heat in the saucepan until the water boils. Drain well, add 100 g/ 3½ oz/½ cup sugar and use a hand-held stick blender or food processor to make a smooth purée. Leave to cool in a bowl. It should be a very thick paste.

Stir in the *paneer* and condensed milk thoroughly and transfer to the non-stick saucepan. Place over medium heat and stir constantly to prevent it from catching. After about 3 minutes, add the 50 g/1¾ oz/¼ cup sugar and keep stirring for another 8–10 minutes or so, keeping the sides of the pan clean with a wooden or silicone spatula. The mixture is done when it looks and feels like a soft dough that stays together.

Scrape the mixture out onto the plate or tray and quickly shape into a slab, about 17 x 17 cm/6½ x 6½ in and 2 cm/¾ in thick. Moisten your fingers to flatten and neaten the top. Alternatively, shape into individual rounds. Leave to cool, then chill until needed, cutting it into squares or half-moons as required.

Serve at room temperature or chilled, decorated with flakes of dried mango.

Chapter
Five

Magical Marzipan

Marzipan

You can, of course, simply mix together ground almonds and icing sugar and bind it with egg white. This will produce a very crude and gritty product, really not worthy of the name marzipan. If you take just a little more time in the preparation and make a syrup or cook the mixture as required, you will be rewarded with something absolutely delicious. In addition to a basic recipe for almond marzipan that should serve you well, I'm giving you a few others, to demonstrate how marzipan and marzipan-like concoctions are made in different places. Each has its own specific flavour and texture characteristics, so one cannot really say which is better than the other. As with so many things in life, it is a question of taste and I suspect that ethnicity will also play a leading role.

Follow the method as described in each recipe and use the freshest possible nuts. Note that the basic recipes for marzipan require a sugar thermometer. If you make the chocolate-dipped versions, keep them at a constant, cool temperature to discourage discolouration. The refrigerator is usually too cold. Apart from that, it's all quite clear sailing to achieve delicious results.

A subtle delicacy

The almond tree (*Prunus amygdalus*) is known to have been cultivated by the ancient Greeks and its botanical name derives from the Greek word for almond. So strong was the connection that the Romans referred to the nut as *Nux Graeca* (Greek nut). It spread through trade and travel to occupy a vast region from the western Mediterranean to Western Asia, journeying even further afield in modern times, to America. Although it was used in savoury preparations, it has always been most highly prized as a key ingredient in cakes, biscuits and confectionery. Marzipan, for instance, is almond in one of its purest and most delightful forms.

Marzipan has a long and illustrious history, but its origins and name are cloaked in mystery and its development shows a tangle of intercultural influences and exchanges. The most popularly held belief is that it originated with the Arabs. The geographical location certainly fits and the Arabs were great traders, who introduced sugar from Asia to the Mediterranean and Western world. Sugar-based nut confections were already a tradition and fine art for Arab cultures when Medieval Europe began to catch on. But when they did, they did so in a grand way: with *subtleties*, a name which is intriguing to say the least, as they brimmed over with magnificence. 'Subtlety' was the name given to the splendid marzipan centrepieces used as table decoration for banquets and other feasts, which were dismantled and eaten at the end of the meal. The beautifully moulded and sculpted figures were used individually or grouped to portray historical or religious scenes, or one that suited the occasion for which it was made. Gilding and colouring were used to great effect. The colouring was extracted from available natural sources, some of them questionable. They included edible leaves for green, saffron or other flower stamens for yellow, saffron and egg yolk for gilding as well as blood cooked with breadcrumbs to produce black. Indigo gave blue, and holly berries or powdered sandalwood yielded red. If the thought currently crossing your mind is that people certainly ate strange things in the past, allow yourself to dwell for a moment on the lists of E-numbers that adorn the tubes and pots of modern food colourings.

By the reign of Elizabeth I, the *subtlety* was going out of fashion and was being replaced by *marchpane*. This was also a presentation item, moulded as cakes in wooden hoops and artistically decorated. Sugar and rose water were mixed to provide a glaze and gilding or gold leaf could be used to add even more beauty. With the passing of the centuries, marzipan has lost none of its allure and not much has changed in its preparation, nor at times in its presentation. Those who have visited Italy may have seen the gorgeously moulded, sculpted and coloured *Martorana* fruit, originally a speciality of the Sicilian convent of the same name, but now copied all over the country. They are often quite garish but some are produced with such skill that it is hard to tell them from the real thing. In Western and Eastern Europe, marzipan figures are still a Christmas speciality and though the mass-produced kind generally lack both flavour and finesse, they are seasonal items that are always in great demand. In Holland, bakers and supermarkets stock marzipan fruit, vegetables and animals in their miniature forms, with one exception. In December almost every counter houses several kilos of moulded pink pig or piglet, whose size diminishes as people buy a piece from snout to tail.

European recipes from the 1660s show that marzipan has not changed vastly in the course of time. The marzipans of old were often flavoured with rose and orange flower waters, a custom that still enjoys enormous popularity in the Middle East. They ranged from simple raw mixtures of nuts, sugar and flower waters to boiled versions and mixtures baked on wafers. In the modern Western world, two main schools of marzipan exist: the German and the French, with some regional variants. For the German method whole almonds and sugar are repeatedly ground together before being cooked and shaped. It produces a fairly coarse product that is delicious for eating but less versatile for uses such as moulding. French marzipan is made by mixing finely ground almonds with a sugar syrup, yielding a smooth and malleable mixture.

But there is more to the world of marzipan and the following section will take you through some of the regional variants as well as a few oddities that, to my mind, admirably fit the category.

Makes just over 550 g/1 lb 4 oz

250 g/9 oz/2¾ cups blanched almonds, finely ground

1 tbsp icing sugar if grinding your own almonds (see left)

300 g/10½ oz/1½ cups granulated sugar

100 ml/3½ fl oz/scant ½ cup water

This is a good all-purpose marzipan. It can be eaten as it is, used to decorate cakes or to stuff dried dates and apricots, or cut into cubes and dipped in chocolate to make a special confection – or whatever else you can think of. The texture depends largely on how the almonds are ground and the finer the nuts, the smoother it will be. You can buy them ready-ground or grind them yourself, adding a tbsp of icing sugar to absorb some of the oil and enable you to grind more finely. Once you've made a block of marzipan, wrap it well and store it in the refrigerator, where it will keep for several weeks.

Almond Marzipan

Put the ground almonds in a heavy-duty electric mixer fitted with a paddle attachment. Put the granulated sugar and water in a small heavy-based saucepan and stir over low heat until the sugar dissolves completely. Attach a sugar thermometer to the pan, increase the heat and bring to the boil. Leave to boil without stirring until it reaches 114°C/237°F (soft ball stage).

Remove the thermometer and pour the syrup over the ground almonds. Mix at medium speed for about 5–7 minutes. Stop when it is smooth and well bound. You want to get the oil from the nuts well combined with the syrup, but if you overmix it, it will become too oily.

Scrape the mixture out of the bowl onto a silicone mat, flatten it into a rough disc and leave to cool completely.

When completely cool, knead well by hand to get rid of the crusted bits. Don't add extra icing sugar; it will only coarsen the marzipan.

Shape the marzipan into a neat block and wrap well in a few layers of clingfilm. Put the marzipan into a plastic bag and store in the refrigerator for up to 6 weeks. Unless otherwise stated, bring the portion you need to room temperature before using.

Pistachio Marzipan

To make pistachio marzipan, use the amounts and method described for Almond Marzipan (see above), substituting the same amount of skinless pistachios for almonds. Grind the pistachios finely with 1 tbsp icing sugar and proceed as for Almond Marzipan. This recipe makes about 575 g/1lb 4 oz.

Situated south of Madrid, Toledo is as famous for its marzipan as its steelwork, and its medieval look is picturesque if rather inconvenient by modern standards. It is definitely a place to be explored on foot. Among the many sights, one finds several 'confiterías' around the main square and in the streets leading off it. Some are simply the foyers of convents, holding a nun and a workaday wooden table stacked with their wares. Chief among these are the absolutely delicious 'mazapán de Toledo'. The rich marzipan is shaped into tiny figures of all kinds and some are filled with 'yemas' (see p.68), making them even more succulent. This recipe is for Toledo-style marzipan, cut into a simple elegant shape.

Makes about 30 rounds, about 1.5 cm/⅝ in thick and 3 cm/1¼ in in diameter

200 g/7 oz/1 cup granulated sugar

5 tbsp water

200 g/7 oz/scant 2¼ cups blanched almonds, finely ground

4 egg yolks, mixed with a good pinch of finely grated lemon zest

icing sugar, for dusting (optional)

Rich Spanish Marzipan

Mazapán al estilo de Toledo

Put the sugar and water in a medium non-stick pan and stir over low heat until the sugar dissolves completely. Attach a sugar thermometer to the pan, increase the heat and bring to the boil. Leave to boil without stirring until it reaches 90°C/194°F (about 5 minutes after it comes to a rolling boil).

Remove the thermometer and stir in the ground almonds. Cook over low–medium heat for 2–3 minutes, stirring constantly. Quickly stir in the yolk mixture (it helps to have someone pour the yolks in for you) and cook for a further 3–4 minutes, stirring constantly. The mixture should come together and look like a soft dough.

Transfer the mixture to a heavy-duty electric mixer fitted with a paddle attachment and beat at medium speed for about 3–4 minutes until smooth but not too dry. Scrape the mixture out of the bowl and flatten it into a rough disc, then lay it on a silicone mat to cool completely.

When completely cool, knead the mixture by hand to get rid of the crusted bits. Don't add extra icing sugar at this stage; it is not necessary with a silicone mat and will coarsen the marzipan. If you don't have a silicone mat, lay the mixture on a sheet of clingfilm instead. Flatten it and cover with another sheet of clingfilm.

Roll the marzipan out to an even thickness of 1.5 cm/⅝ in and cut out neat rounds with a 3-cm/1¼-in fluted cutter. You may need to wipe the cutter clean from time to time and/or dust it with icing sugar. Re-knead the trimmings lightly and re-roll until you have used up all the marzipan. Try to roll and cut as economically as possible; the marzipan gets oily as you continue to handle it.

Leave the marzipan to air-dry at room temperature for an hour or two, then pack it into an airtight container, with sheets of greaseproof paper between the layers. Keep in a cool place and eat within a week.

Makes 16 rounds

50 g/1¾ oz/½ cup walnuts, finely chopped

200 g/7 oz Almond Marzipan (see p.114)

about 250 g/9 oz/9 squares dark chocolate

16 walnut halves

These can be flavoured to suit your taste. Add a little orange zest or finely chopped candied orange peel if you like, or stem or crystallised ginger.

Dipped Walnut Marzipan

Knead the finely chopped walnuts and/or other flavourings into the marzipan and shape it into a neat sausage, about 25 cm/10 in long. Trim the ends and cut the sausage at 1.5 cm/⅝ in intervals to make 16 rounds. Neaten the shape if necessary.

Place the rounds on a wire rack and leave to stand uncovered at room temperature for at least 30 minutes. The surface should feel dry to the touch and not at all oily.

Melt (or temper) the chocolate in a heatproof bowl (see p.25), then drop a piece of marzipan into it. Swirl it around to coat well, then remove it with a dipping or dining fork, tapping the fork several times on the rim of the bowl to get rid of excess chocolate. Deposit the coated round gently onto greaseproof paper and repeat for the rest. Gently place a walnut half in the centre of each one. Don't press, or you will wrinkle the top.

Leave the marzipan to set completely on a wire rack before removing from the paper and storing in an airtight container in a cool place for up to 2 weeks.

If you have ever invested in the fruity marzipan-like French delicacy 'Calissons d'Aix', sold by good 'confiseries' and available directly from France at the click of a mouse, you will know how expensive it is. Try my homemade version instead. The authentic ones use candied melon and that is very difficult to obtain outside of France or Italy, so I replace it with candied citron. If you can't find that either, use more orange. You will need orange flower water and edible paper as well. The good news is that they are easy to make and fairly quick, if you discount the resting time. I cut them simply into rectangles, but you can try cutting them in the typical pointed oval, if you can find a cutter. However, you will then have to do a lot of neatening of the glaze, as the cutter will not be as effective as a knife, and you will also end up with a lot of trimmings.

Makes about 16 bars, about 2.5 x 6 cm/ 1 x 2½ in OR small squares as desired

125 g/4½ oz/scant 1½ cups blanched almonds, finely ground

50 g/1¾ oz/scant ½ cup icing sugar

50 g/1¾ oz/¼ cup caster sugar

100 g/3½ oz candied citron, diced

100 g/3½ oz candied orange peel, diced

1½ tbsp orange flower water

edible wafer paper

For the glaze

100 g/3½ oz/scant 1 cup icing sugar

2 tbsp egg white, as needed

A Kind of Calissons

Put the almonds, icing sugar, caster sugar, citron and orange peel in a food processor and pulse until finely ground. Add the orange flower water and pulse until you get a smooth mixture.

Place a sheet of clingfilm on your work surface. Place the almond mixture on it and flatten it with your hands. Cover with a second sheet of clingfilm and roll out to an even thickness of 1 cm/½ in. (Approx. 22 x 14 cm/8½ x 5½ in.) Remove the top sheet of clingfilm.

Cover the surface completely with edible wafer paper, trimming it to fit. Wrap well with the bottom sheet of clingfilm and leave for 24 hours at cool room temperature.

Next day, sift the icing sugar for the glaze into a small bowl and add enough egg white to make a stiff but spreadable consistency. Mix thoroughly but gently to avoid bubbles. Unwrap the almond mixture and place on a cutting board paper-side-down, otherwise you will spoil the finish if you have to move it later.

Spread the glaze evenly over the surface and leave uncovered for 2–3 hours so that the glaze becomes firm enough to cut through neatly. Use a sharp knife to cut into bars or squares, or as you wish. Make sure that you cut all the way down through the paper and clean the knife frequently between cuts so that it doesn't drag the glaze.

Preheat the oven to 130°C/266°F/Gas Mark ½–1.

Arrange the bars or squares on a baking sheet and leave the glaze to dry in the oven for about 20 minutes. The glaze should barely colour and may still feel slightly soft to the touch until it cools and hardens properly. Leave to cool on the baking sheet, then transfer to a wire rack. They can be eaten immediately and will keep for a few weeks in an airtight container in a cool place.

Makes 16 squares

200 g/7 oz Pistachio Marzipan (see p.114)

200–250 g/7–9 oz/7–9 squares dark chocolate

small pieces of crystallised rose

petals (optional)

You can vary these to suit by cutting the marzipan
into sticks instead and using dark or white chocolate.
White chocolate will, of course, make them sweeter.

Dipped Pistachio Marzipan

Roll out the marzipan to a thickness of 1.5 cm/⅝ in and cut 16 neat squares, re-rolling and using the trimmings too.

Place the squares on a wire rack and leave to stand uncovered at room temperature for at least 30 minutes. The surface should feel dry to the touch and not at all oily.

Melt (or temper) the chocolate in a heatproof bowl (see p.25), then drop a piece of marzipan into it. Swirl it around to coat well, then remove it with a dipping or dining fork, tapping the fork several times on the rim of the bowl to get rid of excess chocolate. Deposit it gently onto greaseproof paper and repeat for the rest.

Gently drop a piece of crystallised rose in the centre of each one. Don't press, or you will wrinkle the top.

Leave to set completely on a wire rack before removing from the paper and storing in an airtight container in a cool place for up to 2 weeks.

Makes about 16 pieces

butter, for greasing

150 g/5½ oz/1 cup untoasted cashews

150 g/5½ oz/¾ cup granulated sugar

110 ml/3½ fl oz/generous ⅓ cup water

edible silver leaf, to decorate (optional)

Although the milk-based 'burfis' are most widely known, there are other kinds too, such as this cashew version, which is more like marzipan than anything else. It is very simple to make, but you will need untoasted cashews, which you can buy from health food shops or Indian grocers, and it is best to make it the day before you need it so that the nutty flavour is able to come to the fore. Embellished with a touch of edible silver leaf, this will make a delicious and eye-catching addition to your sweet plate. The silver has no flavour whatsoever, but adds a nice Bollywood touch. Indian grocers stock it, as do the better suppliers of sugar craft ingredients.

Indian-style Cashew Marzipan

Kaju Burfi

Grease a dinner plate and set aside.

Grind the cashew nuts as finely as you can and put them in a dry non-stick frying pan over medium heat. Stir-fry for about 5 minutes, moving the nuts constantly. They are ready when they start to give off a pleasant, nutty aroma. Do not let them colour. Transfer to a medium bowl and set aside.

Put the sugar and water in a small saucepan and stir over low heat until the sugar dissolves completely. Attach a sugar thermometer to the pan, increase the heat and bring to the boil. Leave to boil without stirring until it reaches 110°C/230°F (thread stage) and remove immediately from the heat.

Remove the thermometer and pour the syrup over the cashews in the bowl. Stir for a minute or so until the mixture starts to bind so that it will hold its shape well when you scrape it out onto the plate, but still be malleable enough to mould and shape. If you continue to mix until it is very stiff, your burfi will be dry and brittle, so take care.

Using a plastic or metal scraper, quickly scrape the mixture out onto the dinner plate and shape it into a square, about 15 x 15 cm/6 x 6 in; it should be 1.5 cm/⅜ in thick. Use the scraper to straighten the edges and to compress the top of the mixture. Make 3 parallel cuts to divide the block into 4 slices, then make as many parallel cuts as needed, at an angle of 45°, to create diamond shapes.

If using the silver decoration, apply a little to the tops of the diamonds and leave to cool.

When cool, loosen the *burfi* carefully from the plate. If it sticks, heat the base of the plate briefly to melt the butter. Store in an airtight container at cool room temperature for a day before serving. It will keep in the container for several days.

Makes 16

16 Amarena cherries (in syrup)

250 g/9 oz Almond Marzipan (see p.114)

200–250 g/7–9 oz/7–9 squares dark chocolate

They look like truffles, but the chocolate covering hides a layer of marzipan that in its turn conceals a flavourful cherry. Amarena cherries are an Italian speciality that are sold in jars with syrup. They have a wonderfully distinctive taste and go very well with anything made from almonds, such as these bites. The remaining syrup can be drizzled or poured over ice cream and other desserts.

Cherry Marzipan Bites

Rinse the cherries and pat them dry with kitchen paper.

Divide the marzipan into 16 equal portions. Flatten each portion and use it to encase a cherry, sealing well. Roll between your palms to form a neat ball and set aside on a wire rack.

Shape the rest in the same way and leave to stand uncovered at room temperature for at least 30 minutes. The surface should feel dry to the touch and not at all oily.

Melt (or temper) the chocolate in a heatproof bowl (see p.25) and drop a ball into it. Swirl it around a little to coat well, then remove it with a dipping or dining fork, tapping the fork several times on the rim of the bowl to get rid of excess chocolate. Deposit it gently onto greaseproof paper and repeat for the rest.

Leave to set completely on a wire rack before removing from the paper and storing in an airtight container in a cool place for up to 2 weeks.

Makes 16

250 g/9 oz Pistachio Marzipan (see p.114)

200–250 g/7–9 oz/7–9 squares dark chocolate

For the filling

100 g/3½ oz/3½ squares dark chocolate

30 ml/2 tbsp double cream

1 tbsp brandy (or replace with cream)

Here is one that looks similar to the Cherry Bites on p.122, but with pistachio marzipan and a 'surprise' chocolate filling instead. You can make the chocolate filling beforehand and keep it chilled for a day or so before using it. Be warned that the brandy gives quite a kick, so replace it with cream if you prefer. Decorate the balls with tiny pieces of gold or silver leaf, or with whole pistachios if you like, or simply wrap them in gold or green foil wrappers.

Pistachio and Chocolate Balls

For the filling, melt the chocolate in a heatproof bowl over a pan of barely simmering water. Warm the cream with the brandy and stir it into the melted chocolate until smooth. Leave to cool completely, then chill until firm.

Shape into 16 balls and keep them chilled or pop them into the freezer for a few minutes. If the balls are not firm enough, they will be harder to coat with marzipan and will get out of shape. If your kitchen is not cool, remove them from the refrigerator or freezer in 2 batches, as needed.

Divide the marzipan into 16 equal portions. Flatten each portion and use it to encase a ball of filling, sealing well. Roll between your palms to form a neat ball and set aside on a wire rack. Shape the rest in the same way and leave to stand uncovered at room temperature for 15 minutes.

Melt (or temper) the chocolate in a heatproof bowl (see p.25) and drop a ball into it. Swirl it around a little to coat well, then remove it with a dipping or dining fork, tapping the fork several times on the rim of the bowl to get rid of excess chocolate. Deposit it gently onto greaseproof paper and repeat for the rest.

Decorate as you wish and leave to set completely before removing from the paper and storing in an airtight container in a cool place for up to 2 weeks.

A few more ways of using marzipan

Cakes

You can dress up a cake by covering it with a layer of Almond Marzipan (see p.114), tinted in an attractive pastel colour. Make sure that the cake is free of crumbs and brush it lightly with warm sieved apricot jam so that the marzipan will stick. If you tint a few small bits in other colours, they can be used to make extra decorations. These can be simple flat shapes such as stars, butterflies, leaves, and flower cut-outs, or you can make roses by pressing small balls of marzipan flat with your thumb and joining them in layers onto a tiny central cone.

Stuffing

Dates, apricots and other dried fruit can be filled with marzipan, and walnut halves can be sandwiched. Use plain Almond Marzipan (see p.114) or tint it as desired. Or use the Pistachio Marzipan (see p.114) for a real Middle Eastern flavour.

Sticks, squares and lozenges

Simply roll out the Almond or Pistachio Marzipan (see p.114) to the desired thickness (or shape into a sausage) and cut into the required shape. A whole nut can be pressed into the tops of squares and lozenges. A little sugar syrup or glucose syrup will help it to stay in place.

Mulberries

These are known as *toot* in Iran and are simply blunt cone shapes of marzipan that are rolled in sugar, with a sliver of pistachio pressed into the wide end to simulate a stem.

Layered squares and spirals

Using two or three colours of Almond Marzipan (see p.114) – for instance, plain, pink and green – you can create a nice effect. Roll out the pieces of marzipan to an even thickness and place them one on top of the other. Press lightly with the rolling pin and cut into squares or roll up to form a sausage and then cut into discs that show the spiral pattern.

Chapter
Six

Nice and
Nutty

A bit of knowledge

Those unfortunate enough to have nut allergies have this delightful option removed from their reach, but on the other hand, nuts are a godsend to those with gluten intolerance because they can be used to replace flour in many recipes. In fact, many of the recipes in this section are flour-free. I find nuts one of the most delicious ingredients and I can honestly say that I have never met a nut I didn't like. There are so many to choose from and all have their own specific flavour. In this section you'll find a selection of nut recipes from several regions, with a few combinations that you may not yet have encountered. Everything is quite straightforward and all you need to know is given in the individual recipes, so I'll just stick to a few basic pieces of advice here.

Selecting and buying nuts

It goes without saying that fresh nuts will give the best flavour. Buy your nuts as freshly as you can from a reliable source. Indian and Middle Eastern grocers have a good turnover and often price their products very attractively. Taste before buying if you are given the option. When selecting pistachios, try to get very green ones. They come in a wide colour range, from cream to bright green; the greener ones will really shine through and give an eye-catching effect. See the Ingredients section for information about coconut (see p.12).

Preparation

Grind, chop or slice the nuts as directed in the recipe. Grinding is best done in a food processor and if you add a small amount of the sugar or flour from the recipe, you will be able to grind finer and drier as some of the oil will be absorbed. If you can buy good-quality blanched ground almonds, do so. They are generally finer than you can achieve at home, with a nice loose texture. If you use only small quantities of walnuts at a time, buy them in their shells and shell as needed. Larger amounts can be bought shelled, preferably in halves. Look for French walnuts. They are more expensive than Chinese or Indian nuts, but the flavour is far better.

Equipment

Make sure that your equipment is scrupulously fat-free for the recipes that use egg whites. Any trace of fat or egg yolk will have an adverse affect. Baking parchment will ensure easy release of the baked items.

Makes 13

2 egg whites

100 g/3½ oz/½ cup caster sugar

1 tsp vanilla extract

150 g/5½ oz/1⅔ cups fine desiccated coconut

⅛ tsp salt

about 100 g/3½ oz/3½ squares dark chocolate, melted (see p.25), optional

These flat and chewy coconut macaroons are excellent on their own, but dipping the bases in dark chocolate makes them quite irresistible.

Coconut Macaroons

Preheat the oven to 160°C/315°F/Gas Mark 2–3. Line a baking sheet with baking parchment.

Whisk the egg whites in a scrupulously clean bowl until foaming. Pour in the sugar while still whisking. Add the vanilla and keep on whisking until soft peaks hold their shape when you pull out the whisk.

Fold in the coconut and salt and use 2 dessertspoons to shape neat little piles on the baking parchment. Leave enough space in between for spreading. Bake for about 20 minutes until just cooked through and light gold on the outside. They will still be soft to the touch but will firm up as they cool. Overbaking will dry them out. Leave to cool on a wire rack.

Store in a jar or tin or freeze for later.

If you are using the melted dark chocolate, spread some on the base of each cooled macaroon and put it on a sheet of baking parchment to harden. Once the chocolate has set properly, the baking parchment can be peeled off.

Makes 16

2 eggs

1 tsp vanilla extract

125 g/4½ oz/½ cup + 2 tbsp granulated sugar

150 g/5½ oz/1⅔ cups fine desiccated coconut

¼ tsp salt

Homemade Dutch coconut macaroons are quick and simple. They are softer on the inside than the chewier and flatter ones with a cracked surface that commercial bakers tend to make. My mother-in-law had quite a sweet tooth and often whipped up a batch of these to supplement the cakes and tarts she baked every week. Production peaked at Passover, as they contain no flour. She always made a depression in the centre of each one as she laid it to rest on its bed of wafer paper and this allowed it to bake more evenly and faster, producing a succulent mouthful. Once baked, they can be dressed up by pouring melted chocolate or ganache into the depressions, or by dipping the bases into melted chocolate, but they are absolutely delicious as they are.

Coconut Kisses

Kokosmakronen

Preheat oven to 180°C/350°F/Gas Mark 4. Line a baking sheet with baking parchment.

Whisk the eggs with the vanilla in a large bowl. Add the sugar, coconut and salt and stir well with a fork to moisten the coconut. Leave to stand for 20–30 minutes to allow the coconut to re-hydrate a little.

Scoop up about 1½ tablespoons of the mixture and press between your palms to compact it into a rough ball. Place on the baking sheet and use your thumb to make a depression in the centre of each macaroon. The outer edges will crack slightly; simply press with your fingers to neaten.

Bake for 12–15 minutes until the tops are tinged with gold and the mixture is cooked through. Overbaking will dry them out. Leave to cool on a wire rack.

Store for a few days in a jar or tin, or freeze as soon as they are cool.

Makes about 24

200 g/7 oz/1⅓ cups pistachios, finely ground

50 g/1¾ oz/generous ⅓ cup plain flour

⅛ tsp salt

125 g/4½ oz/½ cup + 2 tbsp caster sugar

50 g/1¾ oz/3½ tbsp butter, melted

4 tbsp beaten egg (reserve the rest)

1 tbsp water

about 4 tbsp sesame seeds

These delicious cookies are made for special occasions in many Middle Eastern countries. Economical versions rely more heavily on flour for body, but the basic ingredients remain similar while methods for mixing and shaping may vary: the sesame seeds may be toasted and then mixed with honey or not; the pistachios may be finely ground or chopped; the biscuits may be coated with pistachio on one side and sesame on the other. However they are made, they remain a treat to be savoured at the end of a meal or to accompany a cup of tea or coffee.

Pistachio and Sesame Biscuits
Barazek or Barazeh

Preheat the oven to 180°C/350°F/Gas Mark 4. Line a baking sheet with baking parchment.

Mix all of the ingredients, except the reserved egg, 1 tbsp water and sesame seeds, to form a dough. If you have just used a food processor to grind the pistachios, simply add the dry ingredients and pulse to mix, then turn into a bowl and add the butter and egg. Shape into 24 even-sized balls.

On a deep plate, beat the 1 tbsp water into the reserved egg. Scatter 1 tbsp of the sesame seeds onto another plate. If you put it all on the plate at the same time, you will end up using a lot more. Roll each ball in the egg, then in the sesame seeds and arrange on the baking sheet. Keep on adding more sesame seeds as needed.

Flatten each ball with your palm to a diameter of about 4.5 cm/1¾ in and a thickness of 1.5 cm/⅝ in. Bake for 12–15 minutes. They should be slightly chewy, so do not overbake them. Leave to cool on a wire rack.

Store in an airtight container at room temperature for a few days or freeze for later.

Makes 16

175 g/6 oz/1¾ cups walnuts
1 tbsp flour or potato starch
⅓ tsp baking powder
¼ tsp ground cinnamon
100 g/3½ oz/½ cup caster sugar
1 beaten egg, as needed
few tbsp icing sugar

Nutty confections are always in great demand in North Africa. Those who cannot afford more expensive kinds of nuts content themselves with sesame seeds and peanuts, or use flour-based doughs and a restrained amount of pistachios, almonds or walnuts. The height of luxury is to be able to eat a few of the delicious morsels that consist mainly of nuts, such as these walnut macaroons. They are quick and easy if you use a food processor. Use the freshest walnuts you can find, as even a hint of staleness or bitterness will spoil the flavour.

Walnut and Cinnamon Macaroons

Preheat the oven to 180°C/350°F/Gas Mark 4. Line a baking sheet with baking parchment.

Put the walnuts, flour, baking powder and cinnamon into a food processor and pulse until the nuts are very fine. Add the caster sugar and pulse for a few seconds to mix. Transfer to a bowl and knead in enough egg to make a softly malleable mixture. You will need about three-quarters of it. Shape into 16 balls.

Roll the balls thoroughly in the icing sugar and arrange on the baking sheet, spaced well apart. Bake in the centre of the oven for about 13 minutes. The tops will crack as they bake and they will still feel soft to the touch when they are done. They should be slightly chewy in the centre, so do not overbake them. Leave to cool on a wire rack.

Store in an airtight container at room temperature for a few days or freeze for later.

Makes about 36

100 g/3½ oz/²/₃ cup blanched almonds, finely ground

215 g/7¼ oz/generous 1 cup granulated sugar

55 g/2 oz egg white

These are not the slick and trendy French 'macarons' that are one of the latest fads, but rather the more homely, chewy, slightly crackled ones that are very easy to make. They can be eaten as they are or sandwiched with a filling of your choice such as ganache or buttercream and also make an excellent component for trifles and other creamy desserts.

Almond Macaroons

Note that this recipe relies on correct weighing, particularly of the egg whites. If it is too wet, it will spread more than it should and the resulting macaroons will be thin and unattractive.

Preheat oven to 190°C/375°F/Gas Mark 5. Line 2 baking sheets with baking parchment.

Mix all of the ingredients together to a smooth, stiff paste. This will take about 2 minutes using a heavy-duty electric mixer fitted with a paddle attachment or 3 minutes with a vigorous hand and a wooden spoon.

Transfer the mixture to a piping bag fitted with a 16 mm/⅝ in plain nozzle and pipe neat little heaps onto the baking sheets. Space well apart as the macaroons will spread while baking. If you haven't got a 16 mm/⅝ in or similar sized nozzle you can spoon little heaps onto the sheet, or make balls, but the result won't be as neat as the piped ones. Moisten your fingertips and use them to neaten the pointed tops.

Bake for about 10 minutes until light golden brown. Be careful not to overcook them, or you will lose the chewiness. They will have spread considerably and the tops will be slightly crackled. Carefully remove the macaroons from the baking sheets and leave to cool on wire racks.

The cooled macaroons will be crisp on the outside and chewy on the inside. Store in an airtight container. They will stay chewy for a week or so, but will start to dry out and get brittle after that, which some people seem to like too. If, like me, you are a fan of chewiness, keep most of the surplus stored in the freezer and thaw at room temperature.

Makes 16

150 g/5½ oz/1 cup blanched almonds,
finely ground

150 g/5½ oz/¾ cup granulated sugar

2 eggs, beaten

50 g/1¾ oz/½ cup (7–8 tbsp) flaked almonds

For the filling (optional)

125 ml/4 fl oz/½ cup cream (single or double)

125 g/4½ oz/4½ squares dark chocolate,
finely chopped

Simple to make, these almond cookies are
deliciously chewy and are good eaten on their own
or used as an accompaniment to dessert. If you
sandwich them with a filling made of equal
quantities of dark chocolate and cream, they
will be irresistible.

Flourless Almond Biscuits

Preheat the oven to 180°C/350°F/Gas Mark 4. Line a baking sheet with baking parchment.

Mix the ground almonds, sugar and 3 tbsp of the beaten egg together and knead lightly to make a malleable mixture.

Put the reserved beaten egg in a small bowl and scatter the flaked almonds onto a plate.

Divide the almond mixture into 16 portions and roll each into a ball between your palms. Flatten each ball to a diameter of about 5 cm/2 in and dip on both sides into the egg, then press both sides into the flaked almonds and arrange on the baking sheet. Bake in the centre of the oven for 12–15 minutes. The biscuits will be done as soon as the almonds and sides start to get golden brown. They should be slightly chewy, so do not overbake them. Leave to cool on a wire rack.

Store in an airtight container at room temperature for a few days or freeze for later.

All you need to do for the filling, if you wish, is to heat the cream to boiling point, then stir in the finely chopped dark chocolate and wait for it to reach a spreading consistency. Spread onto half of the cooled biscuits and top with the rest.

Makes 16

200 g/7 oz/1⅓ cups blanched almonds, very finely ground

100 g/3½ oz/½ cup caster sugar

2 egg yolks

about 2 tbsp rose water, or as needed

1 egg white

50 g/1¾ oz/½ cup flaked almonds, crumbled onto a plate

Rose water lends a delicate perfume to these almond balls, but if you are not fond of the flavour of roses, substitute water. They make a lovely addition to a teatime or dessert selection and foil cases can be used for an attractive presentation.

Almond and Rose Water Balls

Preheat the oven to 170°C/325°F/Gas Mark 3. Line a baking sheet with baking parchment.

Put the ground almonds, caster sugar and egg yolks in a bowl and add enough rose water to make a malleable paste that is not too soft. Knead well and divide into 16 pieces. Roll each piece between your palms into a ball.

Whisk the egg white lightly in a deep plate to loosen it a little. Dip the balls thoroughly in the egg white, then roll them around in the crumbled almonds to coat.

Arrange on the baking sheet and leave to rest for about 10 minutes. Bake for 12–15 minutes. The almonds should be lightly tinged with gold, and overbaking will make them chewy instead of tender. Leave to cool on a wire rack.

Store in an airtight container. They will be quite yielding when fresh, but the texture will become firmer after a day or two.

Makes about 300 g/10½ oz

150 g/5½ oz/1²/³ cups finely ground
blanched almonds

150 g/5½ oz/¾ cup granulated or
caster sugar

pinch of grated lemon zest (preferably organic)

enough beaten egg to bind

Almond paste is simple to make and this recipe is for paste that is to be baked; it is not suitable for covering cakes. When baked, it gives a moister result than marzipan, which is firmer and closer in texture. It keeps quite well and is a great standby to have in the refrigerator, as you can whip up cookies in minutes (see Pine Nut Clusters p.142 and Quick Almond Lozenges p.144) or add it to other baked desserts. The type of sugar you use will be reflected in the texture and granulated or caster sugar will give the best results in baking. Granulated sugar provides a slightly looser and coarser texture than caster sugar. Icing sugar makes the paste too compact. If you are making a big batch, it is best to leave it neutral or to add just a little lemon zest, but use it cautiously because you don't want it to dominate. Flavourings such as orange zest, vanilla and fragrant flower waters can be added prior to baking.

Almond Paste

Put the dry ingredients in a bowl and mix together. Add the beaten egg, a little at a time and knead until it becomes a firm but malleable mixture. It responds well to kneading, especially once a little of the almond oil starts to dissolve some of the sugar. Do not add too much egg at this stage; it can be added to the matured paste in the correct quantity as described in the recipe you use.

Shape the paste into a block, wrap it well in several layers of clingfilm and refrigerate overnight.

It will keep for at least a fortnight. Use as needed.

Makes 16

300 g/10½ oz almond paste (see p.141)

pinch of orange zest (optional)

1½ tbsp beaten egg, or as needed

125 g/4½ oz/scant 1 cup untoasted pine nuts

Pine nuts are a popular ingredient in sweet and savoury Mediterranean cooking, and oven baking or light toasting brings out their flavour and delicate crispness. They are delicious sprinkled over salads and rice dishes or used in cookies such as these. As this recipe is so easy to make once you have the almond paste to hand, you can halve or double it as the mood takes you. They are a good accompaniment to tea and coffee any time of the day and are also a very pleasant way to end a meal.

Pine Nut Clusters

Preheat oven to 170°C/325°F/Gas Mark 3. Line a baking sheet with baking parchment.

Crumble the almond paste into a bowl. Grate the orange zest over it, if using. Add enough beaten egg to make a softly malleable paste. Shape the paste into 16 balls.

Scatter the pine nuts onto a plate and roll each ball around to coat thoroughly with the nuts, pressing a few into bald spots with your fingers. Be sure to embed them well, or they will fall off later. Neaten the shape of the balls, place them on the baking sheet and flatten the tops slightly. Bake for about 15 minutes until the nuts are light golden brown. Leave to cool on a wire rack.

Store in an airtight container. The pine nuts soften quickly, so they are best eaten within a day or two.

Makes 20 lozenges

300 g/10½ oz almond paste (see p.141)

1 egg yolk

few drops of water, if needed

about 3 tbsp granulated sugar

These Dutch lozenges are ridiculously simple to make and all you need is a quantity of prepared almond paste, an egg yolk, some sugar and a few minutes of time.

Quick Almond Lozenges

Weespermoppen

Preheat the oven to 200°C/400°F/Gas Mark 6. Line a baking sheet with baking parchment.

Crumble the almond paste into a bowl. Add the egg yolk and knead thoroughly to a firmly malleable consistency, adding a few drops of water if necessary. Divide into 2 portions.

Scatter the sugar onto your work surface or a silicone mat if you have one. Roll one portion of the almond paste back and forth in the sugar until you have a sausage about 20 cm/8 in long. Repeat with the second portion.

Cut each sausage into 2-cm/¾-in thick rounds, neaten the shape and press the cut sides lightly into the sugar. Arrange the lozenges on the baking sheet and bake for 8–10 minutes just until the edges are golden brown. The bases will caramelise nicely.

Remove immediately from the baking sheet and leave to cool on a wire rack.

Store in an airtight container for up to a week.

Makes 12

225 g/8 oz/1½ cups blanched almonds,
finely ground

175 g/6 oz/scant 1 cup granulated sugar

2 tbsp cornflour or potato starch

3 eggs

grated zest of ⅓ of a lemon (preferably organic)

icing sugar, for dusting

OR melted dark chocolate (see p.25)

OR icing, to decorate (optional)

Nutty Cakes

Marquesas

Every year just before Christmas, a delivery van stops and deposits an enormous box on our doorstep.

In it reposes a hamper brimming with delicious treats sent by our Spanish friends Nuria and Josep: an astounding assortment of 'turrones' and brittles, Toledo marzipan, fine wines and spirits, wonderfully flavoured Catalan olive oil and much more. Last year there was a box of 'marquesas', small almond cakes with a texture somewhere between marzipan and cake. They are quick and easy to make at home and the potato starch option makes them suitable for a gluten-free diet. If you make them a day or two in advance, they will be even more succulent. Don't stop at almonds. See below for variations.

Preheat the oven to 180°C/350°F/Gas Mark 4.

These cakes are usually baked in small square or rectangular paper cases. Using a 20-cm/8-in square tin with loose paper cases will give an angular, artisan effect. If you prefer neatly uniform round cakes, use a 12-hole muffin tin to hold the cases. For the square tin, put 9 of the empty cases in the tin and leave 3 out. Fill them all, then add the 3 to the tin to make 4 rows of 3, and tweak the papers here and there to create angular cakes.

If you have ground your own almonds in a food processor, leave them there and add the remaining ingredients. Pulse for about a minute, then divide the batter among the cases. If using a heavy-duty electric mixer or a hand whisk, beat the ingredients together vigorously for about 2 minutes, then transfer the batter to the cases.

Bake for 18–20 minutes in the muffin tin (a little longer in the square tin). The tops will barely colour; a skewer inserted into the centre of a cake should come out clean. Don't overbake; the insides should be just cooked through to retain a soft texture.

Dust the cakes with icing sugar just before serving. Alternatively, drizzle with melted chocolate or some thin icing.

Variations

Try them with walnuts, pistachios or hazelnuts. If using walnuts, I recommend a proportion of two parts walnuts to one part almonds, with some cinnamon replacing the lemon zest. Use the full amount of pistachios or replace a third with almonds for a milder flavour for those who find pure pistachios overpowering. Hazelnuts can be used on their own. Untoasted hazelnuts will taste sweeter and light toasting will bring out a little more nuttiness.

Even before I set foot in the region, Cádiz city held a peculiar attraction for me. Having been born and brought up in the New World, I found it quite thrilling to stand by the sea and imagine Columbus setting sail with the Niña, Pinta and Santa Maria (as told in our history books at school) and ending up stumbling upon the West Indies. It was a close-run thing, but when I did explore the region the sweets of Medina Sidonia very nearly outdid Cádiz and Columbus. 'Amarguillos' are a particular speciality of the town and are kept tender with a little mashed sweet or regular potato. They are very simple and pure in flavour and will melt in the mouth if left to mature for a day or two. If you like, you can add a drop or two of almond extract or a small pinch of lemon or orange zest. In the past a few bitter almonds were added, accounting for the name: 'amargo' means 'bitter'.

Makes 16

100 g/3½ oz boiled potato, preferably fresh and floury

1 medium egg

200 g/7 oz/1¾ cups icing sugar, sifted, plus extra for dusting

250 g/9 oz/1⅔ cups blanched almonds, finely ground

2 tbsp cornflour

Almond Delights
Amarguillos

Preheat oven to 200°C/400°F/Gas Mark 6. Line a baking sheet with baking parchment.

Mash the boiled potato with a ricer or mash well with a fork and pass it through a sieve. It should be completely lump-free, or you will have hard bits in the finished product.

Beat the egg and reserve about 2 tsp. Stir the rest into the potato, add the icing sugar and whisk until smooth.

Mix the ground almonds with the cornflour and add to the mixture. Fold it in well with a spatula so that you get something that looks like very soft almond paste. Add the rest of the egg as needed.

Use 2 dessertspoons to make 16 well-spaced mounds on the baking sheet. Moisten your fingers and shape each mound into a fairly neat disc, about 5 cm/2 in in diameter and 2 cm/¾ in high. It is easiest if you flatten the top first with outstretched fingers and then pat the sides into shape, moistening your fingers as necessary.

Bake for 12–15 minutes until set. They should hold their shape quite well. The bottoms will be golden brown, but the tops will remain pale. Remove the sheet from the oven and dust liberally with icing sugar. As soon as they can be handled, place them on a wire rack to cool.

When cool, wrap each one individually in a square of greaseproof paper and store in a glass jar for a pretty effect. Leave to mature for a day or so before eating. They will keep for more than a week in a cool, dry place.

Makes 16

200 g/7 oz/1⅓ cups blanched almonds, very finely ground

100 g/3½ oz/½ cup caster sugar

2 egg yolks

about 2 tbsp orange flower water, or as needed

1 egg white

a few tablespoons of sesame seeds, untoasted or lightly toasted

Flavoured with orange flower water and coated with sesame seeds, these sticks will bring a very North African touch to your table. The mixture is basically the same as for the Almond and Rose Water Balls (see p.140), but changing the flavouring and shape produces a very different article.

Sesame and Orange Flower Sticks

Preheat the oven to 170°C/325°F/Gas Mark 3. Line a baking sheet with baking parchment.

Put the ground almonds, caster sugar and egg yolks in a bowl and add enough orange flower water to make a malleable paste that is not too soft. Knead well and divide into 16 pieces. Roll each piece into a sausage, about 7 cm/2¾ in long with slightly tapering ends.

Whisk the egg white lightly in a deep plate to loosen it a little. Scatter the sesame seeds onto another plate. Dip the sticks thoroughly in the egg white, then roll them around in the sesame seeds to coat.

Arrange the sticks on the baking sheet and leave to rest for about 10 minutes. Bake for 12–15 minutes. Overbaking will make them chewy instead of tender. Leave to cool on a wire rack.

Store in an airtight container. They will be quite yielding when fresh, but the texture will become firmer after a day or two.

Totally Truffles

Techniques

Have you ever felt cheated by shop-bought truffles? I have. Walking into an elegant German *konditorei* one day, I admired the truffles on display: row upon neat row of balls of various kinds of chocolate with a wealth of filling and coating options. I finally managed to decide which to buy and had a box put together. Eagerly unpacking the box at home, anticipation soon melted to disappointment. The seemingly hand-rolled coating was purely cosmetic and the 'truffles' were perfectly pre-moulded spheres with a hole at one end, so that the too soft filling could be piped in and then closed with a dot of melted chocolate. To my mind, a truffle is a bite of delectable ganache with a chocolate, cocoa or nut coating, made all the more attractive by their slightly lop-sided shapes. They are just about the easiest of chocolates to make, so rather than getting sucked in by marketing tricks, try your hand at making your own.

The ingredients

I don't expect that you would even dream of using less than the best quality ingredients, but just in case you forget, I'm reminding you. I use Belgian or Swiss chocolate and fine Dutch cocoa with a deep colour and an intense but not bitter taste. Couverture (which has a high percentage of cocoa butter) is easier to work with than regular bars, but not absolutely necessary. You will simply need to take a bit more care. You may find that some of the fat separates and lodges at the edge of the bowl. (Couverture is less prone to this.) This can be stirred back into the mixture, but don't do it too vigorously once the chocolate starts to set, or it will harden very fast. Take into consideration too that the very high percentage dark chocolates may give a slightly firmer result. My suggestion is to use chocolate containing the following percentages of cocoa solids: dark chocolate 55–70%, milk chocolate at least 35% and white chocolate at least 30%. If you deviate greatly from these, you can expect different results. Callebaut 55% is my standard dark chocolate; it is easy-going and will allow itself to be put to almost any use. Lindt 70% has a wonderful fruity flavour, but needs a little more attention. Green and Black's is also superb. I'll leave it up to you to make wise choices. There's no need to get snobbish and obsessive, but you need chocolate with a high cocoa butter content and good flavour characteristics. Taste is your best guide.

Melting the chocolate

Most of the truffles here are covered with cocoa or another decoration, so you need not temper the coating chocolate; simple melting is enough. An improvised *bain-marie* works even better than a double boiler, as you can use a smaller bowl. Break up the chocolate and put it in a heatproof bowl that fits snugly over a saucepan of boiling water. The bowl should not touch the water and no steam should escape from the sides of the pan. See p.25 for more information on melting/tempering.

Size

As far as size goes, you may find mine on the generous side. I don't like the Malteser-sized kind. Make them smaller if you must, but take into account that you will need a larger amount of coating chocolate to cover the extra numbers you have created. You will also be ingesting more cocoa per bite, which will alter the overall taste experience.

Working temperature

A fairly cool setting is best for making truffles. However, it doesn't always work out that way and that need not deter you. Avoid the most obvious evildoers: sun streaming onto your work surface, an overheated kitchen, mugginess and high humidity. The warmer it is, the more chilling will be needed, but you should still be able to turn out delicious truffles.

Chilling

I find that chilling in stages works best and is quicker and easier in the long run. Instead of leaving the filling to set completely in the bowl in the refrigerator, I leave it there until it will hold its shape, and then make little heaps on a baking sheet lined with greaseproof paper. At this stage, the heaps need not be completely neat. They are then chilled again until completely firm, then quickly re-rolled between your palms to neaten before being rolled or dipped. This saves you from having to struggle with a mixture that is harder in some places than others as the heaps chill more evenly. If you find that the filling is very soft after shaping, chill again until firm.

.... and freezing

It is fine for truffles that are to be rolled in chocolate between your palms to be very cold, so you can even pop them into the freezer for a few minutes to speed up the process, instead of chilling them in the usual way. However, those that are to be dipped should be chilled, not even briefly frozen, or the dipping chocolate will lose its temperature very quickly and it will become difficult to coat them evenly; you may need to reheat the chocolate. The Dutch Cream Truffles (see p.173) are different – follow the instructions in the recipe.

Hand-coating and dipping

Use the method described in the recipe. Hand-coating by rolling between your palms will give a beautifully thin, crisp and brittle coating, just enough to contain the filling and to fix the cocoa. It is quite messy, but not unpleasant. Scrape the excess from your hands on the side of the bowl at regular intervals and keep lots of kitchen paper towels and a damp cloth handy to deal with spills. Dipping uses more chocolate and produces a thicker layer. If the chocolate is too warm, much of it will fall off to make a foot, so keep it between 30–35°C/86–95°F. White chocolate covering a dark filling can sometimes be transparent enough to reflect the filling. If you find this unattractive, you can double-dip them. Leave the first coat to set, then dip them a second time in melted chocolate.

Dipping fork

A two-tined or round chocolate-dipping fork is useful to have because less of the dipping chocolate clings to it than to a multi-tined dinner fork. If you don't have one, use a dinner fork, but make sure that you tap it well and pass it over the rim of the bowl to remove excess chocolate.

Cocoa and rolling

Cocoa for dusting needs to be scattered liberally. You will not use all of it, but an abundant layer makes it easier to coat the truffles. If you are making a subsequent batch of truffles within a day or two, it will still be usable. Sift it and add more as needed. Or use it in a chocolate cake or make a cup of cocoa. After all, you are using the best quality cocoa and why discard what can be reused?

Storage and serving

Pack truffles in layers in airtight boxes with sheets of greaseproof paper separating them. Keep them for up to two weeks in the refrigerator or more than a month in the freezer. If the truffles go 'bald' on thawing (due to moisture), re-dust them lightly with cocoa. Truffles can be eaten straight from the refrigerator, but they are even better if allowed to come to room temperature. The recipes give serving guidelines. Present them in sweet cases if you like, or arrange them on a dish. The sweet cases will minimise cocoa spillage.

Equipment

You need only a few basic pieces of equipment to create gorgeous truffles:
* saucepan for cream
* wire whisk
* wide shallow bowl for chilling filling
* bowl and saucepan for melting coating chocolate in a bain-marie
* a few large teaspoons or small dessertspoons
* chocolate dipping fork or dinner fork (for dipped truffles)
* dinner fork for rolling in cocoa
* a small sheet lined with greaseproof paper for the heaps of filling
* a small sheet for the cocoa
* kitchen paper and a damp cloth
* airtight containers for storage

Makes 20
For the filling

75 ml/2½ fl oz/5 tbsp double cream

3 tbsp unsweetened raspberry purée

175 g/6 oz/6 squares milk chocolate,
finely chopped

75 g/2¾ oz/2¾ squares dark chocolate,
finely chopped

For the coating

20–25 g/¾–I oz/scant ¼–¼ cup
(unsweetened) cocoa powder

75 g/2¾ oz/2¾ squares dark chocolate,
broken into pieces

This fruity truffle is a long-standing family favourite. A few days in the refrigerator brings out even more flavour - if you can bring yourself to leave them for that long. Use seedless purée made from undiluted fruit and without added sugar. If not, you will miss out on the flavour. You can make your own purée by pressing fresh or thawed frozen raspberries through a sieve. Preserves are not suitable.

Raspberry Truffles

Line a small baking sheet with greaseproof paper.

Put the cream in a small saucepan and stir in the raspberry purée. Bring the mixture to the boil and switch off the heat. Scatter in the finely chopped milk and dark chocolate and give the pan a shake so that the liquid covers the chocolate. Leave to stand for 30 seconds or so, then stir thoroughly with a wire whisk until smooth. Transfer to a wide shallow bowl and leave to cool to room temperature then chill in the refrigerator.

As soon as the mixture can hold its shape, use 2 large teaspoons to dip and shape 20 heaps onto the greaseproof paper, they needn't be very neat. Chill again until very firm. At this stage, you can even pop them into the freezer for a few minutes.

Roll the chilled chocolate heaps quickly between your palms to make neat balls and replace them on the greaseproof paper. If they feel soft, chill briefly again.

For the coating, scatter the cocoa onto a small baking sheet. Melt the dark chocolate in a heatproof bowl over a pan of barely simmering water and leave to cool slightly to about 30°C/86°F, or it will form too thin a coat.

Dip a ball of filling partially into the melted dark chocolate and roll quickly between your palms to coat with a thin layer of chocolate. Deposit it gently onto the cocoa and coat the rest in the same way. When all have been sealed with chocolate, use a clean fork to roll the truffles around in the cocoa to coat well. Just push the truffle lightly with the end of the fork, making it turn little somersaults until evenly coated with a layer of cocoa. Shift the coated truffles to one side.

Keep the truffles refrigerated and serve at room temperature. They will keep in an airtight container for at least 2 weeks in the refrigerator and for at least a month in the freezer.

Makes 20
For the filling
125 ml/4 fl oz/½ cup double cream

250 g/9 oz/9 squares milk chocolate,
finely chopped

2¼–2½ tsp instant espresso powder

For the coating
20–25 g/¾–1 oz/scant ¼–¼ cup
(unsweetened) cocoa powder

150 g/5½ oz/5½ squares white chocolate,
broken into pieces

Excellent with or without an after-dinner cup of coffee. Try to get the instant espresso powder, as it is more intense than regular instant coffee granules. Failing that, crush granules before measuring. Note that these need to be dipped before being rolled in cocoa. Hand-coating will make the two colours bleed into each other.

Cappuccino Truffles

Line a small baking sheet with greaseproof paper.

Put the cream in a small saucepan and bring to the boil. Switch off the heat. Scatter in the finely chopped milk chocolate and give the pan a shake so that the liquid covers the chocolate. Sprinkle the 2¼ tsp coffee powder over the chocolate and leave to stand for 30 seconds or so, then stir thoroughly with a wire whisk until smooth. Taste at this stage and add more coffee if needed, stirring it in well.

Transfer the mixture to a wide shallow bowl and leave to cool to room temperature, then chill in the refrigerator.

As soon as the mixture can hold its shape, use 2 large teaspoons to dip and shape 20 heaps onto the greaseproof paper; they needn't be very neat. Chill these again until very firm.

Roll the chilled chocolate heaps quickly between your palms to make neat balls and replace them on the greaseproof paper. If they feel soft, chill briefly again.

For the coating, scatter the cocoa onto a small baking sheet. Melt the white chocolate in a heatproof bowl over a pan of barely simmering water and leave to cool slightly to about 30°C/86°F, or it will form too thin a coat.

Drop a ball of filling into the melted chocolate. Swirl it around a little to coat well, then remove it with a dipping or dining fork, tapping the fork several times on the rim of the bowl to get rid of excess chocolate. Deposit it gently onto the cocoa. When all have been sealed with chocolate, use a clean fork to roll the truffles around in the cocoa to coat well. Just push the truffle lightly with the end of the fork, making it turn little somersaults until evenly coated with a layer of cocoa. Shift the coated truffles to one side.

Keep the truffles refrigerated and serve at room temperature. They will keep in an airtight container for at least 2 weeks in the refrigerator and for at least a month in the freezer.

Makes 20
For the filling
100 ml/3½ fl oz/scant ½ cup double
cream
250 g/9 oz/9 squares dark chocolate,
finely chopped
3 tbsp rum

For the coating
100–150 g/3½–5½ oz dark chocolate
vermicelli (as needed)

Although these look pretty innocent, the rum kick is quite potent. They are the easiest of all to make, as the only coating is chocolate vermicelli. For the best results, use a product that is made from real dark chocolate, not confectionery coating. The amount needed will depend on the thickness of the vermicelli.

Rum Balls

Line a small baking sheet with greaseproof paper.

Put the cream in a small saucepan and bring to the boil. Switch off the heat. Scatter in the finely chopped chocolate and give the pan a shake so that the liquid covers the chocolate. Leave to stand for 30 seconds or so, then stir thoroughly with a wire whisk until smooth. Slowly whisk in the rum and continue to whisk until smooth. Transfer to a wide shallow bowl and leave to cool to room temperature, then chill in the refrigerator.

As soon as the mixture can hold its shape, use 2 large teaspoons to shape 20 heaps onto the greaseproof paper; they needn't be very neat. Chill these again until very firm. At this stage, you can even pop them into the freezer for a few minutes.

For the coating, sprinkle half of the vermicelli onto a plate, adding more later as needed. Roll the chilled chocolate heaps quickly between your palms to make neat balls and replace them on the greaseproof paper. When all have been shaped, roll them one at a time in the vermicelli to coat and set aside on another plate.

Keep refrigerated and serve at room temperature. They will keep in an airtight container for at least 2 weeks in the refrigerator and for about a month in the freezer.

Makes 20
For the filling
125 ml/4 fl oz/½ cup double cream

250 g/9 oz/9 squares white chocolate,
finely chopped

about 1½–2 tsp powdered green tea (*matcha*),
plus extra to decorate (as desired)

For the coating
200 g/7 oz/7 squares white chocolate,
broken into pieces

This combination of powdered Japanese green tea ('matcha') with white chocolate is not only irresistible, it is also lovely to look at, and the amount of tea you add will contribute to both colour and flavour. It will also cut some of the sweetness of the white chocolate. Bear in mind that powdered green tea has quite a high caffeine content, and that the actual strength will also depend on the brand. Taste the mixture and see if you need more before you use the larger amount; use even more if you think it is needed.

Green Tea Truffles

Line a small baking sheet with greaseproof paper.

Put the cream in a small saucepan and bring to the boil. Switch off the heat. Scatter in the white chocolate and give the pan a shake so that the liquid covers the chocolate. Sprinkle 1½ tsp of the powdered tea over the chocolate and leave to stand for 30 seconds or so, then stir thoroughly with a wire whisk until smooth. Taste at this stage and add more tea if needed, stirring it in well. Transfer to a wide shallow bowl and leave to cool to room temperature, then chill in the refrigerator.

As soon as the mixture can hold its shape, use 2 large teaspoons to dip and shape 20 heaps onto the greaseproof paper; they needn't be very neat. Chill these again until very firm.

Roll the chilled chocolate heaps quickly between your palms to make neat balls and replace them on the greaseproof paper. If they feel soft, chill briefly again.

For the coating, melt the white chocolate in a heatproof bowl over a pan of barely simmering water and leave to cool slightly to about 30°C/86°F, or it will form too thin a coat.

Drop a ball of filling into the melted chocolate. Swirl it around a little to coat well, then remove it with a dipping or dining fork, tapping the fork several times on the rim of the bowl to get rid of excess chocolate. Deposit it gently onto the greaseproof paper and repeat for the rest. Leave to set completely before removing from the paper.

Keep the truffles refrigerated and serve at room temperature. They will keep in an airtight container for at least 2 weeks in the refrigerator and for at least a month in the freezer.

Fruity Nutty Truffles

Many types of dried fruit go extremely well with chocolate; chocolate-coated raisins, for example, are popular throughout the world. I'm not a fan myself, finding that the intense sweetness of the raisins largely overpowers whatever chocolate flavour there is. However, there are other combinations that I greatly enjoy, such as the Cheat's Chocolate Panforte on p.185, and these truffles, where cranberries, orange and walnuts are combined with dark chocolate. Instead of being coated with cocoa, they are rolled in powdered pistachios. The pistachios need to be ground to a powder, easily done in a food processor fitted with a sharp blade. A coarser grind will use far more nuts and will result in a more rustic finish.

Makes 20

For the filling

35 g/1¼ oz dried cranberries

35 g/1¼ oz candied orange peel

35 g/1¼ oz/generous ⅓ cup walnuts

100 ml/3½ fl oz/scant ½ cup double cream

175 g/6 oz/6 squares milk chocolate, finely chopped

75 g/2¾ oz/2¾ squares dark chocolate, finely chopped

For the coating

50 g/1¾ oz/⅓ cup pistachios, ground to a powder

75 g/2¾ oz/2¾ squares dark chocolate, broken into pieces

Line a small baking sheet with greaseproof paper.

Chop the cranberries, orange peel and walnuts very finely in a food processor. If you don't have one, chop them by hand with a large, very sharp knife, going back and forth several times until very fine. Set aside.

Put the cream in a small saucepan and bring to the boil. Switch off the heat. Scatter in the finely chopped milk and dark chocolate and give the pan a shake so that the liquid covers the chocolate. Leave to stand for 30 seconds or so, then stir thoroughly with a wire whisk until smooth. Stir in the fruit and nut mixture. Transfer to a wide shallow bowl and leave to cool to room temperature, then chill in the refrigerator.

As soon as the mixture can hold its shape, use 2 large teaspoons to dip and shape 20 heaps onto the greaseproof paper; they needn't be very neat. Chill again until very firm. At this stage, you can even pop them into the freezer for a few minutes.

Roll the chilled chocolate heaps quickly between your palms to make neat balls and replace them on the greaseproof paper. If they feel soft, chill briefly again.

For the coating, scatter the powdered pistachios onto a plate. Melt the dark chocolate in a heatproof bowl over a pan of barely simmering water and leave to cool slightly to about 30°C/86°F, or it will form too thin a coat.

Dip a ball of filling partially into the melted dark chocolate and roll quickly between your palms to coat with a thin layer of chocolate. Put it on the powdered pistachios and coat the rest in the same way. After you have coated 3 or 4 with chocolate, start rolling them in the powdered pistachio, or the nuts will not stick. Use a small spoon to sprinkle some of the nuts onto the truffles, then use a clean fork to roll the truffle around in the nuts to coat well. Just push the truffle lightly with the end of the fork, making it turn little somersaults until evenly coated with a layer of nuts.

Put the coated truffles on another plate. Repeat until all the truffles have been shaped and coated with both chocolate and nuts.

Keep the truffles refrigerated and serve at room temperature. They will keep in an airtight container for at least 2 weeks in the refrigerator and for at least a month in the freezer.

Makes about 24 squares
For the filling

100 ml/3½ fl oz/scant ½ cup double cream

150 g/5½ oz/5½ squares milk chocolate,
finely chopped

50 g/1¾ oz/1¾ squares dark chocolate,
finely chopped

75 g/2¾ oz/½ cup toasted hazelnuts,
ground to powder

1–2 tbsp (unsweetened) cocoa powder

For the coating

20–25 g/¾–1 oz/scant ¼–¼ cup (unsweetened)
cocoa powder

90 g/3¼ oz/3¼ squares dark chocolate, melted

These square truffles are very easy to shape, as they are cut from a block. For the best flavour, toast the hazelnuts well and leave them to cool before grinding them to a fine powder in the food processor. For a less sweet version, switch the amounts of dark and milk chocolate around.

Hazelnut Truffle Squares

Line a 15 x 10-cm/6 x 4-in loaf tin generously with greaseproof paper.

Put the cream in a small saucepan and bring to the boil. Switch off the heat. Scatter in the finely chopped milk and dark chocolate and give the pan a shake so that the liquid covers the chocolate. Leave to stand for 30 seconds or so, then stir thoroughly with a wire whisk until smooth. Stir in the powdered nuts thoroughly and leave to stand for about 5 minutes.

Meanwhile, scatter 1–2 tbsp cocoa over the base of the prepared loaf tin. Pour the filling into the tin and leave to come to room temperature, then chill until firm enough to cut.

Use the paper to lift the block out of the tin. Put it on a flat surface and carefully peel back the sides. Hold a large knife under very hot water, dry quickly and cut the block into 2.5-cm/1-in squares. Hold the knife under hot water and dry before each cut. Separate the squares on the paper and transfer to a small sheet. Chill until firm. You can put it into the freezer for 10–15 minutes to speed up the process, if you wish.

For the coating, scatter the remaining cocoa onto a small baking sheet. Dip a square of filling into the melted dark chocolate and use your palms and fingers to coat without losing the shape. Pay special attention to the base, which will have a layer of cocoa. Just rub on chocolate as needed until it forms a thin layer. Deposit it gently onto the cocoa and coat the rest in the same way. After you have sealed all with chocolate, use a fork to turn them over in the cocoa so that the cocoa layer is on top. Leave to set until the chocolate is firm enough to be handled. Shift a little pile of cocoa to one side. Pick up each square lightly and press the sides into the cocoa.

Keep them refrigerated and serve at room temperature. They will keep in an airtight container for at least 2 weeks in the refrigerator and for about a month in the freezer.

Makes 20
For the filling
100 ml/3½ fl oz/scant ½ cup double cream
175 g/6 oz/6 squares milk chocolate, finely chopped
75 g/2¾ oz/2¾ squares dark chocolate, finely chopped
3 tbsp Grand Marnier liqueur

For the coating
20–25 g/¾–1 oz/scant ¼–¼ cup (unsweetened) cocoa powder
100 g/3½ oz/3½ squares dark chocolate, melted

Here is a log shape for variety. The truffle mixture is soft and packs quite a punch. You need to handle them with a gentle touch, but they are not difficult to shape. Reducing the quantity of Grand Marnier to 30 ml/1 fl oz/2 tbsp will give a slightly firmer and less boozy result.

Boozy Grand Marnier Logs

Line a small baking sheet with greaseproof paper.

Put the cream in a small saucepan and bring to the boil. Switch off the heat. Scatter in the finely chopped milk and dark chocolate and give the pan a shake so that the liquid covers the chocolate. Leave to stand for 30 seconds or so, then stir thoroughly with a hand whisk until smooth. Slowly whisk in the liqueur and continue to whisk until smooth. Transfer to a wide shallow bowl and leave to cool to room temperature, then chill in the refrigerator.

As soon as the mixture can hold its shape, use 2 large teaspoons to shape 20 elongated heaps onto the greaseproof paper; they needn't be very neat. Chill these again until very firm. At this stage, you can even pop them into the freezer for a few minutes.

Roll the chilled chocolate heaps quickly between your palms to make log shapes and replace them on the greaseproof paper. The mixture is quite soft, so chill again until firm.

For the coating scatter the cocoa onto another small baking sheet. Dip a log of filling partially into the melted dark chocolate, and roll quickly between your palms to coat with a thin layer of chocolate, not forgetting the ends. Put it on the cocoa and coat the rest in the same way. When all have been sealed with chocolate, use a clean fork to roll the truffles around in the cocoa to coat well. Just push the log lightly with the end of the fork, making it turn little somersaults until evenly coated with a layer of cocoa. To coat the ends, pick up a log and press both ends lightly into the cocoa. Be gentle, so that you don't damage the thin chocolate layer. Shift the coated truffles to one side.

Keep the truffles refrigerated and serve straight from the refrigerator or remove about half an hour before needed. Room temperature will give a very soft filling, if you prefer that. They will keep in an airtight container for at least 2 weeks in the refrigerator and for at least a month in the freezer.

Makes 20

125 ml/4 fl oz/½ cup double cream

1 tbsp honey

seeds from 1 vanilla pod

200 g/7 oz/7 squares dark chocolate (70% cocoa solids), finely chopped

¼ tsp ground cinnamon

¼ tsp chilli powder

a few tbsp (unsweetened) cocoa powder, for dusting

I really wanted to call these truffles 'Montezuma's Dream', but thought better of it after my tasters burst out laughing when they heard it, as they all immediately substituted 'revenge' for 'dream' in their minds. I still think Montezuma would have liked them, particularly as they contain two ingredients that the Aztecs greatly favoured as flavourings in their cups of bitter frothy chocolate: vanilla beans and chilli pepper. The tiny vanilla seeds give a slight crunch as they pop between the teeth and while these truffles will not have you gasping for breath, they leave the tongue tingling very pleasantly with a satisfying feeling of warmth in the throat. They are quick to make because they do not need to be coated before dusting and are even better after a few days.

Chilli and Vanilla Truffles

Line a small baking sheet with greaseproof paper.

Put the cream in a small saucepan and stir in the honey and vanilla seeds. Bring the mixture to the boil and switch off the heat. Scatter in the finely chopped chocolate and give the pan a shake so that the liquid covers the chocolate. Sprinkle on the ground spices and leave to stand for 30 seconds or so, then stir thoroughly with a wire whisk until smooth. Transfer to a wide shallow bowl and leave to cool to room temperature, then chill in the refrigerator.

As soon as the mixture can hold its shape, use 2 large teaspoons to dip and shape 20 heaps onto the greaseproof paper. Leave them slightly rugged looking.

Dust the truffles generously with cocoa and place them in cases.

Keep the truffles refrigerated and serve at room temperature. They will keep in an airtight container for at least 2 weeks in the refrigerator and for at least a month in the freezer.

Ginger Double Chocolate Truffles

Dried ginger was a valuable import in Roman times and was originally used medicinally, later finding its way to the kitchen. By the Middle Ages it was already common in the West. Elizabethans seasoned their meat with it and added it to sweet confections such as gingerbread. By that time, it was also being brought in by trading ships as stem ginger preserved in syrup. It was spooned up as a sweetmeat. Nowadays we prefer stem ginger in less overwhelming quantities, generally in combination with other ingredients, in cakes and confectionery such as these truffles. The ginger pairs very well with a fruity very dark chocolate and an outer coating of white chocolate adds both contrast and flavour.

Makes 20

For the filling

125 ml/4 fl oz/½ cup double cream

250 g/9 oz/9 squares dark chocolate (preferably 70% cocoa solids), finely chopped

50–60 g/1¾–2¼ oz stem ginger, drained and very finely chopped

For the coating

75 g/2¾ oz/2¾ squares dark chocolate, melted, for sealing

200 g/7 oz/7 squares white chocolate, for dipping

Line a small baking sheet with greaseproof paper.

Put the cream in a small saucepan and bring to the boil. Switch off the heat. Scatter in the finely chopped dark chocolate and give the pan a shake so that the liquid covers the chocolate. Leave to stand for 30 seconds or so, then stir thoroughly with a wire whisk until smooth. Stir in the ginger and transfer to a wide shallow bowl. Leave to cool to room temperature, then chill in the refrigerator.

As soon as the mixture can hold its shape, use 2 teaspoons to dip and shape 20 heaps onto the greaseproof paper, they needn't be very neat. Chill these again until firm.

Roll the chilled chocolate heaps quickly between your palms to make neat balls and replace them on the greaseproof paper. If they feel soft, chill briefly again.

For the coating, dip a ball of filling partially into the melted dark chocolate and roll quickly between your palms to coat with a thin layer of chocolate. Deposit it gently onto the greaseproof paper and coat the rest in the same way.

When the sealing layer has hardened, the truffles can be dipped. Melt the white chocolate in a heatproof bowl over a pan of barely simmering water and leave to cool slightly to about 30°C/86°F. If it is too warm, the layer will be thin and messy because the warm chocolate will cause the dark coating to melt. Drop a ball into the melted chocolate. Give it a quick swirl to coat, then remove it quickly with a fork, tapping the fork several times on the rim of the bowl to get rid of excess chocolate. Deposit it gently onto the greaseproof paper and repeat for the rest. Leave to set completely before removing from the paper and storing in an airtight container in a cool place.

Keep them refrigerated and serve at room temperature. They will keep in an airtight container for at least 2 weeks in the refrigerator and for about a month in the freezer.

Makes just over 24

For the filling

200 ml/7 fl oz/generous ¾ cup whipping cream

100 g/3½ oz/½ cup caster sugar

½–1 vanilla pod

150 g/5½ oz/11 tbsp (scant ¾ cup)
butter, softened

For the coating

35–40 g/1¼–1½ oz/generous ⅓–scant ½ cup
(unsweetened) cocoa powder

250 g/9 oz/9 squares dark chocolate,
broken into pieces

These large, rich oval truffles make a refreshing change from chocolate centres. A chocolate shell holds the creamy white filling in check until it can melt deliciously on your tongue with a characteristic silky mouth-feel. They are extremely popular in Holland - hardly surprising considering that cream, butter and cocoa are all produced here to very high standards. Cream is eaten in copious quantities and can be found on all kinds of cakes and desserts and is used to top coffee as a special treat. In general, the Dutch enjoy their cream whipped with a liberal amount of sugar to very stiff peaks, differing from the British, for instance, who prefer a softer whip, or the Germans and Austrians who often serve it unsweetened. It is almost never used simply poured, and strawberries - or any other fruit - and cream means a thick sweet cloud perched on top of the fruit.

Dutch Cream Truffles
Slagroomtruffels

Note that this method is quite different from the previous recipes and may appear unorthodox. Bear with me, and you will have your reward. The cream mixture and butter both need to be at room temperature.

Put the cream and sugar in a small saucepan. Split the vanilla pod and scrape out the tiny black seeds. Add both seeds and scraped pod to the pan. The amount you use will depend on the freshness and fragrance of your vanilla pod. I find ½ a pod enough. Heat the mixture very slowly, stirring to dissolve the sugar. Switch off the heat as soon as the sugar has dissolved. The cream should not boil, or it will form a skin. Leave to cool to room temperature, removing the vanilla pod just before use.

Use a heavy-duty electric mixer fitted with a whisk attachment to whisk the butter until smooth. Pour the cream mixture in a very slow, thin stream onto the butter while whisking. Scrape down the sides of the bowl a few times as needed. The mixture will look curdled at first, changing to grainy and lumpy afterwards. Keep on whisking at just above medium speed for several minutes until it emulsifies and looks like a smooth and silky buttercream. Stop whisking. The mixture should be able to hold its shape. If it is slightly soft, chill in the refrigerator for a few minutes.

Line 1 large or 2 small baking sheets with greaseproof paper.

Use 2 small dessertspoons to make quenelles that are rounded on top. To do this, dip some of the mixture with one spoon and transfer it to the second spoon. Use the first spoon to shape it into a nicely domed oval, then slide it off (with the aid of the shaping spoon) onto the greaseproof paper. You should have 25 or 26 ovals. Stick a toothpick or cocktail stick vertically into the centre of each oval, all the way down to the bottom. Put the sheet(s) in the freezer and leave the ovals to freeze.

For the coating, scatter half of the cocoa in an even layer on another baking sheet. Melt the dark chocolate in a heatproof bowl over a pan of barely simmering water and leave to cool slightly to about 30°C/86°F, or it will form too thin a coat.

Remove the ovals from the freezer and dip them quickly into the melted dark chocolate, swirling around to coat well. Tap the toothpick rapidly a few times on the side of the bowl to remove excess chocolate and deposit carefully onto the cocoa. You may need to put the bowl of chocolate briefly over the hot water again after dipping about two-thirds of the ovals. When all have been dipped and the chocolate coating has hardened, twist each toothpick gently to remove it. You can apply a little melted chocolate to the hole with a clean toothpick, if you like.

Put the rest of the cocoa in a sieve and dust the truffles generously. Then turn them lightly to dip the narrow rim that has escaped the cocoa so far into the cocoa on the sheet. Arrange on another sheet or platter and chill well before packing into plastic boxes with a sheet of greaseproof paper between the layers.

Refrigerate those that will be eaten within a few days and freeze the rest. Frozen, they will keep for at least a month. Remove them from the refrigerator about half an hour before serving and serve at cool room temperature for the best flavour.

Makes 20

For the filling

125 ml/4 fl oz/½ cup double cream

200 g/7 oz/7 squares dark chocolate, finely chopped

50 g/1¾ oz/1¾ squares milk chocolate, finely chopped

½ tsp ground cinnamon

¼ tsp ground cardamom

generous ⅛ tsp ground ginger

large pinch of freshly grated nutmeg

For the coating

3 tbsp (unsweetened) cocoa powder

1 tbsp icing sugar

1 tsp ground cinnamon

75 g/2¾ oz/2¾ squares dark chocolate, melted

The fragrance and warmth of the spices gives an almost Asian feeling to these truffles. They are coated in slightly sweetened and spiced cocoa, adding a small element of surprise.

Spice Island Truffles

Line a small baking sheet with greaseproof paper.

Put the cream in a small saucepan and bring to the boil. Switch off the heat. Scatter in the chopped dark and milk chocolate and give the pan a shake so that the liquid covers the chocolate. Sprinkle on the ground spices and leave to stand for 30 seconds or so, then stir thoroughly with a wire whisk until smooth. Transfer to a wide shallow bowl and leave to cool to room temperature, then chill in the refrigerator.

As soon as the mixture can hold its shape, use 2 large teaspoons to shape 20 heaps onto the greaseproof paper; they needn't be very neat. Chill these again until very firm. At this stage, you can even pop them into the freezer for a few minutes.

Roll the chilled chocolate heaps quickly between your palms to make neat balls and replace them on the greaseproof paper. If they feel soft, chill briefly again.

For the coating, sift together the cocoa, icing sugar and cinnamon and scatter onto another small baking sheet.

Dip a ball of filling partially into the melted dark chocolate, and roll quickly between your palms to coat with a thin layer of chocolate. Deposit it gently onto the cocoa mixture and coat the rest in the same way. When all have been sealed with chocolate, use a clean fork to roll the truffles around in the cocoa mixture to coat well. Just push the truffle lightly with the end of the fork, making it turn little somersaults until evenly coated with a layer of the mixture. Shift the coated truffles to one side.

Keep the truffles refrigerated and serve at room temperature. They will keep in an airtight container for at least 2 weeks in the refrigerator and for at least a month in the freezer.

Simply Chocolate

Here are a few recipes that involve little more than melting some
chocolate. They are also useful for using up what is left of dipping
chocolate, as you usually need to melt more than you actually use.

Makes 12 of each flavour

100 g/3½ oz/3½ squares dark chocolate

100 g/3½ oz/3½ squares milk chocolate

100 g/3½ oz/3½ squares white chocolate

100 g/3½ oz hundreds and thousands

Here in Holland, bakers, confectioners and elegant patisseries stock these chocolates and it continues to surprise me that people actually buy them - and not that cheaply, either - considering how quick and easy they are to make. I'm not a great fan of food colouring, but sprinkling on the brightly coloured hundreds and thousands is a very cheering task, even for me. The finished discs look like Aboriginal dot painting miniatures, with the added attraction of being edible. Simple though they are, the contrast of melting chocolate with the crispness of the hundreds and thousands provides a very pleasant sensation in the mouth. Needless to say, the quality of the chocolate will make or break them.

Colourful Chocolate Coins

Musketflikken

Melt the 3 kinds of chocolate in separate small heatproof bowls over a pan of barely simmering water. As soon as the chocolate has melted completely, drop it by the teaspoonful onto a sheet of greaseproof paper. If the chocolate doesn't spread out of its own accord, encourage it with the back of the teaspoon. You should aim for 12 coins per kind, each 5 cm/2 in diameter.

Using a clean teaspoon, dip scant spoonfuls of the hundreds and thousands and scatter them as neatly as you can over each coin. If you hold the spoon close to the chocolate and shake gently, you won't lose too much along the way. Leave to harden on the greaseproof paper and repeat the process with the 2 other kinds of chocolate.

When the coins have set properly, peel away the greaseproof paper. Store in a pretty glass jar or dish on the dining or coffee table. They will keep for a few weeks if well covered, but they don't usually last that long.

Makes 8 discs, approx. 6 cm/2½ in
in diameter
150 g/5½ oz chocolate, melted (see page 178)

Your choice of the following (or anything
else you can think of):
few toasted nuts, such as pistachios, hazelnuts,
macadamias, cashews and almonds

untoasted walnut halves

slivered candied orange or other fruit

chopped candied ginger

brightly coloured dried fruit, such as cranberries

silver balls

dried lavender

crystallised rose or violet petals

As with the coins, these thicker chocolate discs
are so easy to create at home. All you need to do
is melt chocolate and decorate it with delicious
and attractive morsels to give it your own
special touch. Use one kind of chocolate,
or make three batches using dark, white and
milk chocolate ones. As far as the decoration
goes, a few suggestions follow, but feel free
to use your own imagination and taste.

Chocolate Discs

Spread a sheet of baking parchment on your work surface.

Deposit 8 generous spoonfuls of the melted chocolate on the baking parchment and
spread lightly to form discs, about 6 cm/2½ in in diameter.

Decorate as you wish, using varying combinations. White chocolate simply begs for
bright combinations like pistachios and cranberries, while dark chocolate will be
happy with almost anything.

Leave to harden before peeling away the paper and arranging them on a serving plate.
Keeping qualities will depend on your choice of decoration, but they should keep for at
least a few days in an airtight container.

Makes 16 medium or 24 small clusters

125 g/4½ oz/generous ¾ cup skinless
hazelnuts, toasted

1½ tbsp finely chopped candied orange peel

150 g/5½ oz/5½ squares milk chocolate

1¼–1½ tsp instant espresso powder*

*If using granules, crush to a powder
before measuring.

This milk chocolate combination blends very
harmoniously and you can adjust the size to suit
yourself. The small ones are just right as an
accompaniment to an after-dinner cup of coffee.
Don't put it on the saucer, though, as it will
melt. Just serve separately in a dish.

Hazelnut Coffee Clusters

Chop the hazelnuts coarsely with a large knife, leaving in the inevitable smaller bits and shavings. Mix in the peel and set aside.

Melt the chocolate in a heatproof bowl over a pan of barely simmering water and sprinkle the espresso powder over it. Stir well to combine before adding the nut and peel mixture. Give it all a good stir to coat the nuts well. They should all be thinly coated with chocolate, with no light surface area visible.

Use 2 dessertspoons or teaspoons to drop 16 portions (or the teaspoons to drop 24 portions) onto a sheet of greaseproof paper, dipping with one spoon and using the second one to slide the mixture off onto the greaseproof paper. Neaten if necessary and leave to set completely before removing from the paper.

Store in an airtight container in a cool place for up to 10 days.

Dark Rice Crispies Clusters

It is almost embarrassing to add this quick-fix treat here, but I love them and would hate to withhold them from you. They are a good way of using up excess melted chocolate and sometimes I even melt some specially for the purpose. The chocolate is the star, but the Rice Crispies play an excellent supporting role and add a light and lovely crunch.

Makes 12 large clusters

125 g/4½ oz/4½ squares dark chocolate

25–30 g/1 oz Rice Crispies

Melt the chocolate in a heatproof bowl and add as much of the Rice Crispies as it will take. (If you are using up leftover melted chocolate, simply add Rice Crispies as needed.) The Rice Crispies should all be thinly coated with chocolate, with no light surface area visible, neither should there be large blobs of chocolate.

Use 2 soup or large dessertspoons to drop 12 generous portions onto greaseproof paper, dipping with one spoon and using the second one to slide the mixture off onto the greaseproof paper. Neaten if necessary and leave to set completely before removing from the paper.

Store in an airtight container in a cool place for up to 10 days.

Cheat's Chocolate Panforte

Makes 1 slab

100 g/3½ oz dried figs, chopped

50 g/1¾ oz dried apricots, chopped

25 g/generous ¾ oz candied orange peel, chopped

25 g/generous ¾ oz dried cranberries

50 g/1¾ oz hazelnuts, lightly toasted

50 g/1¾ oz walnuts

25 g/generous ¾ oz pistachios

200 g/7 oz/7 squares dark chocolate, chopped into small pieces

5 tbsp runny honey

½ tsp ground cinnamon

¼ tsp ground cardamom

pinch of freshly ground nutmeg

'Panforte' was originally an Italian Christmas delicacy, but can now be bought all year round. It hangs halfway between cake and confectionery and was supposedly introduced to Siena by monks more than a thousand years ago. This Tuscan city is reputed to have been one of the first Italian cities to adopt the use of sugar and spices, and up to today it remains closely linked with 'panforte'. Local businesses cash in on the association, and towering stacks of 'panforte' in the shop windows tempt passers-by, who puff and pant their way through the narrow and steeply winding streets, to stop and try some. Dried fruit and nuts of all description, and varying combinations stud the discs and slabs that come in a variety of sizes. Spices are used subtly, flour is used sparingly, and a little cocoa is sometimes added to produce a dark version, 'panforte scuro'. This quick and simple recipe is a cheat's take on the original and needs no baking. The spices give it a decidedly festive flavour and all the good natural ingredients could almost make it qualify as health food. Substitute your own combinations of fruit if you prefer, but do so wisely. Candied ginger, for instance, should be used quite cautiously or it will dominate.

Line a medium-sized loaf tin with non-stick parchment.

Place the figs, apricots, orange peel and cranberries in a bowl. Chop the hazelnuts and walnuts very coarsely and add them to the fruit along with the pistachios and give it a few stirs to distribute everything well. Set aside.

Put some water to boil in the bottom part of a double boiler, or select a saucepan and a medium-sized heat-proof bowl that fits snugly over it. The bowl should not touch the water. Place the chocolate in the top part of the boiler or bowl along with the honey and spices. When the water comes to the boil, reduce the heat and place the top/bowl containing the chocolate over it. Allow the chocolate to melt and stir to combine with the honey. Stir in the rest of the chopped ingredients, remove from the heat and scrape into the prepared tin. Level the top, pressing down well to make a compact slab.

Allow to set before cutting into cubes or small squares. Serve them on a pretty plate or present them in paper cases.

Dates for chocolate lovers

15 August 1502 During his fourth voyage of discovery, Columbus captured two huge canoes belonging to the Maya and seized their cargo: fine cotton garments, war implements, copper bells and foodstuff, including 'almonds'. The almonds were, of course, cacao beans. The Maya and their neighbours the Aztecs enjoyed their chocolate in fluid forms ranging from a bitter foaming liquid to a maize-thickened gruel. Flavourings included vanilla, chillies, allspice and annatto (which also provided a rich red colour) as well as fragrant flowers.

1506 Christopher Columbus died without apparently having tasted chocolate; neither did he take it to Europe.

Early sixteenth century Cacao beans were also used as currency. Nicarao Indians of Nicaragua were equating ten cacao beans with one rabbit and one bean with two sapote fruits. A prostitute could be engaged for eight to ten beans and if one saved up long enough and managed to amass 100 beans, a slave might be bought with them. The cost of living seems to have been higher in the Aztec lands. Shortly after the fall of the Aztec capital Tenochtitlan to the Spaniards in 1521, a porter in central Mexico earned 100 beans a day. A document drawn up in the native language Nahuatl in central Mexico in 1545 shows considerable inflation. Here, a large sapote fruit cost 1 cacao bean; a turkey cock was valued at 200 beans and a turkey hen could be bought for 100 plump beans or 120 shrunken ones. A hare was worth 100 beans, but a small rabbit was cheap by comparison at only 30.

1544 Chocolate is believed to have arrived in Europe with a delegation of Mayan nobles, who were taken to Spain in 1544 by Dominican friars. Among the many gifts they presented to Prince Philip were containers of beaten chocolate and while he may have been gracious enough to taste it, chocolate was not an instant hit or hype.

Seventeenth century Slowly and gradually, chocolate began to make its presence known and by the mid-seventeenth century it had gained wide acceptance at the Spanish court and spread to the rest of Europe. Chocolate houses,

where patrons could enjoy a cup of
the delicious liquid and socialise with their
friends at the same time, soon sprang up in all major
European cities.

1727 A disaster all but wiped out the Criollo plantations in
Trinidad. New plants of the hardy Forastero variety were brought in to
replace them and they hybridised with what few Criollo plants remained
to produce the Trinitario, a bean with many of the fine flavour qualities of
Criollo, while the trees showed all of the sturdiness of the more common Forastero.

1778 Frenchman Doret invented the first chocolate press. Eating chocolate was
dribbling into Europe, made by the Spanish nuns in Mexico whose coffers were soon
brimming from the profits. This luxurious and novel confectionery would have been
rejected by the modern taster as a gritty, greasy and often bitter mouthful. The chocolate
press was to change all that.

1828 Coenraad van Houten invented a wooden screw press that extruded the cocoa butter from
the beans and left behind a fatless mass that could be pulverised to produce what we now know as
cocoa. He further refined the cocoa by adding potash, which neutralised the acid and gave a less
astringent taste, an idea he is said to have copied from the Native Americans, who used wood ash in
their chocolate drinks to make them milder. This process is known today as 'Dutching' and
produces a more mellow cocoa than non-alkalised versions. Coenraad sold his invention to other
European manufacturers, opening the way to the production of an improved kind of chocolate in
which cocoa butter was an important ingredient.

1868 In Great Britain Dr Joseph Fry produced the first confectionery bars in the mid-19th
century and the company started manufacturing boxes of fancy chocolates in 1868.

1879 Swiss chemist Henri Nestlé, who had already discovered a way to make powdered milk,
joined forces with chocolate manufacturer Daniel Peter to make milk chocolate. In the
same year, Rudolph Lindt invented the process of conching: chocolate was passed for
72 hours or more between granite slabs and rollers to produce a smooth and silky
confection, especially when extra cocoa butter was added.

Twenty-first century Criollo remains the King of Beans and accounts for
just ten per cent of world production, followed by the almost equally
wonderful Trinitario at twenty per cent; both are sought after by
those with discerning palates. Most 'ordinary' chocolates
are made from pure Forastero or a blend. Cocoa
butter continues to be a prized ingredient.

Brownie Bites

Equipment

Of all chocolate cakes, brownies give the most satisfying chocolate hit with the least effort, and for something so simple to make and eat, they bring out surprisingly strong feelings in people. Everyone has their own favourite texture and expectations, and the brownie recipe does not exist that will please universally. They come cake-like, fudgy and in-between. Baking powder is sometimes used – a practice abhorred by purists. Whisking the eggs as far as the ribbon stage is done by some, but frowned upon by others because it will give a lighter texture. The most a recipe writer can hope for is to convey what potential bakers can expect as far as flavour and texture go and trust that they will be tempted to choose and try something that will suit them. Bear in mind that these brownies vary as to composition, thickness and texture.

Tin

The tin used for these recipes measures 20 x 20 cm/8 x 8 in at the base, widening slightly to 22 x 22 cm/8½ x 8½ in at the top. If you use a larger tin, your brownies will be flatter and less moist than intended.

Lining

The recipes that include wetter or more delicate ingredients all require the tin to be generously lined with baking parchment, so that the entire brownie can be lifted out. Leave to cool and set sufficiently before lifting it out or it may break. When the tin is lined only on the base, the brownie can be inverted after a few minutes, using an upturned wire rack placed over the tin.

Chocolate

As it is such an important ingredient, and there is so much of it, choose your chocolate wisely. I use dark chocolate with around 55% cocoa solids and a fairly high percentage of cocoa butter for these recipes. Going up to 70% or so is fine, but resist the temptation to substitute a really dark 'speciality' chocolate with an absurdly high cocoa percentage. You may end up with a drier brownie that falls short of being sweet enough.

Alcohol

Many of the recipes contain rum or liqueurs. It dissipates during baking, leaving flavour without any significant alcohol value. However, if you prefer not to use it, replace it with the same amount of water, but add it to the batter, not the chocolate.

Whisking

Whisk the eggs with the sugar for a few minutes until the sugar dissolves and the mixture thickens and lightens in colour. Note that this is long before the ribbon stage. If you continue to whisk it to a thick ribbon, your brownie will have a lighter and airier texture and will not be as dense as it might have been.

Timing

The exact baking time depends on your oven, the type of heat and of course the actual temperature. In general, I find the difference between a conventional electric oven and a fan-assisted one negligible. However, in the case of brownies, where the texture is a large part of the finished product, you need to be more precise. A conventional oven may need a few minutes extra to produce the same consistency that a fan-assisted oven will reach a little earlier. Note that these brownies are baked at 170°C/325°F/Gas Mark 3, which means that they cook more gently for a little longer. The recipe timings are merely a guideline so always start testing early enough.

Testing

Always test about 5 cm/2 in from the edge, not in the centre. If you wait until the centre sets before removing it from the oven, the rest will be dry. However, the skewer should come out with a few moist crumbs, not uncooked batter. The brownie will continue to set as it cools.

Portions

A 20 x 20-cm/8 x 8-in brownie will cut into 16 satisfying squares. If you allow the brownie to cool completely, you will be able to cut neatly. Cutting into a still warm brownie gives ragged and crumbling edges. I generally cut as needed, keeping the rest well wrapped in clingfilm.

Storage

Brownies will keep for a few days at cool room temperature, but can also be suitably packed and frozen. I like to cut an entire brownie into quarters for freezing, wrapping the unneeded pieces well in clingfilm before putting them in a plastic box or sturdy freezer bag. If you portion the brownie before freezing, it will dry out faster.

Serving

Some brownie lovers enjoy eating a chilled product. This works best with very gooey brownies and is not my thing. My personal preference is to eat them slightly warm, so that the butter and chocolate are already soft when you take a bite, and the whole flavour just flows smoothly on to your tongue. A few seconds per portion in the microwave will be enough. A simple but attractive way to present the brownies is to use cupcake papers, plain or coloured. If you are serving a few kinds at once, you can use different papers to distinguish them.

Makes 16

175 g/6 oz/scant ¾ cup butter, cubed, plus
extra for greasing

150 g/5½ oz/generous 1 cup plain flour, plus
extra for dusting

200 g/7 oz/7 squares dark chocolate, chopped
into small pieces

1 tbsp rum

¼ tsp salt

¾ tsp baking powder

225 g/8 oz/1⅛ cups caster sugar

2 eggs

1 tsp vanilla extract

50–75 g/1¾–2¾ oz/½–¾ cup walnuts, coarsely
chopped or broken (optional)

I think that walnuts and brownie go well
together, but accept that not everyone shares
my opinion. My son, for instance, finds them a
distraction if not a downright hindrance, serving
as an obstacle to the enjoyment of a mouthful
of pure chocolate bliss. The choice is yours.
It might also be useful to note that this recipe
is a little sweeter and more fudgy than the
others in this chapter.

Classic Brownies

Preheat the oven to 170°C/325°F/Gas Mark 3. Grease a 20-cm/8-in square tin, line
the base with baking parchment and dust with flour.

Put the chocolate and butter in a double boiler or in a heatproof bowl over a pan of
barely simmering water and leave to melt, stirring from time to time. Remove from
the heat and stir in the rum. Set aside to cool a little.

Sift the flour with the salt and baking powder and set aside.

Whisk the sugar, eggs and vanilla together until thick and pale. Stir in the melted
chocolate, followed by the flour mixture, and nuts, if using. Mix gently but
thoroughly, making sure that there is not a pool of chocolate at the bottom of
the bowl.

Transfer the batter to the tin, level the top and bake for about 25 minutes. A skewer
inserted about 5 cm/2 in from an edge should come out clean or with moist crumbs,
not wet batter. Do not overbake. Leave the brownie to cool in the tin for about
5 minutes before transferring it carefully to a wire rack to cool completely.

Serve in squares.

Makes 16

200 g/7 oz/scant 1 cup butter, cubed,
plus extra for greasing

150 g/5½ oz/generous 1 cup plain flour, plus
extra for dusting

225 g/8 oz/8 squares dark chocolate, chopped
into small pieces

2 tbsp (unsweetened) cocoa powder

½ tsp baking powder

generous ¼ tsp salt

200 g/7 oz/1 cup caster sugar

3 eggs

2 tsp vanilla extract

The combination of chocolate and cocoa make these brownies dense and intensely chocolatey, with a slightly cake-like texture. Serving them slightly warm will bring out the flavour even better.

Intense Brownies

Preheat the oven to 170°C/325°F/Gas Mark 3. Grease a 20-cm/8-in square tin, line the base with baking parchment and dust with flour.

Put the chocolate and butter in a double boiler or in a heatproof bowl over a pan of barely simmering water and leave to melt, stirring from time to time. Remove from the heat and set aside to cool a little.

Sift the flour with the cocoa, baking powder and salt and set aside.

Whisk the sugar, eggs and vanilla together until thick and pale. Add the melted chocolate, followed by the flour mixture and mix gently but thoroughly. Make sure that there is not a pool of chocolate at the bottom of the bowl.

Transfer the batter to the tin, level the top and bake for about 25 minutes. The top will start to swell and crack towards the end of the baking time, but will settle again as the brownie cools. A skewer inserted about 5 cm/2 in from an edge should come out with moist crumbs, not wet batter. Do not overbake. Leave the brownie to cool in the tin for about 5 minutes before transferring it carefully to a wire rack to cool completely.

Serve in squares.

Makes 16

150 g/5½ oz/scant ¾ cup butter, cubed,
plus extra for greasing

200 g/7 oz/7 squares dark chocolate, chopped
into small pieces

2 tbsp Kirsch

1 jar pitted cherries, well drained (175 g/6 oz
drained weight)

1½ tsp cornflour

175 g/6 oz/1¼ cups plain flour

¼ tsp salt

1¼ tsp baking powder

175 g/6 oz/scant 1 cup caster sugar

2 eggs

You can enjoy this brownie any time of the year
because it uses bottled cherries. Use a firm
variety of cherries and discard any pieces.

Cherry Brownies

Preheat the oven to 170°C/325°F/Gas Mark 3. Grease a 20-cm/8-in square tin, then line so that the paper comes up 5 cm/2 in on 2 sides.

Put the chocolate and butter in a double boiler or in a heatproof bowl over a pan of barely simmering water and leave to melt, stirring from time to time. Remove from the heat and stir in the Kirsch. Set aside to cool a little.

Toss the cherries with the cornflour in a small bowl and set aside.

Sift the flour with the salt and baking powder and set aside.

Whisk the sugar and eggs together until thick and pale. Mix in the melted chocolate, followed by the flour mixture. Mix gently but thoroughly, making sure that there is not a pool of chocolate at the bottom of the bowl. Carefully fold in the cherries, taking care not to mash them.

Transfer the batter to the tin, level the top and bake for 25–30 minutes. A skewer inserted about 5 cm/2 in from an edge should come out with moist crumbs, not wet batter. Do not overbake. Leave the brownie to cool in the tin for about 10–15 minutes before gripping the paper and transferring the brownie with the paper to a wire rack. Leave to cool completely.

Serve in squares.

Makes 16

125 g/4½ oz/9 tbsp butter, cubed, plus extra
for greasing

150 g/5½ oz/5½ squares dark chocolate, chopped

1 tbsp rum

115 g/4 oz/generous ¾ cup plain flour

⅛ tsp salt

¾ tsp baking powder

150 g/5½ oz/¾ cup caster sugar

2 eggs

1 tsp vanilla extract

For the cheesecake topping

250 g/9 oz/scant 1¼ cups cream cheese at
room temperature

1 tbsp cornflour

50 g/1¾ oz/¼ cup caster sugar

1 egg

1 tsp vanilla extract

This brownie offers the best of both worlds:
cheesecake and brownie in a single mouthful.

Cheesecake Brownies

Preheat the oven to 170°C/325°F/Gas Mark 3. Grease a 20 cm/8 in square tin and line so that the paper comes up 5 cm/2 in on 2 sides.

Combine all the cheesecake topping ingredients in a bowl and use a whisk to blend to a smooth, lump-free consistency, then set aside.

For the brownies, put the chocolate and butter in a heatproof bowl over a pan of barely simmering water and leave to melt, stirring from time to time. Remove from the heat and stir in the rum. Set aside to cool a little.

Sift the flour with the salt and baking powder and set aside.

Whisk the sugar, eggs and vanilla together until thick and pale. Mix in the melted chocolate, followed by the flour mixture. Mix gently but thoroughly.

Transfer the batter to the tin. Spoon the cheesecake mixture onto the base in about 8 or 9 blobs, leaving some space in between, so that there is still brownie batter visible. Make a few swirls with a spatula to give a lightly marbled effect, but don't cover the base completely with the cheesecake mixture. Don't worry about the rough surface. The cheesecake mixture will sink a little as it bakes and cools.

Bake for about 25–30 minutes. A skewer inserted about 5 cm/2 in from an edge, in a brown part, should come out with moist crumbs, not wet batter. Do not overbake. Leave to cool in the tin for about 10–15 minutes before gripping the paper and transferring the brownie with the paper to a wire rack. Leave to cool completely. Serve in squares. Store chilled, but serve at room temperature.

Makes 16

175 g/6 oz/1½ sticks butter, cubed, plus extra
for greasing

150 g/5½ oz/generous 1 cup plain flour, plus
extra for dusting

200 g/7 oz/7 squares dark chocolate, chopped
into small pieces

1 tbsp rum

¼ tsp salt

¾ tsp baking powder

200 g/7 oz/1 cup caster sugar

2 eggs

2 tsp vanilla extract

50 g/1¾ oz dried cranberries

100 g/3½ oz/generous ½ cup white chocolate
chips (or a bar, chopped)

Small pieces of white chocolate and tart cranberries
add lots of extra flavour to this brownie.

Cranberry and White Chocolate Brownies

Preheat the oven to 170°C/325°F/Gas Mark 3. Grease a 20-cm/8-in square tin, line the base and dust with flour.

Put the chocolate and butter in a double boiler or in a heatproof bowl over a pan of barely simmering water and leave to melt, stirring from time to time. Remove from the heat and stir in the rum. Set aside to cool a little.

Sift the flour with the salt and baking powder and set aside.

Whisk the sugar, eggs and vanilla together until thick and pale. Mix in the melted chocolate, followed by the flour mixture. Mix gently but thoroughly, making sure that there is not a pool of chocolate at the bottom of the bowl. Fold in the cranberries and chocolate chips.

Transfer the batter to the tin, level the top and bake for 25–30 minutes. A skewer inserted about 5 cm/2 in from an edge should come out with moist crumbs, not wet batter. Do not overbake. Leave the brownie to cool in the tin for about 5 minutes before transferring it carefully to a wire rack to cool completely.

Serve in squares.

Makes 16

150 g/5½ oz/scant ¾ cup butter, cubed, plus extra for greasing

200 g/7 oz/7 squares dark chocolate, chopped into small pieces

1 tbsp rum

100 g/3½ oz/scant ¾ cup plain flour

¼ tsp salt

¾ tsp baking powder

100 g/3½ oz/⅔ cup toasted hazelnuts, very finely ground

200 g/7 oz/1 cup caster sugar

2 eggs

1 tsp vanilla extract

This brownie is in the style of the chocolate and hazelnut cakes of the Piedmont region of Italy, an area renowned for its excellent hazelnuts. Although chocolate goes with just about anything, it partners particularly well with hazelnuts. Buy blanched, skinless hazelnuts and toast them yourself shortly before needed. It takes very little effort that will be richly rewarded.

Hazelnut Brownies

Preheat the oven to 170°C/325°F/Gas Mark 3. Grease a 20-cm/8-in square tin and line so that the paper comes up 5 cm/2 in on 2 sides.

Put the chocolate and butter in a double boiler or in a heatproof bowl over a pan of barely simmering water and leave to melt, stirring from time to time. Remove from the heat and stir in the rum. Set aside to cool a little.

Sift the flour with the salt and baking powder, add the ground hazelnuts and set aside.

Whisk the sugar, eggs and vanilla together until thick and pale. Mix in the melted chocolate, followed by the flour and nut mixture. Mix gently but thoroughly, making sure that there is not a pool of chocolate at the bottom of the bowl.

Transfer the batter to the tin, level the top and bake for about 25–30 minutes. A skewer inserted about 5 cm/2 in from an edge should come out with moist crumbs, not wet batter. Do not overbake. Leave the brownie to cool in the tin for about 10–15 minutes before gripping the paper and transferring the brownie with the paper to a wire rack.

Serve in squares.

Makes 16

175 g/6 oz/1½ sticks butter, cubed, plus extra
for greasing
....

150 g/5½ oz/generous 1 cup plain flour, plus
extra for dusting
....

200 g/7 oz/7 squares dark chocolate, chopped
into small pieces
....

1 tbsp Grand Marnier or Triple Sec
....

zest of 1 fairly large orange (preferably organic)
....

¼ tsp salt
....

¾ tsp baking powder
....

200 g/7 oz/1 cup caster sugar
....

2 eggs
....

1 tsp vanilla extract

I use a little Grand Marnier or Triple Sec to
bring out more orange flavour, but you can use
any good-quality orange-based liqueur.

Orange Brownies

Preheat the oven to 170°C/325°F/Gas Mark 3. Grease a 20-cm/8-in square tin, line
the base with baking parchment and dust with flour.

Put the chocolate and butter in a double boiler or in a heatproof bowl over a pan of
barely simmering water and leave to melt, stirring from time to time. Remove from
the heat and stir in the Grand Marnier. Grate the orange zest over this mixture and
set aside to cool a little.

Sift the flour with the salt and baking powder and set aside.

Whisk the sugar, eggs and vanilla together until thick and pale. Mix in the melted
chocolate, followed by the flour mixture. Mix gently but thoroughly, making sure
that there is not a pool of chocolate at the bottom of the bowl.

Transfer the batter to the tin and bake for about 25 minutes. A skewer inserted about
5 cm/2 in from an edge should come out with moist crumbs, not wet batter. Do not
overbake. Leave the brownie to cool in the tin for about 5 minutes before
transferring it carefully to a wire rack to cool completely.

Serve in squares.

Shortbread Selection

Say 'shortbread' and most people automatically think Scotland and thick and
generous fingers that melt in the mouth. Deservedly so, of course, as the
Scots have charmed the world with the simple perfection of this buttery treat.
But shortbreads are made and eaten in many other parts of the globe and come
in many guises. I have put together some of my favourites based on classic
international traditions as well as a touch or two of my own here and there.

Before You Start

Equipment
A heavy-duty electric mixer fitted with a paddle attachment is the best tool for the recipes that require the butter and sugar to be creamed. A vigorously wielded wooden spoon will make up for the absence of an electric mixer.

Ingredients
As with all the recipes in this book, use good unsalted butter. You will taste it, and much of the flavour of shortbread comes from this simple ingredient. It should be soft, of a spreadable consistency, but not so soft as to be approaching runny.

Handling
Handle the dough as lightly as possible for the best results. Overmixing and kneading will toughen it. You can often proceed with the mixer after adding the dry ingredients, finishing it off by hand, but follow the instructions in the individual recipes. The mixer will be cooler than your hands.

Chilling
Always chill the dough well in the refrigerator before baking, unless the recipe states otherwise. Good chilling will minimise spreading and ensure a neater shape.

Baking
Position the rack just below the centre of the oven. The shortbread need to be spaced well apart so that they will not touch after spreading. Use as many baking sheets as it takes, keeping unbaked batches chilled until needed. Light coloured sheets can be greased. If your sheets are dark, use a sheet of baking parchment as insulation, to prevent the bases from browning too much. Remove carefully with a thin flexible spatula and leave to cool completely on a wire rack.

Add-ins and add-ons
In some recipes, I give suggestions about optional ingredients, such as chopped nuts and crystallised ginger, or chocolate for decoration. Allow yourself to be guided by your instincts, but don't lose sight of the fact that the pure flavours are often the charm of a recipe. Some biscuits don't need more than a powdering of icing sugar; Green Tea Fingers (see p.209) can take a drizzling or half-dipping in white chocolate, but avoid adding enhancements to the dough.

Storage
Shortbread is best eaten fresh or within a few days of baking. It can be stored in an airtight container in a cool place for up to a week, but freezing on the day of baking preserves its freshness best. Remove from the freezer as needed.

Classic Shortbread Fingers

Makes 36

200 g/7 oz/scant 1 cup butter, softened, plus extra for greasing

225 g/8 oz/1⅔ cups plain flour, plus extra for dusting

75 g/2¾ oz/½ cup cornflour

¼ tsp salt

100 g/3½ oz/½ cup caster sugar

For this pure and simple treat, I have used the traditional Scottish proportions of one part sugar to two parts butter to three parts flour. This recipe replaces some of the flour with cornflour for a short texture, but some people prefer more crunch in the form of ground rice or semolina. Note that they are not interchangeable here. For variation, you can add a handful of finely chopped walnuts or stem ginger. Proper chilling will keep some of the spread in check, but these fingers will not have the sharp edges of the commercial product. If you prefer a geometric look, bake as described in the recipe for Double Chocolate Shortbread (see p.215) and cut into fingers instead of bars. Have a look at Petticoat Tails (see p.206) too.

Grease 2 baking sheets.

Sift the flour with the cornflour and salt and set aside.

Use a heavy-duty electric mixer fitted with a paddle attachment to cream the sugar and butter together well. Alternatively, use a vigorous hand. Add the dry mixture a little at a time and stop mixing as soon as you have a very crumbly dough.

Turn the contents of the bowl out onto a lightly floured work surface or a silicone mat. Press lightly with your fingers to make it come together in a ball. It will be quite soft. Gather it up and set to one side while you clean the work surface. If the dough feels too soft to handle, wrap it in clingfilm and chill briefly until it becomes manageable enough to roll out.

Roll the dough out on a lightly floured surface or between 2 sheets of clingfilm to an even thickness of 1 cm/½ in, dusting with flour as needed, and cut into fingers, about 6 x 2 cm/2½ x ¾ in. Press together any trimmings and re-roll as necessary.

Use a bench scraper or thin metal spatula to transfer the fingers carefully to the baking sheets, spacing them well apart as they will spread during baking. Use a fork to prick 3 parallel rows of holes in each finger, then chill for 30 minutes to minimise spread.

Preheat the oven to 150°C/300°F/Gas Mark 2.

Bake the biscuits for 25–30 minutes until the edges just begin to colour. Use a flexible spatula to transfer the biscuits to a wire rack to cool and firm up.

Store in an airtight container in a cool place.

Makes 2 rounds (16 wedges)

butter, for greasing

ingredients as for Classic Shortbread Fingers (see p.205)

caster sugar, for dusting (optional)

No shortbread collection would be complete without Scottish Petticoat Tails. They are usually baked in rounds that have been marked into wedges, and if you look at the entire round, it isn't hard to imagine how the name came about: the fork pricks could be layers of lace and the scalloped edge the swirling hem of an old-fashioned petticoat. An alternative explanation for the name is that it is a corruption of the French petites gatelles that entered Scotland with Queen Mary. Whatever their origin, they are popular as a treat and several traditions are bound to these delicious biscuits. Even in present-day Scotland, few households will be without some of these rounds to offer to New Year's guests, and in former times a beautifully decorated shortbread also served as a bridal cake in remote rural communities. It was broken over the bride's head as she entered her new home and her friends were given the pieces to take home and put under their pillows, much as some people still do with wedding cakes.

Petticoat Tails

Preheat the oven to 150°C/300°F/Gas Mark 2. Grease a baking sheet.

Make the dough as described in Classic Shortbread Fingers (see p.205).

Divide the dough into 2 portions and flatten each with a rolling pin or by hand to an even round with a diameter of 15 cm/6 in and a thickness of about 1¼ cm/½ in. Press any cracks together with your fingers.

Place the rounds on the baking sheet and neaten the edges, then crimp them with a fork. Use a sharp knife to mark each round into 8 wedges, cutting to about halfway though the cake. Prick 3 parallel rows of holes in each wedge with the fork and bake for about 1 hour, or until pale golden brown and cooked through. If you skimp on the baking time, the centre will stay soft. As a safeguard, you can also separate the wedges with a knife after 45 minutes and return them to the oven for 10 minutes. If you don't take this previous option, cut all the way to the bottom of the wedges as soon as you take the cakes out of the oven.

Dust the rounds with caster sugar, if you like, and leave them on the sheet until they are firm enough to transfer to a wire rack to cool completely.

Store in an airtight container.

Makes 24, depending on size

250 g/9 oz/generous 1¾ cups plain flour, plus extra for dusting (optional)

4 tsp *matcha*

⅛ tsp baking powder

¼ tsp salt

150 g/5½ oz/scant ¾ cup butter, softened

100 g/3½ oz/½ cup caster sugar

1 egg yolk

white or dark chocolate, melted, for dipping, optional

I love 'matcha', Japanese green tea powder, as much for its beautiful colour as its specific flavour. In these buttery biscuits, both are very evident. They can be cut into fingers, but simple leaves are very attractive; use an unfussy cutter to avoid overbrowned edges.

Green Tea Fingers

Line a baking sheet with baking parchment.

Mix the flour with the *matcha*, baking powder and salt and set aside.

If possible, use a heavy-duty electric mixer fitted with a paddle attachment to cream the butter and sugar together until lightened in colour. If not, use a wooden spoon and be very thorough. Beat in the egg yolk, then add the dry ingredients and knead briefly by hand or in the mixer until it all comes together and stays together. If the dough feels too soft to handle, wrap it in clingfilm and chill briefly until it becomes manageable enough to roll out.

Roll the dough out on a lightly floured work surface or between 2 sheets of clingfilm to an even thickness of 1 cm/½ in, dusting with flour as needed, and cut into fingers about 6 x 2 cm/2½ x ¾ in. Alternatively, cut into ovals and make veins with a knife. Press together any trimmings and re-roll as necessary.

Use a bench scraper or thin metal spatula to transfer the fingers carefully to the baking sheets, spacing them well apart as they will spread during baking. Use a table fork to prick 3 parallel rows of holes in each finger and chill for 30 minutes to minimise spread.

Preheat the oven to 180°C/350°F/Gas Mark 4.

Bake the biscuits for 25–30 minutes until the edges just begin to colour. Use a flexible spatula to transfer the biscuits to a wire rack to cool and firm up.

If dipping in chocolate, leave one half of the finger/leaf free for a colour contrast.

Store in an airtight container in a cool place.

Makes about 30

250 g/9 oz/generous 1¾ cups plain flour
½ tsp baking powder
⅛ tsp salt
150 g/5½ oz/scant ¾ cup butter, softened
100 g/3½ oz/½ cup caster sugar
1 egg yolk
grated zest of ½ a lemon (preferably organic)

These rounds are made from refrigerated dough
that can be prepared up to a day or two in
advance and sliced and baked as needed. Even
if you plan to bake them straightaway, be sure
to chill the dough well, or the biscuits will
not hold their shape. If two sheets will not fit
in your oven at the same time, bake them in two
batches, keeping the unbaked dough chilled.

Lemon Rounds

Preheat the oven to 180°C/350°F/Gas Mark 4. Line 2 baking sheets with baking
parchment.

Mix the flour with the baking powder and salt and set aside.

If possible, use a heavy-duty electric mixer fitted with a paddle attachment to cream
the butter and sugar together until lightened in colour. If not, use a wooden spoon
and be very thorough. Beat in the egg yolk and lemon zest. Add the dry ingredients
and knead lightly until it all comes together and stays together.

Transfer the dough to a large sheet of baking parchment or greaseproof paper and
shape into a sausage. Use the paper to help you roll the sausage into a neat cylinder,
about 28–30 cm/11–12 in long.

Chill the dough in the paper for at least an hour, or until it is firm enough to slice.

Unwrap the dough and use a sharp knife to cut it into 1-cm/½-in thick rounds.
Neaten the edges with your fingers and space them evenly and well apart on the
baking sheets.

Bake for about 15 minutes, or until the outer edges are golden brown. Transfer the
rounds to a wire rack to cool and firm up.

Store in an airtight container.

Makes 25

75 g/2¾ oz/generous ⅓ cup butter, softened,
plus extra for greasing

125 g/4½ oz/scant 1 cup plain flour, plus extra
for dusting

¼ tsp baking powder

¼ tsp salt

65 g/2¼ oz/¼ cup + 2 tbsp caster sugar

1 tbsp beaten egg

1 tsp vanilla extract

50 g/1¾ oz/½ cup walnuts, finely chopped

These thin squares are delicious eaten fresh but even better after a day or two, when the walnut aroma will have blended fully with the other ingredients. Pecans, which have a milder flavour, also work well. And although the thinness gives an attractive snap, there's nothing to stop you from making them thicker, or in another shape. Remember to adjust the baking time accordingly.

Walnut Thins

Preheat the oven to 180°C/350°F/Gas Mark 4. Grease a baking sheet.

Combine the flour, baking powder and salt in a bowl and set aside.

Beat the butter and sugar until lightened and fluffy, by hand or with a heavy-duty electric mixer. Beat in the egg and vanilla. Knead in the dry ingredients and walnuts to form a dough.

Turn the dough out onto a lightly floured work surface and roll out to a 20 x 20-cm/8 x 8-in square. Neaten any untidy edges by pressing with a scraper or metal ruler. Cut the square into 5 strips, each 4 cm/1½ in wide, then repeat at right angles so that you end up with 25 x 4-cm/1½-in squares.

Transfer the squares to the baking sheet and bake for 10–12 minutes, or until the edges are golden brown. Transfer to a wire rack to cool.

Makes 16

90 g/3¼ oz/6 tbsp butter, softened, plus extra for greasing

100 g/3½ oz/scant ¾ cup plain flour

50 g/1¾ oz/generous ⅓ cup cornflour

½ tsp ground cardamom

scant ¼ tsp salt

75 g/2¾ oz/⅔ cup icing sugar, sifted, plus extra icing sugar, for dusting

1 tbsp rose water

Pale, tender shortbreads that melt in the mouth are very much a Middle Eastern speciality. They come plain, flavoured with spices, nuts or flower waters, with cornflour for tenderness or fine semolina for crunch. I have flavoured these with rose water and cardamom, and the perfume will linger deliciously in your mouth. My husband, a pragmatic Dutchman, was moved to remark that the flavours caress the tongue. Good rose water is essential. Enjoy them with a cup of tea or add them to a dessert plate – for instance, fresh summer berries with a dollop of crème fraîche.

Rose Water and Cardamom Biscuits

Preheat the oven to 150°C/300°F/Gas Mark 2. Grease a baking sheet.

Sift the flour with the cornflour, cardamom and salt and set aside.

Beat the butter until smooth. Add the icing sugar a little at a time and continue to beat until light and fluffy, using a heavy-duty electric mixer fitted with a paddle attachment or a vigorously wielded wooden spoon. Add the flour mixture in 3 or 4 batches, putting in the rose water with the last batch. Continue to beat until soft and smooth.

Divide the dough into 16 portions and roll into balls. Arrange the balls well spaced out on the baking sheet. Do not flatten them. They will flatten themselves gradually as they bake, ending up about 6 cm/2½ in in diameter. Bake for about 25 minutes. Only the edges should colour a little, while the dough stays creamy white. They will be soft and will firm up as they cool. Dust the biscuits with more icing sugar while still on the baking sheet, then use a spatula to remove them carefully and leave to cool completely on a wire rack.

Store in an airtight container.

Makes 18 bars

200 g/7 oz/scant 1½ cups plain flour

50 g/1¾ oz/½ cup (unsweetened) cocoa powder

25 g/1 oz/scant ¼ cup cornflour

¼ tsp salt

200 g/7 oz/scant 1 cup butter, softened

125 g/4½ oz/generous 1 cup icing sugar

1½ tsp vanilla extract

60 g/2¼ oz/2¼ squares white chocolate, melted

This simple but oh so satisfying chocolate biscuit is my favourite. The intensely chocolatey flavour is complemented by a decoration of creamy white chocolate, which also looks very pretty against the dark background. If for some reason you don't want such a wonderful chocolate blast, reduce the cocoa by 2 tbsp and increase the flour by the same amount. It is easy to prepare, as it is baked in a tin and portioned afterwards.

Double Chocolate Shortbread

Preheat the oven to 170°C/325°F/Gas Mark 3. Generously line a 20 x 20-cm/8 x 8-in baking tin.

Mix the flour with the cocoa, cornflour and salt and set aside.

If possible, use a heavy-duty electric mixer fitted with a paddle attachment to cream the butter and icing sugar together until lightened in colour. If not, use a wooden spoon and be very thorough. Beat in the vanilla, then add the dry ingredients and knead briefly by hand or in the mixer until it all comes together and stays together.

Press the dough evenly into the tin and use a fork to prick 6 parallel rows of holes all the way to the base. Bake for 35–40 minutes until cooked through. The top will still feel slightly soft. As soon as you remove the tin from the oven, use a thin metal spatula to cut the biscuits into 6 rows of 3. Lift the paper with the bars out of the tin and transfer to a wire rack. After 5–10 minutes, slide the now firmer bars off the paper onto the rack itself. Separate them and leave to cool completely.

To decorate, press them together to form a square again and drizzle the melted chocolate back and forth over the bars with a spoon, or use a piping bag fitted with a very small plain nozzle if you prefer. You want thin lines of white chocolate with open spaces in between, so move quickly back and forth.

Once the chocolate has set properly, they can be stored in an airtight container.

Makes 16

125 g/4½ oz/9 tbsp butter, softened,
plus extra for greasing

250 g/9 oz/generous 1¾ cups plain
flour

50 g/1¾ oz/¼ cup fine semolina

¼ tsp salt

1 tsp baking powder

75 g/2¾ oz/⅔ cup icing sugar

1 egg, beaten with 1 tsp vanilla extract

16 unskinned almonds or hazelnuts

Syrup is poured over these small shortbread mounds as soon as they come out of the oven, giving them a unique texture that is loose, soft and crunchy, all at the same time. Enjoy them Turkish style with lots of hot tea.

For the syrup

200 g/7 oz/1 cup granulated sugar

150 ml/5 fl oz/⅔ cup water

¾ tsp lemon juice (strained volume)

Syruped Turkish Shortbreads

Sekerpare

Preheat the oven to 180°C/350°F/Gas Mark 4. Grease a baking sheet with sides.

Mix the flour, semolina, salt and baking powder in a bowl and set aside.

Beat together the butter, icing sugar and beaten egg until smooth and creamy. Add the flour mixture and knead lightly to make a softly malleable dough.

Divide the dough into 16 pieces and shape each piece by hand into a ball. Arrange the balls on the baking sheet, leaving enough room for them to spread a little. Press a nut firmly into the centre of each one; elongated nuts should be in a vertical position and only half visible, and bake for about 20 minutes until light golden brown.

Make the syrup while the mounds are baking. Put the sugar, water and lemon juice in a heavy-based saucepan over medium heat. Bring to the boil while stirring to dissolve the sugar. Lower the heat and leave to simmer for 5 minutes. Remove from the heat and set aside. Use about 250 ml/9 fl oz/generous 1 cup for the shortbreads, or to taste.

Remove the mounds from the oven and slowly pour the syrup over them. Move the mounds to one side of the sheet and tilt the sheet so that the excess syrup runs into one corner. Spoon this syrup over the mounds again and repeat once more, so that they are well saturated. Re-position any of the nuts that come loose.

Eat as soon as the shortbreads have cooled, or store in an airtight container for a few days.

Friesian Hazelnut Spice 'Thumbs'

Friese Dumkes

Literally 'Friesian Thumbs', these nutty, spicy
biscuits are a traditional speciality from the
northern Dutch province of Friesland and it's not
hard to see how they got their name. The biscuits
are now sold by most bakers in the region and few
people bother to make what was originally a simple
homemade treat, whipped up fresh in next to no time
to accompany cups of hot milky coffee. In some
areas aniseed is added with a generous hand.

If you like aniseed and would like to try that
twist, add half a teaspoon of ground aniseed and
one teaspoon of whole aniseed to the spice mixture.
The chocolate-dipped option is not traditional, but
it adds a whole new dimension to this simple treat.
I like dark chocolate, but there's nothing to stop
you from using milk or white instead, as long as
it has good melting qualities.

Makes 24

125 g/4½ oz/scant 1 cup plain flour, plus extra
for dusting

⅛ tsp salt

½ tsp ground cinnamon

¼ tsp ground ginger

¼ tsp ground cardamom

⅛ tsp ground allspice

75 g/2¾ oz/¼ cup + 2 tbsp caster sugar

50 g/1¾ oz/⅓ cup hazelnuts, finely chopped

60 g/2¼ oz/¼ cup (generous ½ stick)
butter, softened

1 egg yolk

1½–2 tbsp water, as needed

100 g/3½ oz/3½ squares dark chocolate,
chopped into small pieces (optional)

Preheat the oven to 180°C/350°F/Gas Mark 4. Line a baking sheet with baking parchment.

Sift the flour with the salt and spices and stir in the sugar and hazlenuts. Add the butter, egg yolk and water (as needed) and knead lightly until it all comes together. Roll the dough out to a thickness of 1 cm/½ in, dusting lightly with flour if necessary, and cut into 2 x 5-cm/¾ x 2-in fingers.

Arrange the fingers on the baking sheet and bake for about 15 minutes. Remove from the sheet and leave to cool on a wire rack.

For the optional chocolate dipping, melt the chocolate in a large teacup or small, narrow bowl in the microwave, using 30-second bursts of power and stirring well as soon as you see signs of melting. Alternatively, melt the chocolate in a heatproof bowl over a pan of barely simmering water and transfer it to a smaller cup or bowl if necessary. A small, narrow container makes it easier to coat more of the biscuit with chocolate in a single movement.

Spread a large sheet of baking parchment on your work surface. Dip one end of each biscuit into the chocolate, so that almost half of it is covered with chocolate. Place on the baking parchment and leave to firm up.

Once completely firm, lift carefully from the paper and eat immediately or store in an airtight container. They will keep for at least a week.

Chapter
Eleven

A Tartlet
or Two

Before You Start

There are people who like a generous amount of pastry with their filling. Others look on the pastry as a mere formality, much as in medieval times when the pastry shells or 'coffins' were elaborate but largely inedible receptacles for a lavish filling. Once it had served as an eye-catching table decoration and the contents had been eaten, it was disposed of. Whatever your personal preference may be as to the ratio of pastry to filling, common sense is still required. Small pastries that have a short cooking time need a thinner layer of pastry than a large tart. If the filling is very liquid, the pastry must have the right consistency in order to stay crisp and is then usually pre-baked. And most important of all, the two should combine harmoniously and not compete for attention. It is fine for you to experiment or to use your own better recipe, but if you are aiming for the result described, it is a good idea to follow my recipe.

Working temperature

Pastry tends to turn sticky very quickly in a warm environment and you may find that it needs less liquid in the summer than in the winter. Try to work very quickly if your kitchen is warm or use a food processor for the first part, as hand contact will warm the ingredients faster. Chilling and resting will improve the texture and make the pastry easier to handle.

Ingredients

Everything you need to know is usually given in the recipe, but here are a few items that need attention.

Unless otherwise stated, butter should always be chilled and cubed. Use good unsalted butter for the best flavour.

When nuts are used to replace flour in a recipe, always grind the nuts as finely as you can to a powdery consistency.

Plain flour is generally used, but some pastries use a little baking powder. This will have a tenderising effect as well as making the pastry increase in volume, so the result will be softer than a pastry without baking powder.

Equipment

A silicone mat is virtually non-stick and allows you to use less flour when rolling. An added attraction is that it keeps the mess confined to a small area.

I use plain wooden rolling pins that season themselves beautifully with use. Although you can buy rolling pins with plastic rings at the ends to enable you to roll pastry evenly to a required thickness, I prefer flat wooden measuring sticks that come in pairs in various thicknesses. They can be bought, but you can also make them yourself as long as you ensure that they are completely flat and even – 3 mm/⅛ in, 5 mm/¼ in and 1 cm/½ in are useful thicknesses, with a length of 30 cm/12 in. You place them parallel, on either side of the pastry, within the range of the rolling pin. The rolling pin will not be able to go lower than the thickness of the stick. If you use a 3 mm/⅛ in pair and the pastry should be 2.5 mm/scant ⅛ in, remove the sticks and give the pastry an extra roll.

A flour dredger is useful, but a sieve will do if you don't have one.

Tin dimensions are given when a specific size and volume is required, such as the 10-cm/4-in (2-cm/¾-in high) fluted tart tins used for the Chocolate Pecan Tarts (see p.237). When a recipe specifies a 12-hole muffin tin, you can of course also use 2 x 6-hole ones, but pay attention to the volume. They should hold 75 ml/2½ fl oz/ ⅓ cup or 90 ml/3 fl oz/scant ½ cup. 75 ml/2½ fl oz/⅓ cup will allow the pastry to come all the way to the top; 90 ml/3 fl oz/scant ½ cup should have the pastry just fall short of the top; don't pull or stretch the pastry, unless you want a thinner layer.

A pastry tamper keeps your fingernails from tearing the pastry, especially when you line a small cavity. It looks like a wooden pestle with completely flat ends that are each of a different size. They are usually made to fit into muffin and mini-muffin tins. A narrow jar or glass with a completely flat base will also work, or even the blunt end of a rolling pin. Line the cavity loosely with the pastry, then use the tamper to press it into place properly.

Paper cases (cups) and pie weights or baking beans are needed for blind baking – i.e. wholly or partially cooking a pastry shell without the filling. The paper cases are simply lifted out with the weights when you reach the correct stage. Ceramic pie weights can be bought in tins and a tin is usually enough for 12 small shells or a large pie. You can also use dried beans or even rice instead, discarding them after a few uses.

Plain and fluted cutters in a few sizes are useful to have and a 10-cm/4-in plain one is essential. They can be bought singly or in sets.

You probably already have your own favourite pastry brushes, but you might like to bear in mind that old-fashioned soft bristle brushes allow you to manoeuvre better than silicone ones for brushing melted chocolate. Either type is fine for egg washing.

A thin and flexible metal spatula makes it easy to loosen and lift a piece of pastry from your work surface without tearing it.

And, of course, a wire rack is absolutely essential.

This is a basic shortcrust pastry that can be used for any number of things. Remember that the pastry will be only as light as your treatment of it.

Makes 300 g/10½ oz

200 g/7 oz/scant 1½ cups plain flour

scant ¼ tsp salt

100 g/3½ oz/7 tbsp butter, chilled and cubed

about 4 tbsp cold water, as needed

Shortcrust Pastry

Put the flour and salt in a large bowl. Rub in the butter with your fingertips until the mixture resembles fine breadcrumbs. It can also be made in a food processor up to this stage. Pulse until well blended, then transfer to a bowl. Add enough water to make it all come together. Do this with your fingertips and don't overwork the pastry.

Shape the dough into a flat disc, wrap it in clingfilm and chill for about 30 minutes.

Proceed as directed in the recipe.

Makes 350 g/12⅓ oz

200 g/7 oz/scant 1½ cups plain flour

scant ¼ tsp salt

50 g/1¾ oz/scant ½ cup icing sugar, sifted

100 g/3½ oz/7 tbsp butter, chilled and cubed

1 egg yolk, beaten with 2 tbsp cold water

Sweet pastry makes a crisp background for a number of tartlets in this chapter. Once you have made the pastry, proceed as directed in the recipe you are using.

Sweet Pastry

Mix the flour, salt and icing sugar together in a bowl. Rub in the butter with your fingertips until the mixture resembles fine breadcrumbs. You can also put the ingredients in a food processor and pulse a few times then turn out into a bowl for the next stage. Add the egg yolk mixture, reserving the last teaspoon or so; add the reserved egg only if you are sure that the pastry won't become too wet. If you need more liquid, add a few drops of cold water. Mix with a few swift strokes of your fingertips until it comes together.

Shape the dough into a flat disc, wrap it in clingfilm and chill for about 30 minutes.

Makes 12

1 quantity Sweet Pastry (see opposite)
or Nut Pastry (see p.226)
butter, for greasing
plain flour, for dusting

Pre-baked pastry shells are good to have as a
standby and can be stored in the freezer for
a quick dessert. Sweet Pastry and Nut Pastry
are particularly good and you can fill them
with all kinds of creams, desserts and fruit,
depending on your mood and the season.

You will need 12 paper cupcake or muffin cases
and ceramic pie weights (baking beans),
dried beans or rice.

Pre-baked Pastry Shells

Make and chill the pastry as directed (see opposite or p.226).

Preheat the oven to 180°C/350°F/Gas Mark 4. Grease a 12-hole muffin tin.

Remove the dough from the refrigerator and roll out to a thickness of just under 3 mm/⅛ in, then cut out 12 circles with a plain 10 cm/4 in cutter, re-rolling the trimmings as necessary.

Line the muffin tin neatly with the pastry, pressing it against the sides and ensuring that it comes all the way to the top of each cavity. I use a 12-hole muffin or bun tin that holds 75 ml/2½ fl oz/⅓ cup per cavity. If you use one that holds 90 ml/3 fl oz/ scant ½ cup, don't pull the pastry all the way up unless you want a slightly thinner layer. Chill again for 30 minutes or put in the freezer for about 7 minutes.

Place a paper case on top of each pastry shell and fill with baking beans, dried beans or rice. Bake for 15 minutes, then remove the paper cases and weights and bake for a further 5–10 minutes, or until the pastry is cooked through. Twist the pastry shells free after a few minutes and leave to cool on a wire rack.

Store in an airtight container at cool room temperature for a few days, or freeze for up to a few months.

Makes 375 g/13¼ oz

100 g/3½ oz/⅔ cup almonds, pistachios or walnuts, very finely ground	
115 g/4 oz/generous ¾ cup plain flour	
50 g/1¾ oz/scant ½ cup icing sugar	
¼ tsp salt	
100 g/3½ oz/7 tbsp butter, chilled and cubed	
scant 2 tbsp beaten egg, or as needed	

This pastry needs a little more care than all-flour pastry, but is well worth the effort. The nuts must be ground to a powder, as they replace part of the flour in the recipe and if they are too coarse, the pastry will fall apart more easily. One of the good things about it is that tears and accidental cuts are easily repaired. Always use a generous amount of dusting flour and, if possible, roll out on a dusted silicone mat, removing the cut rounds with a flexible metal spatula. Once you have made the pastry, proceed as directed in the recipe you are using.

Nut Pastry

If using a food processor to grind the nuts, add the dry ingredients to the nuts and pulse again until well combined. Add the butter and pulse until the mixture looks like fine breadcrumbs, then transfer to a large bowl. If doing it by hand, mix the dry ingredients before rubbing in the butter with your fingertips until you get the same texture. Add enough beaten egg to moisten the dry ingredients and knead lightly in the bowl to form a dough. Use the egg sparingly, as there is not much flour to absorb it; the nuts will not absorb any.

Shape the dough into a flat disc, wrap in clingfilm and chill until it firms up enough to roll.

Proceed as directed in the recipe.

Crunchy Nut Tarts

Makes 12

1 quantity Sweet Pastry (see p.224)

butter, for greasing

plain flour, for dusting

125 g/4½ oz/½ cup + 2 tbsp caster sugar

40 g/1½ oz/2 tbsp golden or light corn syrup

60 ml/4 tbsp double cream

40 g/1½ oz/3 tbsp butter

75 g/2¾ oz/½ cup pistachios

75 g/2¾ oz/½ cup macadamias,
in large pieces

75 g/2¾ oz/½ cup cashews

Use well-toasted nuts for a good crunch and make combinations or just take your favourite nut. Macadamias will give the most crunch, while cashews will be on the softer side. I find that they work well in combinations such as this one, with some bright green pistachios thrown in for contrast.

Make and chill the pastry as directed (see p.224).

Preheat the oven to 180°C/350°F/Gas Mark 4. Grease a 12-hole muffin or bun tin.

Remove the dough from the refrigerator and roll out on a lightly floured work surface to a thickness of just under 3 mm/⅛ in. Cut out 12 circles with a plain 10-cm/4-in cutter, re-rolling the trimmings as necessary. Line the muffin or bun tin neatly with the pastry. I use a 12-hole muffin or bun tin that holds 75 ml/2½ fl oz/⅓ cup per cavity. If you use one that holds 90 ml/3 fl oz/ scant ½ cup, don't pull the pastry all the way up unless you want a slightly thinner layer. Chill again for 30 minutes or put in the freezer for about 7 minutes.

Place a paper case on top of each pastry shell and fill with baking beans, dried beans or rice. Bake for 15 minutes, then remove the paper cases and weights and set aside.

Put the sugar, syrup, cream and butter into a medium heavy-based saucepan and stir over low heat until the sugar dissolves completely. Undissolved sugar will make your caramel grainy. Attach a sugar thermometer, bring to the boil, then reduce the heat and leave to boil, stirring gently from time to time, until it reaches 112°C/234°F (soft ball stage).

Remove the pan from the heat and stir in the nuts, then spoon the filling into the pre-baked pastry shells and return to the oven for a further 8–10 minutes until the pastry is cooked through. When the tarts have cooled a little, twist them carefully out of the tin and leave to cool completely on a wire rack.

They will keep in an airtight container at cool room temperature for a few days, but freeze them if you want to keep them longer.

The delectable Canadian butter tart somehow managed
to elude me during my years at university in Nova
Scotia. Perhaps a good thing, as I'm quite sure
that I would have formed a lifelong attachment and
this rich treat is not a thing to be eaten on a
daily basis. It wasn't until years later that my
sister in Ontario introduced me to these tarts
that are held to be one of the few authentically
Canadian baking specialities. They may look like
mini pecan pies, or even treacle tarts, but a
single bite will disabuse you. I find that the
flavour is more like butterscotch and the texture
is beautifully creamy. The nuts and raisins are
optional and the tarts are just as good without
them. Note that the raisins will also make them
sweeter. The pastry has a pleasant tang that goes
well with the sweet filling. However, you can
substitute shortcrust pastry if you prefer.

Butter Tarts

Makes 12 tarts
For the pastry
85 g/3 oz/6 tbsp butter, chilled and cubed, plus extra for greasing
200 g/7 oz/scant 1½ cups plain flour, plus extra for dusting
¼ tsp salt
1 egg yolk
2 tsp cold water
½ tsp lemon juice
75 g/2¾ oz/⅓ cup sour cream

For the filling
2 eggs
¼ tsp salt
175 g/6 oz/scant 1 cup soft light brown sugar
1 tsp vanilla extract
115 g/4 oz/8 tbsp butter
50 g/1¾ oz/scant ½ cup chopped walnuts or pecans, or raisins, or a mixture (optional)

Preheat the oven to 180°C/350°F/Gas Mark 4. Grease a 12-hole muffin tin well.

To make the pastry, put the flour and salt in a food processor and pulse a few times to mix. Add the butter and pulse until the mixture resembles fine breadcrumbs. Combine the egg yolk, water and lemon juice and add to the flour along with the sour cream. Pulse until the pastry comes together. You can also do the entire job by hand if you prefer; mix lightly with your fingertips. Wrap the pastry in clingfilm and chill for about 20 minutes while you prepare the filling.

For the filling, put the eggs, salt, sugar and vanilla in a mixer bowl and whisk briefly to loosen the eggs. Melt the butter and pour it over the eggs while whisking. Continue to whisk for 2–3 minutes until smooth. Set aside.

Roll the pastry out on a lightly floured work surface to an even thickness of 3 mm/⅛ in and cut out 12 circles, about 9 cm/3½ in in diameter, re-rolling the trimmings as needed. Use the pastry circles to line the muffin tin, pressing them neatly against the sides with your fingers. If using nuts and/or raisins, divide them over the pastry shells. Give the filling a good stir and spoon evenly into the shells so that they are about three-quarters full. Bake for 15 minutes, then lower the temperature to 165°C/329°F/Gas Mark 3 and bake for a further 5 minutes until the pastry colours and the filling sets.

As soon as the tarts are cool enough to handle, transfer them to a wire rack to cool. Don't eat them straight from the oven – the filling will burn you! They are best eaten fresh, but can be frozen for later if necessary.

Makes 12

For the pastry

100 g/3½ oz/7 tbsp butter, chilled and cubed, plus extra for greasing

125 g/4½ oz/scant 1 cup plain flour, plus extra for dusting

75 g/2¾ oz/½ cup blanched almonds, finely ground

scant ¼ tsp salt

50 g/1¾ oz/¼ cup caster sugar

1 tsp vanilla extract

1 egg yolk, beaten with 2 tsp cold water

For the filling

250–300 g/9–10½ oz fresh cherries, pitted

100 g/3½ oz/generous 1 cup ground almonds

2 tbsp cornflour

100 g/3½ oz/½ cup caster sugar

2 eggs, well beaten

1 tbsp Kirsch (may be replaced by cream)

50 ml/1¾ fl oz/scant ¼ cup double cream

The region where I live, the Betuwe, has been noted for its fruit for many centuries and cherries, strawberries, raspberries, redcurrants, plums, apples, pears and more are all available direct from the growers. The cherry season is always welcomed as a sign of summer and in common with the rest of the villagers we eat freshly picked cherries until they come out of our ears. The Dutch are passionate about agricultural innovation and the last decade or so has seen many of the surrounding orchards replanted with 'modern' varieties, mainly shorter trees that make picking easier. I view all of these developments with mixed feelings. It's not that the new kinds are not delicious. Most are, although some seem to have been bred for their ability to travel well and have firm – even hard – skins. My small gripe is that they are all huge, making them less suitable for small tartlets like these. When filling them, you will have to use your discretion and make allowances for the size of your cherries.

Cherry and Almond Tarts

Preheat the oven to 180°C/350°F/Gas Mark 4. Grease a 12-hole muffin tin. This lovely almond pastry is a variant of Nut Pastry (see p.226). It is really good in this recipe, but if you prefer something more straightforward, use the recipe for Sweet Pastry on p.224 instead.

To make the pastry, mix the flour, ground almonds, salt and caster sugar together in a bowl. Rub in the butter with your fingertips until the mixture looks like fine breadcrumbs. You can also put the ingredients in a food processor and pulse a few times then turn out into a bowl for the next stage. Add the vanilla. Add the egg yolk mixture, reserving the last teaspoon or so; add the reserved egg only if you are sure that the pastry won't become too wet. If you need even more liquid, add a few drops of cold water. Mix with a few swift strokes of the fingers until it comes together.

Shape the dough into a ball, wrap in clingfilm and chill for about 30 minutes.

For the filling, reserve the cherries and combine the dry ingredients in a bowl. Add the liquids and stir very thoroughly until smooth. Set aside until needed, giving it a good stir again before using.

Roll out the pastry on a lightly floured work surface to a thickness of just under 3 mm/⅛ in. You will need to dust well with flour because the pastry is quite delicate and may stick. The good news is that tears are easily mended, by pressing the pastry together. Cut out 12 circles with a plain 10-cm/4-in cutter, re-rolling the trimmings as necessary. Once the bulk of the circles have been cut out of the main sheet, I find it easier to take the trimmings intended for the last four or so and press them together, dividing the resulting ball into the correct number of smaller balls. This makes it easier to roll each to the right size and means that the pastry does not get overworked as you keep on pressing trimmings back together. Line the muffin tin neatly with the pastry, mending any tears as you go along.

Spoon a portion of the filling (about 1½ tbsp) into a cavity and top with 3 large or 4 small cherries. There should be about 5 mm/¼ in of pastry still visible. If the filling rises all the way up, decrease slightly for the following ones. It is far better to have a few tbsp of unused filling than to have your tartlets spill over. Bake for about 20 minutes until the pastry is golden brown and the filling has set.

Eat warm or cold, with optional whipped cream, crème fraîche or ice cream.

Makes 12 pastries

butter, for greasing

1 quantity Sweet Pastry, see p.224

beaten egg, as needed

250 g/9 oz almond paste (see p.141)

plain flour, for dusting

100 g/3½ oz/3½ squares dark chocolate, chopped into small pieces

During a spring break spent on the Danish island of Fynen, the bracing sea winds often sent us scuttling off in search of warmth and refreshment. Fortunately, there were always bakeries and tearooms somewhere near by and these triangular pastries cropped up in almost all of them. Their shape is meant to imitate Napoleon Bonaparte's 'tricorne', hence the name. These hats are definitely worth eating.

Napoleon's Hats
Napoleonshatte

Make and chill the Sweet Pastry, see p.224.

Preheat the oven to 180°C/350°F/Gas Mark 4. Lightly grease a baking sheet.

Knead enough egg into the almond paste to make it softly malleable, then divide it into 12 portions, shape them into balls and set aside.

Remove the chilled pastry from the refrigerator and roll out on a lightly floured work surface to a thickness of about 2.5 mm/⅛ in. Use a plain or fluted 10-cm/4-in cutter to cut out 12 circles. Place an almond paste ball in the centre of each circle. Moisten the edge of the pastry and bring it up around the almond paste to form a triangle, with the sides standing up straight and some of the paste visible in the centre. Press the points together with your fingers to seal well. Bake for about 20 minutes, or until the pastry starts to colour a little. Leave to cool on a wire rack.

Melt the chocolate in a small heatproof bowl over a pan of barely simmering water and dip the points of triangle into the chocolate to coat them by about 2 cm/¾ in. Use a spoon to help as the chocolate level goes down. Keep a damp cloth nearby and clean your fingers before you pick up each new pastry. Put the pastries on a sheet of baking parchment and leave the chocolate to harden.

They are best eaten fresh. They can be frozen, with minimal loss of flavour and texture, but the chocolate may become slightly dull.

Makes 8

50 g/1¾ oz/3½ tbsp butter, plus extra
for greasing

1 quantity Sweet Pastry, see p.224

150 g/5½ oz/½ cup golden or dark corn syrup

100 g/3½ oz/½ cup caster sugar

125 g/4½ oz/4½ squares dark chocolate,
finely chopped

plain flour, for dusting

3 eggs, beaten with 1 tsp vanilla extract

125–150 g/4½–5½ oz/1¼–1½ cups pecan halves
(9 per tart)

These tarts are a twist on American pecan pie, which is usually a single large pie. Traditional ones do not use chocolate, but rely on dark corn syrup, sugar and eggs as a backdrop for the nuts. European cooks can more readily lay their hands on golden syrup – either type of syrup will do here, but golden syrup will give a little more sweetness. You can chop up the nuts and mix them into the filling, but if you take an extra minute to arrange the pecan halves on top of the filling, they will remain crunchy, contrasting with the gooey filling, and will look very pretty into the bargain.

Chocolate Pecan Tarts

Preheat the oven to 180°C/350°F/Gas Mark 4. Grease 8 x 10-cm/4-in fluted tart tins, at least 2-cm/¾-in high, well and arrange them on a baking sheet.

Start making the filling just before you remove the pastry from the refrigerator. Put the butter, syrup and caster sugar in a saucepan over medium heat and stir until the mixture warms up and the butter melts. Stir in the chocolate and remove from the heat. Stir thoroughly until homogeneous. A whisk is more effective than a spoon. Set aside while you roll out the pastry.

You may look at the amount of pastry and have doubts as to whether it will be enough. If you use the method I describe, it will be. Divide the pastry into 2 halves. Roll each half out on a lightly floured work surface to make a rough square, about 25 x 25 cm/10 x 10 in. Cut each square into 4 smaller squares and use them to line the tart tins in the following frugal but efficient way: take a square and place it over the tin. Press the pastry gently against the side, then fold down the excess that sticks out over the tin to make the side slightly thicker than the base. Run your finger around the pastry to neaten it to the same thickness all around the circumference. This pastry is easy to work with, so you can pinch off bits from one place to patch another with no ill effects. Just make sure that the pastry comes all the way up the side of the tin or you may lose a little filling.

Whisk the eggs into the chocolate mixture, a little at a time, until smooth. Spoon the filling into the pastry shells. There should be about 5 mm/¼ in left between the filling and the top of the pastry. Arrange the pecans on top of the filling. Aim accurately; once they come into contact with the sticky filling, they will be messy to pull out again. Put the first 4 at the points of the compass and fill in the spaces, adding the last one in the centre.

Bake for about 25–30 minutes until the pastry is golden brown and crisp and the filling has set. The filling will bulge in the centre, but it will subside as the tarts cool.

Leave the tarts in the tins until they are cool enough to handle, then remove them and leave to cool on a wire rack.

Makes 12

butter, for greasing

I quantity Sweet Pastry, see p.224

200 ml/7 fl oz/generous ¾ cup double cream

200 g/7 oz/7 squares dark chocolate (55% cocoa solids), finely chopped

I egg + I egg yolk

scant I tbsp cornflour

100 g/3½ oz/½ cup caster sugar

2 tsp vanilla extract

Who can resist a dark, intense chocolate tart, eaten warm or cold? Eat them as they are, or with a scoop of ice cream or dollop of whipped cream. You could also put a few raspberries on top of the tarts and dust lightly with icing sugar. When I accidentally prepared too much filling, I decided to bake the excess in foil muffin cups, rather than make more pastry. It is my favourite serendipitous creation to date. It turned into that irresistible soft and succulent warm dessert the French call 'moelleux', which are usually underbaked so that the insides spill out deliciously when your spoon breaks through. Spoon the mixture into eight small greased ramekins or handle-less porcelain teacups and bake for seven minutes for a fairly fluid centre and ten for a firmer, but still soft, dessert. Serve hot or warm, accompanied by a cold contrast.

Intense Chocolate Tarts and Moelleux

Preheat the oven to 180°C/350°F/Gas Mark 4. Grease a 12-hole muffin or bun tin.

Make the pastry and pre-bake the shells for 15 minutes as described in Pre-baked Pastry Shells (see p.225). While the cases are pre-baking, make the filling.

Put the double cream in a small saucepan and bring to the boil. Remove from the heat and add the chopped chocolate. Leave to stand for about 5 minutes.

Meanwhile, whisk the remaining ingredients together so that the cornflour and sugar dissolve properly. This will take only a minute or two using a hand whisk. Gently stir the liquid in the saucepan until smooth, then whisk it into the egg mixture. Set aside and give it a whisk again before using.

When the pastry shells have pre-baked, remove the tin from the oven and remove the paper cases and weights. Fill each shell with the chocolate filling, leaving about 5 mm/¼ in free at the top. Be careful not to spill the mixture onto the edges, or it will look untidy. Return to the oven and bake for a further 10 minutes, or a little longer. They are done when the centres barely wobble when you give the tin a shake. There will be a few cracks and the chocolate in the crevices will look shiny and uncooked. The cracks will subside as the tarts cool and the chocolate will continue to set.

When the tarts have cooled a little, twist them carefully out of the tin and serve warm or leave to cool completely on a wire rack.

This dessert can be lifted from good to gorgeous simply by finding tasty mangoes, fresh or canned. This is not always an easy task in temperate zones. Ethnic greengrocers are your best bet, not especially because they know more about tropical fruit, but more because they are generally very obliging in following up specific tips and requests from customers. From time to time my Turkish greengrocer stocks what he labels as 'honey mangoes', although I can't vouch for the accuracy of the name. His labelling can be erratic and I strongly suspect that he blithely camouflages gaps of knowledge with bursts of creativity. These sweet mangoes are small, flat and elongated, with an intensely orange flesh and yellow-orange skin. They look very much like Ataulfo and Carabao mangoes, but any truly tasty ones will do. 'Shrikhand' is a popular Indian dessert that uses drained yogurt. Using firm-textured Greek-style yogurt saves this step. Don't forget to paint the pastry shells with chocolate, or they will become soggy.

Makes 12 (but is easily decreased)

1 quantity pre-baked Nut Pastry Shells, made with pistachios (see p.225)

85–100 g/3–3½ oz/3–3½ squares white chocolate, melted

480 g/1 lb ripe mango, fresh or canned

150 g/5½ oz/¾ cup granulated sugar

500 g/1 lb 2 oz/scant 2¼ cups Greek-style yogurt

whole pistachios, to decorate

Pistachio Cups with Mango Shrikhand

Prepare and bake the pre-baked Nut Pastry Shells as directed (see p.225).

When the pastry is cool, use a pastry brush to coat the insides of the shells with the melted white chocolate. Be gentle but thorough and leave no gaps. Leave to set before using. The pastry shells freeze quite well, so you can use as many as you want fresh and freeze the rest before or after they have been coated with chocolate. The filling is also easily decreased to half or less. If you prefer, simply halve the entire recipe.

If using canned mangoes, drain well and pat dry before weighing. Purée the mango with the sugar and transfer to a small heavy-based saucepan. Bring slowly to the boil and leave to simmer for 5 minutes while stirring. It will spit a little from time to time, so wear oven mitts. Set aside to cool, then chill.

When the mango purée is well chilled, whisk 250 g/9 oz of it into the yogurt. Cover and chill until needed, along with the remaining purée. Both can be left overnight.

When ready to serve, fill the pastry shells with the *shrikhand*, leaving about 5 mm/¼ in free at the top. Spoon over the remaining mango purée, top with about 3 pistachios and serve immediately. Once you've spooned out the filling, you can bite into the pastry cup.

Luscious Coconut Tarts

Even if you are not normally a fan of coconut, I urge you to try these luscious tartlets. The soft cake-like pastry base with tart apricot jam and sweetly tender filling make a melt-in-the-mouth combination, especially when they are still slightly warm from the oven. They originated in South Africa where they are best known as 'Hertzog Cookies' (or 'Hertzoggies') and 'Smuts Cookies'. As the story goes, either one or the other was made in South African kitchens, and the kind you made showed your political affiliation. Both Hertzog and Smuts were leaders from the First World War until after the Second and often worked together for the common good of the country, but the outbreak of the Second World War split them irrevocably apart. Hertzog favoured a position of neutrality for South Africa, bordering on pro-German sympathies according to some reports. Smuts held exactly the opposite view and declared war on Germany as soon as he replaced the deposed Hertzog as Prime Minister in 1939.

This recipe is in the Smuts tradition. Both types have a soft pastry base topped with apricot jam, but while the Hertzog version of the filling is very plain, using only egg white, coconut and sugar, the Smuts one is richer and more tender. South Africans usually bake them in patty tins, producing smaller tartlets. That doesn't mean that they eat them sparingly, though, as recipes are generally designed to produce several dozen.

Makes 12
For the pastry

75 g/2¾ oz/5 tbsp butter, chilled and cubed, plus extra for greasing

175 g/6 oz/1¼ cups plain flour, plus extra for dusting

1 tsp baking powder

¼ tsp salt

25 g/1 oz/2 tbsp caster sugar

1 egg yolk, beaten with 2 tbsp cold water

For the filling

1 egg + 1 egg white, well beaten with 1 tsp vanilla extract

50 g/1¾ oz/3½ tbsp butter, melted

100 g/3½ oz/½ cup caster sugar

125 g/4½ oz/generous 1⅓ cups desiccated coconut

¼ tsp salt

1 tbsp water

about 3 tbsp apricot jam*

*Apricot jam gives a tart contrast, but raspberry jam is almost as good as long as it is not too sweet.

Preheat the oven to 180°C/350°F/Gas Mark 4. Grease a 12-hole muffin or bun tin.

For the pastry, mix the flour, baking powder, salt and caster sugar together in a bowl. Rub in the butter with your fingertips until the mixture looks like fine breadcrumbs. You can also put the ingredients in a food processor and pulse a few times, then turn out into a bowl for the next stage. Add the egg yolk mixture, and an extra teaspoon cold water if needed. Mix with a few swift strokes of the fingers until it comes together. Shape the dough into a ball, wrap in clingfilm and leave to rest at cool room temperature while you put together the filling.

Put all of the filling ingredients, except the jam, in a bowl and mix well to combine. Set aside while you roll out the pastry.

Roll out the pastry on a lightly floured work surface to a thickness of 3 mm/⅛ in and cut out 12 circles with a plain 7.5-cm/3-in cutter, re-rolling the trimmings as necessary. Line the muffin or bun tin neatly with the pastry and spoon ¾ tsp apricot jam into each one. Give the coconut filling a good stir and spoon it out evenly over the jam. Neaten with your fingers if necessary. Bake for 20–25 minutes, or until the pastry is cooked through and the tops are golden brown in most places. Leave the tarts in the tins until cool enough to handle, then remove them and leave to cool on a wire rack.

Even if you plan to eat them warm, leave them to cool a little, or the hot jam will burn your mouth. For freezing, I wrap each one individually in clingfilm and pack them into freezer bags or boxes. Freeze as soon as they are cool.

Makes 12 pastries

butter, for greasing

I quantity Shortcrust Pastry, see p.224

I small can (about 235 g/8½ oz)
sweetened bean paste, e.g. *adzuki*

plain flour, for dusting

I egg yolk, beaten

a few poppy or black sesame seeds
(not nigella!), optional

For sheer visual beauty in pastries, few can beat
the Chinese. These, for instance, are cut to look
like chrysanthemum flowers. They are usually filled
with sweet bean paste, made from red, black and
'adzuki' beans. They are absolutely delicious
and can be bought from Asian shops. I prefer
the Japanese versions because they are in general
not over-sweet and have more texture to them.
If you find the thought of bean paste too exotic,
use pistachio or almond paste. You might like
to colour the almond paste for contrast.

Chrysanthemums

Preheat the oven to 180°C/350°F/Gas Mark 4. Lightly grease a baking sheet.

Make and chill the Shortcrust Pastry, see p.224.

Divide the bean paste into 12 portions. Divide the pastry into 12 pieces and roll each piece out on a lightly floured work surface into a circle, about 9 cm/3½ in in diameter. Top each piece of pastry with a portion of filling, moisten the edges and pinch into a ball to seal. Flatten slightly to a diameter of 5 cm/2 in, sealed side down.

Use a small round 2-cm/¾-in cutter or a bottle cap to press very lightly into the top of the pastry so that you see a faint circle in the centre. Use a sharp and pointed knife to cut right through the pastry from the edge of the circle to just under the base. Do this at scant 1 cm/½ in intervals, all the way around.

Place the pastry on the baking sheet and press lightly with your fingers to flatten it to about 6 cm/2½ in. The 'petals' will separate. Brush the centre of the flower with beaten egg yolk and scatter on a few poppy or black sesame seeds if you like. Bake for about 20 minutes. Leave to cool on a wire rack.

Moulded Nut Pastries

Ma'amoul

In the Middle East, pastries known as 'ma'amoul'
are moulded in intricately cut traditional wooden
moulds or the soulless modern plastic ones now
on the market. There are three basic traditional
shapes, each corresponding to a particular
filling: oval for pistachio, round and domed
for walnut, or round and flat for date. Those
who have no moulds shape them by hand and
sometimes use special tweezers (like those
used for crimping marzipan) to decorate them.

Here is a cheat's way for the Western baker
to make attractively shaped 'ma'amoul': bake
them in fancy tartlet tins. I use oval fluted
tins, about 8 x 5 cm/3¼ x 2 in for the pistachio
version and round fluted 6.5-cm/2½-in ones for
the walnut ones. If you don't have similar tins,
just make sure that the filled raw pastry barely
comes up to the top of the tin, or you will
have an uneven finish. At a pinch you can even
use bun or muffin tins, which will make plainer
but no less delicious pastries. This recipe
gives a dozen of each kind, so if you only
want to make one kind, or half the amount,
adapt it accordingly.

Makes 24 pastries

For the pastry

150 g/5½ oz/scant ¾ cup butter, chilled and
cubed, plus extra for greasing

300 g/10½ oz/scant 2¼ cups plain flour,
plus extra for dusting

90 g/3¼ oz/generous ¾ cup icing sugar,
sifted, plus extra for dusting

¼ tsp salt

2 egg yolks, beaten with
50 ml/1¾ fl oz/scant ¼ cup cold water

For the pistachio filling

100 g/3½ oz/⅔ cup pistachios, finely ground

60 g/2¼ oz/scant ⅓ cup caster sugar

1 egg white, as needed

For the walnut filling

100 g/3½ oz/1 cup walnuts, finely ground

60 g/2¼ oz/scant ⅓ cup caster sugar

¼–½ tsp ground cinnamon (optional)

1 egg white, as needed

Preheat the oven to 170°C/325°F/Gas Mark 3. Grease 12 round and 12 oval fluted high-sided tartlet tins.

For the pastry, mix the flour, icing sugar and salt in a large bowl. Rub in the butter with your fingertips. Alternatively, put these ingredients into a food processor and pulse until the mixture resembles fine breadcrumbs. Transfer to a large bowl. Add the egg yolk mixture, reserving the last teaspoon or so; add the reserved egg only if you are sure that the pastry won't become too wet. If you need even more liquid, add a few drops of cold water. Mix with a few swift strokes of your fingers until it comes together. Shape into a ball, wrap in clingfilm and chill for about 30 minutes.

For the fillings, mix the ingredients in 2 separate bowls. Add about three-quarters of an egg white to each bowl, enough to make a softly malleable paste, then divide each filling into 12 portions and set aside.

Divide the pastry in half and each half into 12 pieces. Roll or flatten out on a lightly floured work surface to a circle about 8 cm/3¼ in in diameter. Place a portion of filling in the centre and bring up the edges around it, pinching to seal neatly and well. Place the filled pastry sealed side down in the tin and press with your fingers to flatten the top and push it into the grooves of the tin at the same time. Arrange the tins on a baking sheet and bake for about 20 minutes, or until cooked through and still quite pale in colour for a tender pastry, or a little longer for a firmer one.

Unmould as soon as the tarts can be handled and leave to cool on a wire rack. Dust generously with icing sugar before serving.

These tarts can also be frozen for later; in that case, dust prior to serving.

Makes 16

40 g/1½ oz/3 tbsp butter, softened

125 g/4½ oz/½ cup + 2 tbsp soft dark
brown sugar

50 g/1¾ oz/generous ⅓ cup plain
flour

⅛ tsp salt

½ tsp ground cinnamon

50 g/1¾ oz/½ cup flaked almonds

1 tbsp water

I find tulips or baskets made from a delicate wafer batter exactly that: delicate. They have the annoying quality of going soggy as soon as they are filled, leaving you with next to nothing to enjoy. These crunchy cinnamon flavoured lace baskets will hold their own far better. They are not difficult to make, but you will need to have everything ready and work quickly to shape them before they harden and break. They can be made in advance and filled with creams and fruits or nuts of your choice shortly before serving. Don't use anything too runny because it will seep through the 'lace'. My favourite way is very simple: put a scoop of delicious vanilla ice cream in the basket and top with a large shard of Macadamia or Spiced Peanut Brittle (see p.53 or p.50). Alternatively, top with a raspberry or strawberry and a mint leaf.

Cinnamon Lace Baskets

Preheat the oven to 200°C/400°F/Gas Mark 6. Cut out 32 squares of baking parchment, about 10 x 10cm/4 x 4 in.

Put all of the ingredients in a bowl and knead lightly to break up the almonds and make a soft dough. Divide the dough into 16 pieces and roll each piece to a ball between your palms. Place each ball on a square of baking parchment and flatten slightly. Arrange 5–6 at a time on a baking sheet and bake just above the centre of the oven for 6–7 minutes. They will spread and flatten as they cook.

Remove the baking sheet from the oven and top each lace round with another square of baking parchment, then position it over the cavity of a 12–16-hole muffin tin* and use your hand together with a pastry tamper, the blunt end of a rolling pin (or a narrow glass or jar with a base slightly smaller than the base of the muffin cavities) to ease it down gently into the cavity. The sides will pleat and the base should rest firmly at the bottom, so give it a few extra presses if necessary. Work quickly to complete the batch. Bake and shape the remaining dough in the same way.

When cool and hard, remove the baking parchment. They can be stored in an airtight container for up to 2 weeks and can be frozen for much longer in a sturdy plastic container. Fill just before serving.

* If you don't have 16 cavities available, wait about 5 minutes between batches to allow the ones in the tin to harden enough to be removed.

Deliciously Dainty

And to end it off, here are a few little cakes that I couldn't resist sharing.
Everything you need to know is given in the recipe and as far as equipment
goes, you might like to take a look at the general information on baking
equipment on p.21. I hope you'll enjoy these last few treats. They range
from plain(ish) to fancy and all have their own special points.

This recipe is based on Portuguese 'bolos de arroz', small cakes that are a popular snack and breakfast item, accompanied by cups of excellent coffee. Rice flour gives them a unique texture that is light and loose and seems to dissolve on the tongue, making the first bite a surprise. Traditional 'bolos de arroz' are sometimes flavoured with a pinch of lemon or orange zest, but I have chosen fragrant cinnamon sticks that add aroma and visual appeal. 'Fragrant' is crucial here, or you will end up with little noticeable extra flavour, so I use some ground cinnamon in the topping too. The cakes should be eaten fresh, so make small batches, unless you are catering for a large group.

The Portuguese are extremely fond of cinnamon and cinnamon sticks make unexpected appearances. Breakfasting with the locals in a small café on the bank of the Douro, I selected a little cake with an upright cinnamon stick in the centre. There were no ground spices in the batter, but the aroma from the stick permeated the cake, producing a subtle spiciness. In another café, I unwrapped the elongated object that rested on the saucer next to my coffee and took a bite. It was not the chocolate or cookie that I had expected it to be, but an unadorned stick of cinnamon! The amused waiter came over to tell me that I was meant to stir my coffee with it. We live and learn.

Makes 6 cakes

75 g/2¾ oz/½ cup rice flour (regular non-glutinous)

50 g/1¾ oz/generous ⅓ cup plain flour

I tsp baking powder

⅛ tsp salt

75 g/2¾ oz/5 tbsp butter, softened

75 g/2¾ oz/¼ cup + 2 tbsp caster sugar

I egg, lightly beaten with ½ tsp vanilla extract

2 tbsp milk

I tbsp brandy or rum

I tbsp granulated sugar + ¾ tsp ground cinnamon, combined

6 cinnamon sticks

Fluffy Cinnamon Rice Cakes

Preheat the oven to 170°C/325°F/Gas Mark 3. Line a 6-hole muffin tin with paper cases.

Sift the flours with the baking powder and salt and set aside.

Beat the butter until smooth. Add the caster sugar and beat until light and fluffy. Add the egg to the creamed mixture, a little at a time, beating well and scraping down the sides of the bowl after each addition. Fold in the flour mixture in 3 batches, adding the milk and brandy or rum with the second batch.

Spoon the batter evenly into the paper cases and sprinkle ½ tsp of the cinnamon sugar over each one. Stand a cinnamon stick upright in the centre of each cake.

Bake for about 20 minutes, or until cooked through. The tops will have cracked to show veins of soft, pale cake between the darker crunchy topping. Leave to cool on a wire rack and serve fresh.

Makes 12 cakes

For the cake

butter, for greasing

plain flour, for dusting

3 eggs

125 g/4½ oz/½ cup + 2 tbsp caster sugar

¾ tsp vanilla extract

125 g/4½ oz/scant 1 cup plain flour, sifted with

¾ tsp baking powder

scant ¼ tsp salt

2 tbsp milk

For the syrup

150 g/5½ oz/¾ cup granulated sugar

125 ml/4 fl oz/½ cup water

3–4 green cardamom pods

2 cinnamon sticks

finely pared zest of ½ a medium organic orange

100 ml/3½ fl oz/scant ½ cup rum or brandy

To serve

crème fraîche, whipped cream, fresh custard or mango *shrikhand* (see p.240)

Tipsy Cakes
Borrachos

Called 'drunkards' in Spain, these cakes are good with tea or coffee and make a delicious dessert. They are generally baked in a slab and cut into slices or squares for decorating and serving. Sadly, many Spanish bakers' idea of a finishing touch is to coat each portion with thick gluey custard. Those with more of an eye for elegance bake them in individual tins and use whipped cream as a filling or decoration, and home cooks like to serve them in a pool of homemade custard. I like a dollop of crème fraîche (lightly sweetened if you like) and whatever decoration is at hand, usually bright berries and mint. If you have a few extra minutes to spare, mango 'shrikhand' (see p.240) makes a great partner. The cakes should be nicely moistened without being wet and they can be eaten fresh, but the flavour will improve if they are left to stand for a day or two. Those who want more of a kick can sprinkle an extra teaspoon or so of alcohol onto their cake.

Preheat the oven to 180°C/350°F/Gas Mark 4. Grease a 12-hole muffin tin and dust with flour.

Use a heavy-duty electric mixer to whisk the eggs, sugar and vanilla extract together until thick and pale. The mixture should fall off the whisk in thick ribbons. Fold in the flour, baking powder and salt and gently but thoroughly mix in the milk.

Spoon the batter into the cavities – they should be about three-quarters full – and bake for about 20 minutes until dark golden brown. Pale cakes will have less flavour.

Make the syrup while the cakes are baking. Put the sugar, water, spices and pared orange zest in a heavy-based saucepan over medium heat. Bring to the boil while stirring to dissolve the sugar. Lower the heat and leave to simmer for 5 minutes. Remove from the heat, add the rum or brandy and set aside. Sieve into a small jug when ready to use.

Turn the baked cakes out upside down onto a tray. Pour the warm syrup slowly and evenly over the cakes. They should absorb all of the liquid. Leave upside down to cool, then pack in an airtight container and leave to mature for a day or so.

Serve as desired. If you are not going to use all the cakes within a few days, freeze them (unsyruped) while fresh. The sieved syrup can be kept in the refrigerator for more than a week. Warm it and pour it over the thawed cakes, then leave them for a few hours to let the flavours develop.

Madeleines

It is surprising how much mystique can surround one tiny and quite simple cake, and it has become almost inevitable to mention Proust and the madeleine in the same breath. In the first volume of his novel 'À la Recherche du Temps Perdu' (In Search of Lost Time), the narrator raises to his lips a spoonful of lime flower tea in which he has soaked some madeleine crumbs and is overwhelmed by ecstasy at the taste.

Although you can now find them in various flavours and compositions, the 'Madeleine de Commercy' is held to be the classic version. The cake called 'quatre-quarts' by the French and 'pound cake' by English speakers had long been a speciality of that town and came to form the basis of the dainty shell-shaped madeleine. In the early eighteenth century, the Polish king Stanislas Leszczynski lived in exile in France and his castle at Commercy was one of his favourite residences. There are various stories surrounding the origin of the madeleine, most linked in some way to Stanislas. One version tells of a pastry cook in his employ abandoning his ovens and leaving the sweet-toothed king to fend for himself. In search of some delicacy to satisfy his craving, he pounced enthusiastically upon the small cakes being eaten by one of his servants and consequently gave them her name. Another variant recounts how Madeleine Paumier saved the day at one of the king's banquets when the intended dessert failed; she quickly baked some 'quatre-quarts' batter in small moulds and the grateful Stanislas named the cakes after her. Their fame spread rapidly once Stanislas introduced them to the French court after the marriage of his daughter Marie to Louis XV.

Commercy remains the madeleine capital and every summer, there is a gathering of the 'Compagnons de la Madeleine' who take their mission very seriously, even donning special robes for the occasion. This fraternity was created in 1963 by master madeleine makers, with the admirable aim of making the madeleine known and appreciated in every possible place, and to protect and maintain the quality of the 'Véritable Madeleine de Commercy'.

The recipe follows overleaf.

Madeleines

A madeleine must be baked in a scalloped mould or it becomes simply another small cake. Choose well-shaped, nicely detailed moulds and take into account that dark tins will brown the cakes faster than lighter coloured ones, especially in the ferocious heat that madeleines require. Freshly baked, they are very tender on the inside with a slight bite to the crust. They become more compact after a day or two, but remain equally delicious. If you find them less than moist, you could always imitate Proust's protagonist and do a little dipping and soaking of your own.

Note: The batter needs to mature for at least half an hour.

Makes 12

100 g/3½ oz/scant ¾ cup plain flour, plus extra for dusting

I tsp baking powder

large pinch of salt

zest of ⅓ of an orange or lemon (preferably organic)

85 g/3 oz/6 tbsp butter, melted and cooled slightly, plus extra for greasing

I tbsp runny honey

2 eggs

½ tsp vanilla extract

85 g/3 oz/scant ½ cup caster sugar

Sift the flour with the baking powder and salt and set aside. Grate the citrus zest over the melted butter, stir in the honey and set aside.

Put the eggs, vanilla extract and sugar in a large mixer bowl and whisk until the mixture is pale and fairly thick. Use a balloon or other large hand whisk to fold in the flour mixture. Do not whisk, but use the whisk as you would use a spoon, to make gentle circles or figures of eight. When most of the flour has been incorporated, blend in the butter gently but thoroughly. Stop mixing as soon as there are no more streaks left in the batter.

Cover the bowl with clingfilm and refrigerate or set aside in a very cool place for at least 30 minutes, but not more than 12 hours. I use it after 45 minutes or so. The baking powder will have started to work, aerating the batter and it will set a little. Do not stir it.

Preheat the oven to 220°C/425°F/Gas Mark 7. Grease a 12-hole madeleine tin and dust with flour*.

Spoon the batter evenly into the tin, level the top and bake in a searingly hot oven just until cooked through, about 8 minutes. A skewer inserted into the middle of the cake should come out clean. Overbaking will make them dry. Serve as soon as they are cool, or pack into an airtight container and eat within three days.

*The best way to prepare the muffin tin is to brush the cavities well with melted butter, then flour them thoroughly, tapping the tin to remove any excess.

Makes 6

125 g/4½ oz/9 tbsp butter, softened, plus extra for greasing

150 g/5½ oz/generous 1 cup plain flour, plus extra for dusting

1¼ tsp baking powder

⅛ tsp salt

125 g/4½ oz/½ cup + 2 tbsp caster sugar

3 eggs, lightly beaten with 1 tsp vanilla extract

2 tbsp milk

To decorate

about 4 tbsp fine desiccated coconut

4 tbsp seedless raspberry jam, warmed

halved glacé cherries

angelica or other green decoration, such as mint leaves

Simple, but delicious and attractive, the English Madeleine seems to have vanished from the tea table. The buttery batter is cooked in tall, pail-shaped dariole moulds, coated with raspberry jam and coconut and the traditional decoration is a glacé cherry half flanked by two small green 'leaves' of angelica. Angelica is the candied stalk of the Angelica archangelica. In Britain, its main use is in confectionery and cakes, adding both colour and flavour. You could just as easily substitute small mint leaves if angelica is difficult to obtain.

The towering shape contributes to the charm, but you can adapt to suit. This recipe will make six tall, domed cakes which are trimmed after baking. If you prefer, you could use eight moulds of the same size for a squatter version, or a larger number of smaller moulds, even a muffin tin at a push. Adjust the baking time and decorating requirements accordingly.

English Madeleines

Preheat the oven to 170°C/325°F/Gas Mark 3. Grease 6 dariole moulds (175 ml/ 6 fl oz) and dust with flour.

Sift the flour with the baking powder and salt and set aside.

Beat the butter until smooth. Add the sugar and beat until light and fluffy. Add the beaten eggs to the creamed mixture, a little at a time, beating well and scraping down the sides of the bowl after each addition. Fold in the flour in 3 batches, adding the milk with the third batch.

Spoon the batter evenly into the dariole moulds and bake for about 20 minutes, or until a skewer inserted into the centre of the cakes comes out clean. Grip the moulds firmly with a folded cloth and gently turn the cakes out onto a wire rack. Stand them on their bases and leave to cool.

When the cakes are cool, trim the domed tops to make them flat. Scatter the desiccated coconut onto a plate. Brush the cakes thoroughly with the warm jam, leaving the cut side free. Prick this side (which will now be the base) with a fork and roll in the coconut so that as much as possible clings to the jam. You should be able to see a red background glow, but there should be no bald spots. Transfer to a serving plate and decorate with a halved cherry and 2 angelica 'leaves' or other greenery.

Eat within a day or two or freeze when they are fresh, adding leaves just before serving.

All
About Pineapples

I always felt that I knew quite a lot about pineapples; all sorts of things, from seeing how they grow on prickly plants with tough waxy leaves in the tropics, how to clean them and prepare them for the table (including rubbing the flesh with a little salt to bring out more flavour), the fact that gelatine will not set with fresh pineapple, its use as a meat tenderiser and even the little known fact that the fibre from the leaves of the plant is used to make beautiful semi-transparent silk-like fabric in the Philippines – I even own several garments and accessories made from it. But there is so much more to the pineapple. I suppose that you could hazard a guess that it is yet another delicacy we owe to Christopher Columbus, but did you know, for instance, that pineapple juice mixed with sand cleans boat decks very effectively? Or that the bromelian contained in its leaves is used to stabilise latex paint? Or even that they come in largely varying sizes, from dwarf to 5 kg/11 lb each? And I bet that not many people know that workers in pineapple processing plants must wear gloves lest their hands get tenderised to the point of decomposing.

The pineapple (*Ananas comosus*) is native to Brazil and is indeed one of the many new foods Columbus introduced to Europe on returning from his voyages of discovery. The plant had spread from Brazil to the Caribbean and was found and enjoyed by the sailors on Guadeloupe in 1493, on the second voyage. The botanical name is derived from the Brazilian Tupi Indian word *nana* or *anana*, meaning 'excellent fruit' and continues to be reflected in several languages, among others French, German, Portuguese, Russian, Hebrew, Turkish, Arabic and Malay.

Its English name of pineapple came about in a tangled way, first adopted from the Spaniards who found that it bore a great resemblance to the pine cone and named it *piña*. It seems that the suffix 'apple' was added in the English language to make a distinction between the tropical fruit and the pine cone and to emphasise the fact that it was a good thing to eat, as apples were known to be. In my native Guyana where pineapples grow abundantly and apples are an imported delicacy and not something most people readily

identify with,
the fruit is simply called
'pine', there being no other kinds of pines,
trees or cones, to cloud the issue. Interestingly, the word
'pineapple' was first recorded in English in 1398 and was used
at that time to denote the pine cone; the term pine cone did not
appear in written form until 1694.

European gardeners managed to grow the fruits in hothouses as early
as the 1520s, although it was to take more than a century for them to
refine the skills and conditions involved. They were a great delicacy and
were often used whole in all their natural beauty to decorate banquet tables.
It appears that pineapples could also be rented for this purpose, if one could
not afford to buy them outright. The fruit came to be associated with hospitality
and friendship and became a well-loved motif in architectural, artistic and
domestic objects. They were engraved and carved into buildings, moulded into
metal decorations and woven into all sorts of household linen and furnishings.

Main world growers include Thailand, the Philippines, Brazil, Costa Rica, Hawaii
and Ivory Coast. The quality of supermarket pineapples has improved vastly over the
years and modern refrigeration and transportation techniques mean that we can enjoy
them quite ripe. This is more important than it sounds, as pineapples, unlike most other
fruits, do not continue to ripen after being picked; they start to deteriorate almost
immediately and low temperatures can combat that to a great extent. Some fruit is canned
at the point of origin, most notably in Hawaii.

The raw fruits are not only delicious to eat on their own, but can be added to salads or
cooked with spicy ingredients to give a wonderful contrast. Being extremely rich
in vitamin C and fibre, they are good for one's health and are said to alleviate
laryngitis, pharyngitis and cystitis. They are also a diuretic and have
some antiseptic and vermifugal properties, also helping against
rheumatoid arthritis, sciatica and obesity. Tasty and
healthy at the same time, what more could
we ask for?

Pineapple Chunks

With just a little extra patience you can turn
a slab of cake into very attractive and tasty
individual treats. It goes without saying that the
pineapple should be flavourful. Canned pineapple
is fine, but pineapple canned in syrup will not be
as good as that canned in its own juice. Diehard
chocoholics will insist that dark chocolate makes
a better glaze, but I find that it overwhelms the
pineapple. Go with the white chocolate, or do as
I do to humour the dark chocolate faction: dip
half or part of the batch in dark chocolate and
the rest in white. Make them a day in advance
for the best flavour.

Makes 16 chunks

150 g/5½ oz/scant ¾ cup butter, softened,
plus extra for greasing

150 g/5½ oz/generous 1 cup plain flour, plus
extra for dusting

200 g/7 oz flavourful pineapple (fresh or
canned), puréed

50 g/1¾ oz/½ cup fine desiccated coconut

2 tbsp rum

1¼ tsp baking powder

¼ tsp bicarbonate of soda

¼ tsp salt

150 g/5½ oz/¾ cup caster sugar

2 eggs, lightly beaten

2 tbsp milk

To finish

400–450 g/14 oz–1 lb white chocolate (with a
high percentage of cocoa butter)

2 whole candied pineapple slices*

*Try to find whole slices of candied pineapple
for the decoration. They are far better than the
minute and sugary chunks and will add to
both the appearance and flavour of the cakes.

Preheat the oven to 170°C/325°F/Gas Mark 3. Grease a 20-cm/8-in square tin, line the base with baking parchment and dust with flour.

Mix the puréed pineapple, coconut and rum together and set aside while you assemble the rest of the ingredients. Stir it again before use.

Sift the flour with the baking powder, bicarbonate of soda and salt and set aside.

Beat the butter and sugar until creamy and lightened in colour. Add the beaten eggs, a little at a time, beating well after each addition and scraping down the sides of the bowl regularly. Gently fold in the flour and pineapple mixture in 3 alternating batches, starting with the flour. Add the milk with the last batch of flour. Transfer the batter to the tin and bake for 35–40 minutes until the cake is light golden brown and a skewer inserted into the centre comes out clean. Leave it in the tin for a minute or two, then invert onto a wire rack, peel off the baking parchment and leave to cool.

When the cake is completely cool, cut it into 4 strips. Trim off a triangular piece from the end of a strip and cut the rest into 4 'chunks' that look like wedges with the thin end lopped off. This end should measure just over 2 cm/¾ in and the wide top end should be about 6 cm/2½ in. Remember to make each cut in the opposite direction, or you will end up with diamond shapes. Eat the trimmings straightaway or freeze them to make a trifle type dessert later.

Brush each chunk completely free of crumbs and neaten any ragged edges, or this will all be visible after glazing. Set aside, right side up, and put a sheet of baking parchment on your work surface.

Chop the chocolate finely and melt it in a small heatproof bowl over a pan of barely simmering water. Prick a chunk of cake with a fork and dip it into the chocolate so that all but the top is coated. Tap the fork on the edge of the bowl to allow any excess to fall off. Use a second fork to help slide the coated cake carefully onto the baking parchment, uncoated side down. Coat the rest in the same way. As you get nearer the end, you may have to use a spoon to help coat the cake.

Cut the pineapple slices into suitable chunks and use to decorate the tops, one chunk per cake.

Leave the chocolate to harden completely, then arrange the cakes in a single layer in an airtight container and leave for a day. You can also freeze a portion for later. The maturation time brings out more flavour.

Makes 8

For the cake

30 g/1 oz/2 tbsp butter, melted and cooled slightly, plus extra for greasing

100 g/3½ oz/scant ¾ cup plain flour, plus extra for dusting

¼ tsp baking powder

¼ tsp salt

3 eggs

100 g/3½ oz/½ cup caster sugar

½ tsp vanilla extract

For the buttercream filling

150 g/5½ oz/scant ¾ cup soft butter

175 g/6 oz/1½ cups icing sugar, sifted

3 tbsp maraschino liqueur

To decorate

about 400 g/14 oz marzipan

red food colouring (optional)

These attractive and rich little layer cakes are a Dutch pastry-shop staple and are easy to make at home. Maraschino liqueur (not the syrup from the bottle of cherries!) is popular with professional bakers in Holland and it imparts a subtle flowery fragrance, but feel free to flavour the buttercream as you choose, or simply leave out the alcohol and use a little milk instead. The marzipan can be tinted pink or left plain. Make them a day in advance to allow the flavours to mature and the marzipan to soften a little.

Marzipan Fancies

Preheat the oven to 180°C/350°F/Gas Mark 4. Grease a 20-cm/8-in square tin well and dust with flour.

Sift the flour with the baking powder and salt and set aside.

Put the eggs, sugar and vanilla extract in a large mixer bowl and whisk until the mixture is very thick and pale. When the whisk is lifted the mixture should fall in thick ribbons, not in a stream. Use a balloon or other large hand whisk to fold in the flour mixture. Do not whisk, but use the whisk as you would use a spoon, to make gentle circles or figures of eight. When most of the flour has been incorporated, blend in the butter gently but thoroughly. Stop mixing as soon as there are no more streaks left in the batter.

Transfer the batter to the tin, level the top and bake for about 20 minutes until golden brown and cooked through. A skewer inserted into the middle of the cake should come out clean and the cake should spring back lightly if pressed with a fingertip. Don't overbake, or it will be dry. Loosen the cake from the sides of the tin and invert onto a wire rack to cool.

For the buttercream, put the butter in a heavy-duty electric mixer fitted with a paddle attachment and beat it for a minute at medium speed. Add the sifted icing sugar and beat well for about 5 minutes until light and fluffy. Start at very low speed to prevent clouds of icing sugar from wafting around, then gradually increase to a fairly high speed. Add 1 tbsp maraschino (or other flavouring) and beat for another minute; it should have a soft spreading consistency.

Cut the cake horizontally into two even layers, then cut away a third of the cake vertically. Reserve 6 tbsp of the buttercream. Sprinkle 1 tbsp of maraschino over one large layer and spread half of the remaining buttercream over it. Repeat with the second large layer, then lay the two small layers next to each other on top of this. You will now have a three-layer cake. Wrap and chill until the buttercream firms up.

Meanwhile, if you would like to tint the marzipan pink, add enough food colouring and knead it in. Divide into two portions. Roll out each portion thinly between layers of clingfilm and trim to a rectangle, about 18 x 52 cm/7 x 20½ in. Cut each sheet into 4 pieces, about 9 x 26 cm/3½ x 10½ in.

Remove the cake from the refrigerator and trim off any untidy edges. Cut the cake into 8 almost-square portions. Spread a dab of the reserved buttercream on all 4 sides of each cake; you just need a thin smear somewhere in the middle that will hold the marzipan in place.

Put a cake on your work surface and press a length of marzipan against one side, beginning exactly in a corner. Fold the marzipan around the cake, patting it into place. Lay the cake on its side so that the excess marzipan is on the work surface and trim away, leaving about ½ cm/¼ in. Press against the other end to seal and stand the right way up. There should be a lot of marzipan at the top of the cake. Use your fingers to bring the 4 sides inwards so that they touch in the centre and 4 pleats form, one in each corner. Looking from the top, it should look like a parcel with a double bow on top.

Refrigerate for at least a few hours (preferably overnight) before serving, covered and away from strong smells. They can also be frozen in an airtight box.

Serve at room temperature for the best flavour. I find them rich and satisfying enough to be shared by two people, but bigger eaters may prefer to have a cake to themselves.

Makes 16 cubes
For the sponge cake
50 g/1¾ oz/3½ tbsp butter, melted and cooled slightly, plus extra for greasing
125 g/4½ oz/scant 1 cup plain flour, plus extra for dusting
25 g/1 oz/generous 3 tbsp cornflour
¼ tsp baking powder
¼ tsp salt
4 eggs
150 g/5½ oz/¾ cup caster sugar
1 tsp vanilla extract

For the glaze
500 g/1 lb 2 oz dark chocolate, finely chopped
250 ml/9 fl oz/generous 1 cup milk

To finish
about 150 g/5½ oz/1⅔ cups fine desiccated coconut

This Australian favourite has been around since the end of the nineteenth century and is said to have been named after Lord Lamington, Governor of Queensland from 1895–1901. Their popularity remains undiminished and they are a hot item for both home bakers and pastry shops. Using real chocolate to coat the cubes instead of the more common cocoa icing makes them absolutely irresistible and very much worth the time the dipping and coating takes.

Lamingtons

Preheat the oven to 180°C/350°F/Gas Mark 4. Grease a 21-cm/8½-in square tin and dust with flour.

Sift the flour with the cornflour, baking powder and salt and set aside.

Use a heavy-duty electric mixer to whisk the eggs, caster sugar and vanilla extract until thick and pale. It should fall off the whisk in a ribbon rather than a thin stream. Gently fold in the flour mixture in 2 batches using a balloon whisk. Add the melted and slightly cooled butter with the second batch of flour and mix just until there are no more streaks of flour or butter apparent in the batter.

Transfer the batter to the tin and level the top. Bake for 20–25 minutes. When you press the top of the sponge with a fingertip, the indentation you create should slowly regain its original shape. Turn out onto a wire rack to cool.

For the glaze, put the chocolate and milk in a heavy-based saucepan over low heat. Stir gently to melt the chocolate. As soon as the mixture is homogenous, remove it from the heat and leave to cool slightly, but don't allow it to thicken too much or it will be difficult to use.

Cut the sponge into 16 cubes and brush free of crumbs. Hold each cube on a fork over the bowl or pan of glaze and use a spoon or small jug to pour the glaze over the cake so that the top and 4 sides are coated. Spills and excess will fall into the bowl or pan to be reused. Arrange the cubes on a wire rack or a sheet of baking parchment.

When the glaze has almost set, put the desiccated coconut on a plate. Tilt each cube gently with a toothpick and prick the bottom on a fork. Press each glazed side lightly in the coconut to coat and leave to set in a cool place away from strong smells.

These delightful macaroon and truffle morsels are a popular Scandinavian treat. They were named after the French actress Sarah Bernhardt (1844-1923), who achieved great fame in her own country and later graced the stages of many European and American cities, even venturing as far afield as Havana. She went on to act in some of the first motion pictures and enjoyed a long and successful career, remaining undaunted by the loss of a leg to gangrene in later life. An air of notoriety always clung to her, mainly due to endless affairs and dalliances with noblemen and other highly placed society figures, including Edward VII while he was Prince of Wales. Her many eccentricities included sleeping in a coffin, and she claimed that this helped her to prepare better for dramatic roles.

Makes 12

For the truffle filling

75 ml/2½ fl oz/5 tbsp double cream

25 g/1 oz/2 tbsp butter

150 g/5½ oz/5½ squares dark chocolate, finely chopped

For the macaroon base

100 g/3½ oz/⅔ cup blanched almonds, finely ground

125 g/4½ oz/½ cup + 2 tbsp granulated sugar

35 g/1¼ oz egg white

To finish

225 g/8 oz/8 squares dark chocolate, finely chopped

12 silver balls or crystallised flower petals, to decorate

Sarah Bernhardts

Preheat oven to 150°C/300°F/Gas Mark 2. Line a baking sheet with baking parchment.

Make the truffle filling first. Heat the cream and butter in a small saucepan until it starts to boil. Scatter in the chocolate and remove it from the heat. Give it a good shake so that the liquid covers the chocolate. Leave to stand for a minute or two, then stir until smooth. Cool and chill until thick enough to hold its shape, but don't let it get too hard, or it will be difficult to shape.

For the macaroon base, mix all of the ingredients together to a smooth paste. Divide the mixture into 12 equal portions. Roll each portion into a ball and arrange them on the baking sheet. Moisten your fingers and flatten each one neatly to a disc about 5 cm/2 in in diameter. They will not spread much while baking. Bake for 15–20 minutes. The tops should stay pale and the bottoms will be golden brown and they should give a little to the touch.

Remove from the oven, leave to stand for a minute or two, then carefully loosen the macaroons from the baking parchment. Leave to cool on a wire rack.

When the macaroon bases have cooled, put a portion of the truffle filling on each one. Spread it out a little, then use a small palette knife to make a conical shape so that the top ends in a point. Try to keep the base free of smears. Chill until firm.

Melt the chocolate in a small heatproof bowl over a pan of barely simmering water. Dip the truffle part into the melted chocolate, holding each one by the macaroon base, keeping the base as smear-free as you can. Decorate as you wish.

They can be served as soon as the chocolate has set. Keep leftovers covered and refrigerated, but serve at room temperature so that the filling is nice and succulent.

Chocolate and Marzipan Cakes

You can use either Pistachio or Almond Marzipan
(see p.114) for these cakes. If I happen to have
both in the refrigerator at the same time, I make
half a dozen of either kind. The Pistachio Marzipan
is so attractive that you could easily find yourself
wanting to dispense with the chocolate glaze, adding
even more colour with fragments of bright pink
crystallised rose petals or whole petals if your
budget permits. If you have any Almond Marzipan left
over, you can colour it and make simple flowers and
leaves to decorate the cakes; bought decorations as
listed below are also fine.

Makes 12

For the cake

100 g/3½ oz/7 tbsp butter, softened, plus extra
for greasing

125 g/4½ oz/scant 1 cup plain flour, plus extra
for dusting

20 g/¾ oz/scant ¼ cup (unsweetened)
cocoa powder

70 ml/2½ fl oz/generous ¼ cup boiling water

1¼ tsp baking powder

scant ¼ tsp salt

150 g/5½ oz/¾ cup caster sugar

2 eggs, beaten with 1 tsp vanilla extract

To finish

about 500 g/1 lb 2 oz Almond or Pistachio
Marzipan (see p.114)

50 g/1¾ oz seedless raspberry or smooth apricot
jam, warmed

100 ml/3½ fl oz/scant ½ cup double cream

175 g/6 oz/6 squares dark chocolate, chopped
into small pieces

pistachios, silver balls or crystallised flowers, to
decorate

Preheat the oven to 180°C/350°F/Gas Mark 4. Grease a 12-hole bun or muffin tin and dust with flour*.

For the cake batter, combine the cocoa and boiling water in a small bowl and stir well to remove any lumps. Sift the flour, baking powder and salt together in another bowl and set aside.

Put the sugar and butter in a large mixer bowl and cream well. Beat in the beaten eggs in 3 batches, scraping down the sides of the bowl after each addition. Continue to beat until light and fluffy. Use a balloon whisk to mix in the cocoa, then gently fold in the flour mixture in 2 batches. Stop mixing as soon as there are no more streaks.

Spoon the batter into the bun or muffin tin and bake for about 20 minutes until a skewer inserted into the centre of a cake comes out clean. Note that they will puff up a bit while baking, but will subside later quite neatly. Transfer them carefully to a wire rack to cool completely.

To finish, roll out the marzipan between two sheets of clingfilm to a thickness of 2 mm/$\frac{1}{16}$ in and cut out 12 circles, about 11 cm/4$\frac{1}{4}$ in in diameter. Re-roll and re-cut the trimmings as necessary. Brush the sides and bottoms of the cooled cakes lightly with the warm jam and place them bottoms up on the rack. Cover each cake with a marzipan circle. The easiest way to do this is to drop a marzipan circle over the cake and invert it into one hand so that the exposed side is facing upwards. Use your other hand to pat and press the marzipan into place, smoothing out the inevitable pleats. If they are too thick, snip off the excess with a pair of scissors and smooth with your fingers. This step is not absolutely necessary, but it will allow you to glaze the cakes more smoothly and evenly. Note that these trimmings fall under the category of cook's perks, as they will most likely have some jam on them and cannot be re-rolled or kept.

Put the cream in a saucepan and bring to the boil. Scatter in the chocolate and remove from the heat. Leave to stand for about 2 minutes, or until the chocolate melts, then stir until homogenous. Drop a generous spoonful of the mixture over the top of each cake and spread with a palette knife so that it covers the marzipan. Decorate as desired. If you are making both pistachio and almond versions, use two different decorations so that you can recognise them later.

Once the chocolate has set, they can be stored in an airtight container for a few days in the refrigerator. Serve at room temperature. They can also be frozen, but the glaze may discolour slightly.

*My tin has cavities that hold 75 ml/2$\frac{1}{2}$ fl oz/$\frac{1}{3}$ cup. If yours deviates, make allowances accordingly. When you cover the cakes with marzipan, measure the two sloping sides plus the diameter of the base (which is now the top) and cut the marzipan to that diameter.

Makes 12 squares

For the filling

200 ml/7 fl oz/generous ¾ cup double cream

200 g/7 oz/7 squares dark chocolate, chopped into very small pieces

1½ tbsp brandy, rum, Grand Marnier or Cointreau

For the cake

35 g/1¼ oz/generous ⅓ cup (unsweetened) cocoa powder

125 ml/4 fl oz/½ cup boiling water

100 g/3½ oz/scant ¾ cup plain flour

1 tsp baking powder

¼ tsp salt

100 g/3½ oz/7 tbsp butter, softened

150 g/5½ oz/¾ cup caster sugar

2 eggs, lightly beaten with 1¼ tsp vanilla extract

This cake, with thin cake layers and a melt-in-the mouth filling, is chocolate heaven to my children. When they were younger, we used to spend part of every summer in America, in the small town where my sister and her family, as well as my parents, lived. One of the local supermarkets offered first-class gourmet cakes and we found an intense chocolate cake that was to die for. It became a firm favourite and I was encouraged by the children to re-create it at home in Holland, where it remains an evergreen. The liquor in the filling is a later addition; if you prefer you can substitute an equal amount of extra cream at the beginning.

Divine Chocolate Squares

Preheat the oven to 180°C/350°F/Gas Mark 4. Line a baking sheet, about 28 x 35 cm/11 x 14 in with sides, with baking parchment.

Make the filling first, as it needs to stand for a while to reach the correct consistency. Put the cream in a saucepan and heat it to boiling point. Remove from the heat and scatter in the chocolate pieces. Give the pan a shake so that all the chocolate is covered with cream and leave to stand for 2–3 minutes. Stir gently until smooth, then stir in the flavouring liquor thoroughly. Overbrisk stirring will create air bubbles. Leave to cool to an easily spreadable consistency while you make the cake. It can also be chilled briefly if it takes too long at room temperature. A spoonful of filling lifted and allowed to fall should do so in soft blobs, not a stream, but if it hardens too much it will start to set and will not give an attractive finish.

For the cake, put the cocoa and boiling water into a small bowl and stir well to make a lump-free paste. Set aside.

Sift the flour with the baking powder and salt and set aside.

Use a heavy-duty electric mixer fitted with a paddle attachment to cream the butter and sugar together well until lightened and fluffy. Add the beaten eggs in 3 or 4 batches, scraping down the sides of the bowl after each addition. Fold in the flour mixture in 3 batches, alternating with the cocoa. Make sure that all the flour has been absorbed each time before adding the liquid, or you may get a few lumps.

Transfer the batter to the tin, level the top and bake for about 15 minutes, or until a skewer inserted into the centre of the cake comes out clean. Remove from the oven and top with a sheet of baking parchment. Invert a wire rack onto the baking parchment. Grip the two sides of the rack and tin firmly and invert quickly. Leave the cake to cool on the baking parchment, then cut into 3 equal rectangles. If you cut straight through the paper, you can then re-invert the pieces onto the filling with the paper attached before peeling the paper away carefully. This is useful, as the layers are thin and fragile.

Put one cake layer on a work surface lined with a large piece of clingfilm. Spread a third of the filling onto it, levelling it so that it comes neatly and evenly to the sides. Top with a second layer of cake and repeat until all 3 layers and all the filling has been used. The last third goes on top of the cake.

Leave to set before cutting into 12 squares. Do this shortly before serving to keep it as moist as possible. To cut it neatly, hold a knife under very hot water for a few seconds, dry it quickly and cut. Hold the knife under hot water and dry it after each cut. That way, the warm knife melts the chocolate and easily slips through, leaving no ragged edges. It needs no decoration, but you can of course do so if you like. Use walnut halves, sugar flowers, dragees or silver balls or whatever tasteful item takes your fancy.

Keep any uneaten cake refrigerated, suitably covered and away from strong smells. Bring to room temperature for serving so that the filling is nice and soft.

A last Word

Now that we have reached the end, I would like to leave
you with this word:
'enjoy'.

Enjoy preparing these sweets.

Enjoy meeting old favourites and making
new discoveries.

Enjoy eating them.

Enjoy thinking about them and even dreaming about them.

Enjoy sharing them with others.

Because, without enjoyment, sweets become
quite pointless.

Index

Bibliography

Academia de la Cocina Española. *La Repostería de los Monasterios*. Oviedo: Ediciones Nobel S.A., n/d.

Achaya, K.T. *A Historical Dictionary of Indian Food*. New Delhi: Oxford University Press, 1998.

Ayto, John. *The Diner's Dictionary*. Oxford: Oxford University Press, 1993.

Bates, Margaret. *The Scottish and Irish Baking Book*. London: Pergamon Press, 1965.

Bennani-Smirès, Latifa. *La Cuisine Marocaine*. Casablanca: Al Madariss, 1998.

Carmona, Julio. *Los Dulces del Convento: Recetas del monasterio de Santa María del Socorro de Sevilla*. Barcelona: Scyla Editores, 2005.

Charrette, Jacques & Vence, Céline. *Le Grand Livre de la Pâtisserie et des Desserts*. Paris: Albin Michel, 1995.

Coe, Sophie D. and Michael D. *The True History of Chocolate*. London: Thames and Hudson Ltd., 1996.

Corriher, Shirley O. *CookWise: the hows and whys of successful cooking*. New York: W. Morrow and Company Inc., 1997.

Corriher, Shirley O. *BakeWise: the hows and whys of successful baking*. New York: Scribner, 2008.

Davidson, Alan & Knox, Charlotte. *Fruit: A Connoisseur's Guide and Cookbook*. London: Mitchell Beazley, 1991.

Davidson, Alan. *The Oxford Companion to Food*. Oxford: Oxford University Press, 1999.

Délices du Maroc. EDL, 2003.

Halıcı, Nevin. *Nevin Halıcı's Turkish Cookbook*. London: Dorling Kindersley, 1989.

Hartley, Dorothy. *Food in England*. London: Futura, 1985.

Kiple, Kenneth F. & Coneè Ornelas, Kriemhild (eds.) *The Cambridge World History of Food*. Cambridge: Cambridge University Press, 2000.

Larousse Gastronomique. Paris: Librairie Larousse, 1984.

Leeming, Margaret. *A History of Food: From Manna to Microwave*. London: BBC Books, 1991.

Lenotre, Gaston. *Desserts Traditionnels de France*. Paris: Flammarion, 1999.

Martínez Llopis, Manuel. *La Dulcería Española: Recetarios histórico y popular*. Madrid: Alianza Editorial, 1999.

Mason, Laura. *Sugar-Plums and Sherbet: The Prehistory of Sweets*. Totnes: Prospect Books, 1998.

McGee, Harold. *On Food and Cooking*. London: HarperCollins, 1991.

Minifie, Bernard. *Chocolate, Cocoa and Confectionery*. New York: Van Nostrand Rhinehold, 1989.

Nicolello, I. & Foote, R. *Complete Confectionery Techniques*. London: Hodder & Stoughton, 1994.

Pagrach-Chandra, Gaitri. *Windmills in my Oven: a Book of Dutch Baking*. Totnes: Prospect Books, 2002.

Pagrach-Chandra, Gaitri. *Warm Bread and Honey Cake*. London: Pavilion, 2009.

Richardson, Tim. *Sweets: A History of Temptation*. London: Bantam Press, 2003.

Roos, Jeanne. *Het Snoepers Leesboek*. Haarlem: Magazijn de Bijenkorf, 1991.

Sexton, Regina. *A Little History of Irish Food*. Dublin: Gill and Macmillan, 1998.

Soler, Emilio. "La única y verdadera historia del turrón". *Information bulletin Universidad de Alicante* 06/04/03.

Stoll, F.M. & de Groot, W.H. *Recepten Huishoudschool Laan van Meerdervoort's-Gravenhage*. The Hague: De Gebroeders van Kleef, 1950.

Toussaint-Samat, Maguelonne. *History of Food*. Oxford: Blackwell, 1992.

Acknowledgements

I owe thanks to many people for various things ranging from information, recipes, hospitality and support. My friends all over the world are always willing to provide whatever it is I require, whenever I need it. A great big thank-you to Sri and Roger Owen, Pia Lim-Castillo and Quincy Castillo, Gina Lim, Nevin Halıcı, Aylin Tan, Filiz Hösukoğlu, Mary Işin, Pearly Ramnauth, Franka Philip, Colleen Sen and Jayant Sukhadia. Very many thanks to my agent, Charlotte Bruton, for looking after everything so well. And a huge thank-you to my husband Henk and our children Judy and Leon, whose candid opinions about my food keep me sharp. (And they hardly complained when meals contained more sweet than savoury components.)

Once again it has been a real pleasure to work with the team from Pavilion. Thanks to Becca Spry for nudging me in this direction, and to my commissioning editor Emily Preece-Morrison who has excelled herself yet again in creating a book that even surpassed my expectations. Many thanks to copy editor Kathy Steer and production manager Laura Brodie. The amazing talents of photographer Yuki Sugiura, home economist/food stylist Aya Nishimura, props stylist Wei Tang and their assistants, and the fantastic job done by book designers Georgina Hewitt and Laura Woussen created the effect you see before you.

Thank you all!

First published in Great Britain in 2012 by
PAVILION BOOKS
10 Southcombe Street
London, W14 0RA

An imprint of the Anova Books Company Ltd

Design and layout © Pavilion, 2012
Text © Gaitri Pagrach-Chandra, 2012
Photography © Yuki Sugiura, 2012

Commissioning editor: Emily Preece-Morrison
Jacket and concept design: Georgina Hewitt
Layout designer: Laura Woussen
Photographer: Yuki Sugiura
Food stylist: Aya Nishimura
Prop stylist: Wei Tang
Copy editor: Kathy Steer
Proofreader: Kate Turvey
Indexer: Patricia Hymans

ISBN 978-1-86205-937-5

A CIP catalogue record for this book is available from the
British Library.

10 9 8 7 6 5 4 3 2 1

Reproduction by
Rival Colour Ltd, UK
Printed and bound by
1010 Printing International Ltd, China

www.anovabooks.com